CONFESSION OF FAITH

ACCOUNT OF OUR RELIGION, DOCTRINE AND FAITH

GIVEN BY PETER RIDEMAN
OF THE BROTHERS
WHOM MEN CALL
HUTTERIANS

*Be ready always to give an answer to every
man that asketh you a reason of
the hope that is in you.*
1 Peter 3:15

PLOUGH PUBLISHING HOUSE

 Rifton, New York

Originally published in 1545 as
Rechenschaft unserer Religion, Lehr und Glaubens,
von den Brüdern, so man die Hutterischen nennt,
ausgangen durch Peter Rideman

Second German Edition (1565) from which this translation was made,
located in the British Museum, London. No. 3908a8

Published in German by The Plough Publishing House, England, 1938

First English Edition translated by the Society of Brothers and
published in Great Britain by Hodder and Stoughton, Ltd.
in conjunction with The Plough Publishing House, 1950

Second English Edition published by
The Plough Publishing House, 1970

SBN 87486-202-7
Library of Congress Catalog Card No. 74-115840
Printed at the Plough Press, Farmington, Pa., U.S.A.

REGISTER OF THE ARTICLES AND POINTS
CONTAINED IN THIS BOOK;
ALSO ON WHICH PAGE EACH IS MOST
QUICKLY TO BE FOUND

FIRST COME THE 12 ESSENTIALS OF THE
CONFESSION OF FAITH

5

END OF THE REGISTER OF THE
FIRST PART OF
THIS BOOK

REGISTER OF THE SECOND PART OF THIS BOOK

END OF THE REGISTER

FOREWORD

SINCE it is right, good, agreeable and well-pleasing to God to confess one's faith, and since, besides, blessedness lieth therein, as Paul saith, "For with the heart man believeth unto righteousness, and with the mouth confession is made unto salvation,"[1] we in our simplicity desire to give expression to our faith and to testify to what is in our hearts and our whole religion; above all, however, we desire to do this since there is so much blasphemy against the truth, which truly shall not pass by void and unpunished.

In order that no man, including the authorities— who, perhaps at the instigation of others, have already stretched out and laid their hand upon the Lord's people of peace—may bring further guilt upon themselves by violating the apple of the Lord's eye,[2] we desire to give an account of our faith, doctrine and life as much in sequence as is possible, through which we believe every man should see and recognize sufficiently that we are not heretics and seducers, as we are blasphemously called, who have deserted the Church that is in Christ Jesus; nor have we founded another faction or sect outside the same; on the contrary, we have drawn near and committed ourselves utterly to her, to serve God and Christ therein with a pure, unblemished and blameless conscience. Firstly, we want to consider the twelve essentials of the confession of the Christian faith, which include the omnipotence of the Father, the righteousness and justice of the Son and the grace of the Holy Spirit; that the Church is accepted by God through Christ and gathered together by the Holy Spirit; what the Church of Christ and community of saints is, as well

9

as what faith is and whence it cometh; concerning doctrine and what we teach about God; what idolatry is; that God created man in his likeness, and what God's likeness is; also how man forsook the same and fell into sin, through which he is led to death.

We want also to show what sin and original sin is, and to what extent it harmeth and destroyeth. Then we want also to say how man findeth God and his grace again in Christ: to speak of remorse, repentance and what true repentance is and how the truly repentant man is grafted once more into Christ; of God's covenant, of the old covenant, the law, the gospel and the new covenant; of child baptism and certain reasons given by those who baptize children; but also of the true baptism of Christ and of his Church; of how one baptizeth, and who should baptize and teach; also of election to and the diversity of offices in the Church.

We desire thereafter to speak of the misuse of the Lord's supper, as well as of Christ's true usage, not forgetting community of goods; we want also to speak of separation; also of marriage and adultery; of government, war and taxes; as well as of the taking of oaths and making of clothes.

Then we want to speak of whether a Christian can go to law or pass judgment, as well as of the taking of oaths; of greeting, the giving of the hand and of embracing; also of prayer, singing, fasting and celebrating; as well as of trading, innkeeping and the drinking of healths. Then we want also to speak of meetings, of the education of children, of exclusion from and re-acceptance into the Church; and lastly of the whole life, walk, dress and adornment of Christians. In all this we strive with all zeal to have a blameless conscience, both before God and man, and should like, in so far as it is possible and in our power, to draw and move all men to renounce their ungodly nature, and turn with their whole hearts to God and his Christ.[1] May God the Almighty grant his blessing and bring to pass the desire of his servants to his glory.

We must now confess that we have received all this from no human being, but from the Lord in heaven, from whom cometh every good and perfect gift.[2] Therefore do we give and ascribe the honour to him alone, for it is his alone; and say that he who resisteth this resisteth the gifts of God. For ourselves, however, we cannot work against but only for the truth, by which, with God's help, we mean to stand unto our end to his glory. Amen.

THE FIRST PART

NOW FOLLOWETH THE CONFESSION OF OUR FAITH, DOCTRINE AND LIFE

WE ACKNOWLEDGE GOD

Firstly, we confess that there is one God, who hath being in himself and through himself, who hath neither beginning nor end, who possesseth all power whether in heaven, on earth or in the abyss; for which reason also the word "God" befitteth, belongeth and is due to him alone. Although there are others that are named "gods," that is, "the mighty,"[1] there is but one God and mighty power over them all, so much greater than all others that there is no power that proceedeth not from him, being lent and given the others by him.

So great is his power that he hath brought into being, formed, modelled and made all things[2] and still preserveth all things, which, even as they have come into being through him, have also their end in him, so that all other gods or mighty powers must truly be ashamed and appalled before him, and tremble, bow down and give him alone the honour. For his hand is strong: he shattereth and maketh again, he humbleth and he exalteth, he killeth and maketh alive whom he will.[3] Therefore is he alone rightly named God and given honour, as he himself saith, "Hear, O Israel, the Lord thy God is one,"[4] and again "I am the Lord thy God,[5] and beside me there is none other."[6] Thus we acknowledge one God.

We confess that this our one God, because he is so great, is everywhere and in all places at once, and that he filleth all things both in heaven and on earth with his glory;[7] which divine glory, strength, omnipotence and Godhead is shown, seen and recognized in the works of his hands.[8] Therefore, as day—a work of his hands—when it hath dawned shineth and enlighteneth everywhere, and as air filleth and pervadeth the whole creation and is in all places at once,[1] even so and still more doth the Creator of the same show himself faithfully, honestly and well in all the works of his hands, in each in its own measure.

Therefore is this one, eternal, almighty God the one eternal and unchanging truth, which hath being in itself and remaineth eternally unchanged;[2] which poureth itself into believing souls, maketh us like, similar and conformable to itself,[3] that we may live and walk in it and testify to the truth within us in word and life.[4]

THE ALMIGHTY FATHER

God, who is eternal truth, is the enemy of all untruth and deceit, the enemy of all that hath a false, purely outward and feigned appearance. Therefore he will not be named Father of those who are disobedient and believe not his word,[5] as the word saith, "If I am your Father, where is mine honour?"[6] and in another place, "This perverse and crooked generation hath lost his favour and they are not his children on account of their sin."[7] For God, who is a Spirit, desireth to be worshipped and honoured in spirit and in truth.[8] But they who have not the same Spirit can neither honour nor worship him,[9] as David showeth in the words that he speaketh: "Unto the wicked God saith, 'Why dost thou take my covenant in thy mouth and declare my law, seeing thou hatest discipline, and castest my word behind thee?'"[10] From this it becometh clear and evident that God will not be worshipped and honoured by the unbelieving, unjust and sinners, nor will he hear their prayer.[11]

Moreover, every sinner who remaineth and con-

16

tinueth in sin, and yet nameth God Father, speaketh what is not true, since it is written as is said above: "They are not God's children on account of their sins."[1] Now, he who with untruth calleth God Father revileth and abuseth God, who is truth, from whom no lie can come,[2] even as did the Jews when they said "We have one Father, God," to whom Christ saith: "If God were your Father, ye would love me: for I proceeded forth and came from God; neither came I of myself, but he sent me. Why do ye not understand my speech? Even because ye will not hear my word. Ye are of your father the devil, and the lusts of your father ye will do. He was a murderer from the beginning, and abode not in the truth."[3] Thus no one can name God Father in truth who hath not given himself to him as a child.

Therefore the Father, in grace and fatherly love and constancy, sendeth his Son from heaven that he may bring us again to be his children and to the true inheritance. Now he, when he came, gave to all who received him, and still receive him, power to become children of God.[4] These, and not the world, he teacheth that they should call him Father when he saith: "When ye want to pray use not vain repetitions, as the heathen or unbelievers do: for they think that they shall be heard for their much speaking. Be not ye therefore like unto them: the Father knoweth what things ye have need of, before ye ask him. After this manner therefore pray ye: 'Our Father which art in heaven.' "[5]

Here, as hath been said, Christ teacheth not the world to call God Father, but the disciples whom he hath chosen from the world,[6] that is those who name him Father not only with the mouth but with a sincere heart in power and truth, and who also in their whole life show themselves to be his obedient children. Of such saith he further, "I say not unto

17

you, that I will pray the Father for you: for the Father himself loveth you, because ye have loved me, and have believed that I came out from God."[1]

OUR FATHER

We, however, confess God to be our Father because he in his grace hath received and chosen us through Christ to be his property.[2] For this reason also hath he sent his Word from heaven, and made us, who were dead through the disease of sin, alive again.[3] He hath begotten us again to an immortal hope,[4] in that he hath led and grafted us into the divine character and nature,[5] sealing us, after we believed the gospel, with the promised Spirit.[6] This Spirit now worketh, doeth and perfecteth everything in us, quenching, eradicating and killing the sin that we have by nature, so that the true, good, right and holy, which he bringeth with him and planteth in us, may take root, grow and bring forth fruit.

Thus this same Holy Spirit of God assureth us through the working of his strength in us that we are God's children.[7] Through him we may well dare with joy and certainty to name him Father, and approach and cry to him in good confidence for all we desire, since we know that he loveth us,[8] and in Christ hath given us all things,[9] and that his ear is open to our cry and attentive to grant our request.[10]

Therefore we, having experienced his fatherly grace, have yielded ourselves in obedience to his will as children to our Father, that he may use all our members according to his own will and good pleasure. This his work we, as his obedient children, desire with a willing and attentive heart to endure and suffer, to let him guide our whole life and control our heart, mouth, eyes, ears, hands, feet and all our members, so that now not we, but he, the Lord, may

18

live and do everything in us.[1] He also careth for us as a father for his children and doth shower upon and fill us with all good things. Therefore is God our Father and we his children.[2]

WHO HATH MADE HEAVEN
AND EARTH

We also confess that God hath made and created heaven and earth and all that is therein from naught, for his honour and glory.[3] For since God was one and alone, he could be known by none but himself, which thing was not sufficient for his glory and divinity, as he could be praised by none.

In order therefore that his glory, majesty and divinity might be seen, known and praised, he created heaven and earth and all that is therein;[4] and made heaven his throne and seat,[5] but gave the earth with all that adorneth it to men, and made them lords of the same, that in it they might learn to know the Creator and Workmaster. Paul, likewise, saith that God's eternal power and Godhead are to be seen in his works from the creation of the world onwards, if one perceiveth and payeth heed and attention to them.[6] Thus it is evident that all of God's creatures, whatever they may be, are given and presented to man, to teach him and lead him to God.

But as soon as man became perverse and turned away from God, the creation, too, became perverse for him, so that what had formerly served for his profit, good and well-being, now on the contrary serveth for his injury. As the wise man saith, "Honey, milk, butter, oil, wheat, corn, flour, bread, cakes, gold, silver, bronze and iron are all made for good to the believer, but to the unbelievers and sinners they are all changed and turned into evil."[7]

Thus, though they should lead him to God, they on the contrary lead and point away from him; and yet it is not now the creation, but the evil will, the taking wrongly and misusing by men, through which they have completely ruined themselves and have become vain, as it is written, "Vain and arrogant are all men who have no knowledge of God; who, out of the good things that are seen, could not know him who is, of himself, from all eternity, and in the created works have not acknowledged and known their Workmaster."[1]

That is the first book, written by God's own finger and given and presented to all of us men, that we may learn therefrom; a book that all men, without exception, can read, be they poor or rich, mighty or lowly, noble or vulgar, learned or unlearned. For all creatures show, point to and prescribe obedience to God, for they all wait upon their Workmaster, obey him and yield their fruit at the right season in accordance with his command. So the disobedient and transgressors of God's commandments are without excuse, for they have known there is a God, yet have not served or thanked him as God, but have sought vain things. Wherefore their foolish heart is darkened, so that thinking themselves wise they have become fools, and have changed the glory of the incorruptible God into a likeness of corruptible man or some other creature.[2] For this reason we fully believe that all such creatures of God, made and created by him to his honour[3] but used by man to his dishonour and shame, will be a witness against those selfsame men at the last judgment to condemn them, so that God's judgment will truly come upon them, and they will then receive even as they have deserved.

WE BELIEVE IN GOD, OUR
ALMIGHTY FATHER

After we had looked around us in every direction,
and found everything to be without strength and
power, so that neither counsel nor help is to be found
save in the one eternal and almighty God, in whom we
found strength, power, might, glory and overflowing
goodness, who can indeed help, protect and give
counsel, we clove, entrusted and gave ourselves to
him that we might receive of his strength and thereby be unburdened and made free, in part, of our
weakness, that we might live unto his righteousness.[1]
We believe firmly and confidently that in him we
have every good gift and eternal life, since we find
we have him who is eternal life.[2] Now since we find
all this in him, we believe in him alone, and place our
heart with complete trust in him, and cleave to him
alone, leaving all things else, and depending on him
with such surety that we know that in him we have
all things.[3] For since he himself, his nature and character, is eternal life and he hath made us partakers
and sharers of the same through the sealing of our
faith with his Holy Spirit, which is the security of
our inheritance; and since we now through his grace
—to him be praise!—are conscious of his working in
us, we are certain and confident of all his promises
and assurances,[4] and firmly believe that he who
cannot lie will fulfil the same, as surely as if they
were already fulfilled.[5] Therefore we also say with
Paul, "Who shall separate us from the love of God?
shall tribulation, or distress, or persecution, or
famine, or nakedness, or peril, or imprisonment or
the sword? For, as it is written, for thy sake we
are killed all the day long; we are counted as sheep
for the slaughter.[6] Nay, in all things we are more
than conquerors through him that loved us. For

I am certain that neither death nor life nor anything created can separate us from the love of God."[1]

It is not, however, as though we of ourselves are so strong, but we firmly and confidently believe that the power and strength which we have found in God hath overcome death, the world, sin and the devil and will keep us faithful, godly and immovable unto the end, to God's glory.

WE ACKNOWLEDGE ALSO JESUS CHRIST, THE ONLY BEGOTTEN SON OF GOD

We have said and acknowledge that God is one,[2] and apart from him there is none that remaineth of himself unchanging in his clarity and who liveth for ever;[3] for he is truth, and that is his name in all eternity.[4] Therefore we acknowledge also his Son, who was in the Father before the world was made, and in whom it was prepared; who modelled all things together with the Father—that is the Word that in the beginning was with God,[5] through whom all things were created, are maintained and shall be completed.[6] Thus, we have the Father and the Son— not, however, two, but one God, for the Son is not without the Father nor is the Father without the Son, for they are not two but one, the Son in the Father and the Father in the Son.[7]

JESUS

This Word proceeded from the Father that the harm wrought by the transgression of Adam might be healed, and the fall restored;[8] he took upon himself human nature and character, became man, became flesh,[9] that even as through a man death came, even so resurrection from the dead and salvation might come through a man.[1]

Now since in him and in none other is salvation,[2] he brought his true name with him: the name given him by the angel before he was conceived in his mother's womb—"Jesus," that is Saviour.[3] He is the Saviour who hath robbed death of its power, torn its bond and snare asunder and set us, his people, free.[4]

CHRIST

Now, since death, which could be crushed and over-powered by the strength of no hero or giant, nor by any human strength, held such sway over us that we were not able to be free, a power other than human strength was necessary. Therefore the Word, that is God himself,[5] although he took upon himself human nature, lost naught of his strength, through which all things were created, that death might thereby be overwhelmed and overcome.

For although the Word put on human nature and became flesh,[6] yet doth the divine nature remain completely in the same, as Paul testifieth, "In him dwelleth all the fullness of the Godhead bodily and in essence."[7] Hence is he also named "Christ" or the anointed of God, as is written of him, "The Spirit of the Lord is upon me; therefore hath he anointed me and sent me to preach the gospel."[8] Thus hath he alone the power to overcome death, and to quicken whom he will[9] and to give of his fullness to whomsoever and in what abundance he will.[10] And those who take from and receive of him become through him likewise "God's anointed" or Christians—failing this, they have the name in vain.

That is the only begotten Son of the Father, come as a light into the world that he might lighten and make bright the darkness in which we were bound and by which we were encompassed,[1] as it is written, "The people which sat in darkness saw great light; and to them which sat in the region and shadow of death a great light is sprung up."[2] And he also himself testifieth, "I am the light of the world; he that believeth in me shall not walk in darkness, but shall have the light of life."[3]

He is the only begotten in that he proceeded in a unique way from the Father, being quite different from all other created things, in that he hath inherited a better name than the angels.[4] For he is the unique power of God by means of which all his holy angels and all other created things were formed, moulded and given shape, therefore hath he from the Father the birthright of the first-born, that every knee should bow and confess that he is Lord, to the glory of God, the Father.[5]

SON

Now, since the Word proceeded forth from Truth and was spoken by Truth it is named the Son, but the Truth which spoke is named the Father, as that from which the Word came. Now it came from God,[6] yet it remained in him,[7] for he is everywhere and in all places, filling the earth with his breadth and with his height reaching unto heaven. A word which proceedeth from a man breaketh away from him because he is weak, but the word that proceedeth from God because of his strength, greatness and power remaineth for ever and ever in him, and can in no way break away from him. Thus are the Word and Truth, or the Son and Father, one;[8] yea, one strength and one nature (although there are two names) [1] which up-holdeth all things, [2] in which also we live and move and are, and without his strength can no one have being; [3] and it is the Son, the brightness of the glory of the Father and the likeness of his nature, who hath now taken us captive into his obedience and leadeth us in his way, teacheth us his character, ways and goodness that he may thereby become more and more known to the children of men. [4]

WE CONFESS CHRIST TO BE LORD

As we know right well that no one can call Jesus Lord except in the Holy Spirit, [5] and that all those who confess him in truth to be Lord must be children of his Spirit or have the same, and since we are not un-aware of his grace which hath been given us by God through him and experienced by us, we likewise con-fess him to be Lord; as, indeed, he truly is, for all power is given him by the Father, not only in heaven but also on earth and in the abyss. [6] For this reason also all unclean spirits fear and tremble before him, [7] for he hath overcome and bound them, and taken from them their power and delivered and set free the prey, namely us, whom they had held captive in death. [8]

But none may in truth give or ascribe to him such glory and honour except he experience such a victory in himself, namely that Christ hath overcome the devil in him also, and rent and removed his snare, that is sin; delivered him, set him free and reconciled him with God. For whosoever else may do so, speaketh not from truth but out of delusion and from an improvised faith, or because others say so, [9] therefore is Christ not confessed to be Lord as is said above by Paul, no man can say that Christ is Lord but by the Holy Spirit. [10] For he in whom Christ is thus to overcome must surrender himself whole-heartedly to him, and endure and suffer his work. Since, however, this is not so, Christ worketh not in the same; therefore doth he remain forever in his sins.

OUR LORD

We confess Christ to be our Lord, since he himself hath bought us with his own blood to be his possession.[1] For through his victory over and overthrow of the devil in his death, he hath liberated, set free and redeemed us from the bonds of the same and reconciled us with God his Father.[2] He hath made of us a royal priesthood for himself and his Father,[3] as well as his dwelling place.[4] He hath now begun to work his work in us that sin, from which he hath redeemed us (though indeed it stirreth within us), may not take control of us and continue to destroy us and lead us to death.[5] Now since he controlleth, ruleth over and useth our members according to his will and thus showeth himself, liveth and doeth all things in us, and since we have completely surrendered our members to him, to wait upon him, to endure his working and to suffer his will, he is rightly our Lord. As Paul saith, "To whom ye yield yourselves servants to obey, his servants ye are to whom ye obey."[6] But such obedience is not the work of men but of God, and this work we find in ourselves (to him be praise!).[7] So in the strength of the same Spirit we call him Lord in truth, and that rightly, for so he is, as he himself saith, "Ye call me Master and Lord: and ye say well; for so I am."[8]

CONCEIVED OF THE HOLY SPIRIT

Now, when the time of compassion drew nigh in which God wanted to fulfil his promise and have mercy on the lost human race, he sent his Word, which was in the beginning in and with him,[1] by means of Gabriel his messenger, to a virgin whom he had aforetime chosen.[2] She, as soon as she believed, was sealed with the Holy Spirit,[3] even as was then told to her: "Power from on high will overshadow thee, and the Holy Spirit will come down from above into thee, therefore also that holy thing which shall be born of thee shall be called the Son of God."[4]

Thus the Holy Spirit worked together with her faith, so that the Word which she believed took from her human nature and became a living fruit.[5] Thus was fulfilled that which God had proposed and undertaken to do, that it might be revealed through what means and in what wise and way God wanted to send his Christ into the world.[6]

For since sin was brought into the world by Adam[7] and passed upon all who were born in a human way of him[8] (as they were commanded by God to multiply, that is, by the mingling of the seed of man and woman),[9] it was necessary that he who was to take away and destroy the sin that had entered the world[10] should have another origin than a human one. Thus we were conceived in the weakness of the flesh and human failing, but he was conceived in the power of God.

For through the mingling and coming together of the Holy Spirit with Mary's faith the Word was conceived and became man.[11] He brought not his human nature with him from heaven, but received and took it from Mary. Therefore doth Paul distinguish the two natures of Christ in this way, "Who was of the seed of David in the flesh, but declared with power a Son of God in the Spirit that maketh holy, from the time that he arose from the dead onwards."[12]

Now, since he entered the world in a way other than the way of Adam, he is likewise a different human being—yea, even one who led and completed his life in the power of God without any inclination to sin.[1] And because he is stronger in power than we and not only we, but even the angels are surpassed by his strength and power, for in him dwelleth really all the fullness of the Godhead.[2] God laid upon him our weakness,[3] as it is written: "For God made him, who knew no sin, to be sin for us,[4] that we being freed from sin might live unto righteousness, for this cause was he sent into the world."[5]

BORN OF THE VIRGIN MARY

Thus we confess that Mary conceived and bore this, her fruit, without loss of her virginity;[6] that during and after his birth she was as much a virgin as she was before, completely untouched;[7] and she, we confess, bore the Saviour of the world,[8] the comfort and hope of all believers and the glory of God the Father;[9] nor was he someone invented and imaginary, but a true and real man,[10] who in all things (sin only excepted) was tempted and tested,[11] proving himself thereby to be really man.[12]

SUFFERED UNDER THE POWER OF PILATE, CRUCIFIED, DEAD AND BURIED

We confess also that, after he had finished the Father's work for which he was sent and had declared to men the Father's name[13] and taught them repentance and faith in God,[14] by the considered counsel of the Father he was given over into the hand

28

of sinners, who, after greatly dishonouring and torturing him, put him to the most disgraceful death, namely that on the cross.[1]

We confess with Peter likewise, that he was put to death in the flesh,[2] that is, in so far as he came of the seed of David,[3] and of Mary, but was made alive in the Spirit;[4] and we say that it was not the divine but the human nature of Christ that died—the divine, that is his nature in so far as it came from heaven, forsook and left the human, that the scripture might be fulfilled which saith, "Thou didst make him for a little while suffer want of God, and didst crown him again with glory and honour."[5] The apostle likewise speaketh the same saying, "For we see that it is Jesus who for a little while suffered the want of angels or of God, and through suffering and death was crowned with glory and honour, for through the grace of God he tasted death for us all."[6] Now, since our transgression and sin so moved the Father[7] that he laid the same upon him and for them gave him into death,[8] we confess that our sins have crucified him. Therefore all who still continue in sin cease not to crucify and mock the Son of God.[9] For he came to take away our sin and destroy the work of the devil.[10] Those, however, who permit not the same to be taken from them, but remain for ever therein, mock his coming into the world and count the blood of the covenant of God an unholy thing; for this reason is his suffering and death no comfort to them but a cause of eternal judgment.[11]

Again, he was taken down from the cross and laid in a grave,[12] that the word which was spoken by him might be fulfilled: "Except a corn of wheat fall into the ground and die, it abideth alone: but if it fall into the ground and die, it bringeth forth much fruit."[13] And for this reason was he laid in the earth and rose again—that all who have fallen asleep and

29

lie in the earth might through him arise and come
forth; as it is written: "The hour is coming, in the
which all that are in the graves shall hear his voice
and shall come forth; they that have done good,
unto the resurrection of life; and they that have
done evil, unto the resurrection of judgment and of
damnation."[1]

DESCENDED INTO HELL

That he might fulfil all things,[2] we confess that he
also went down to the lowest parts of the earth
(namely to the place of captivity, where they are
kept who aforetime believed not the word which was
spoken to them) and proclaimed to the spirits in
prison that the word of salvation had now been sent,[3]
which had previously been resolved upon by God[4]
and promised to men,[5] that all who believe it whole-
heartedly might thereby be set free; and that he had
now, in accordance with the promise given to the
fathers, destroyed the power of death, hell and the
devil, which had for so long betrayed and deceived
them.[6]

ON THE THIRD DAY ROSE
FROM THE DEAD

We confess also that, after he through his death
had destroyed the power of death,[7] he rose again
from the dead through the power of the Father, and
became the first-fruits of them who are to inherit
blessedness,[8] for it was impossible for death to hold
him. As David saith of him, "I have set the Lord
always before my face, for he is at my right hand that
I might not be moved. Therefore is my heart glad
and my tongue rejoiceth, for my flesh also shall rest
secure and in hope. For thou wilt not leave my soul

30

in hell; neither wilt thou suffer thine Holy One to see corruption."[1]

Thus we confess him to be risen from the dead; and that he died and rose again, that he might be Lord of the dead and living.[2] For after he had overcome the devil and death and had risen again,[3] he was given by the Father power, might and royal dignity,[4] as he himself also saith, "All power is given unto me in heaven and on earth."[5]

He was also seen for several days of his disciples, who had before been chosen to be his witnesses,[6] and after his resurrection he ate and drank with them,[7] and gave them the command to gather his bride, community and church, to proclaim repentance and the forgiveness of sins to all nations[8] and to establish the obedience of faith in his name.[9]

ASCENDED INTO HEAVEN, SITTETH AT THE RIGHT HAND OF HIS ALMIGHTY FATHER

We confess also that he ascended up above all heavens,[10] and sat down at the right hand of the strength, might, power, glory and radiance of the Father,[11] which the Word had of him before the foundation of the world was laid.[12] He had, however, divested himself of the same, laid it aside and left it, in that he came into the world in the form of a poor and lowly servant, as Paul saith, "He thought it not robbery to be equal with God, but divested himself of his glory, and took upon himself the form of a servant and became like any other man and was found in fashion as a man."[13]

When, however, he had performed and finished his task, he said, "Glorify thou me again, O Father, with the glory that I had with thee before the world was."[1] For the Word divested himself of radiant glory, became man and took upon himself human nature; and this same human nature, because of its weakness, died, and now in the strength of God liveth and reigneth from eternity to eternity.[2]

Thus hath he received of the Father power, might and birthright, for as the Father hath eternal life in himself, so also hath the Son in himself, and can also give the same to whom he will: that is, to all those who believe in his name, as it is written,[3] "This is the Father's will, which hath sent me, that every one which seeth the Son, and believeth on him, should not be lost but have eternal life."[4]

Because, however, he hath sat down at the right hand of the power of God, and at the same time because he knoweth well our weakness—for he himself (although without sin) was tempted in all manner of ways[5]—is he become our mediator, advocate and reconciler, representing us before the Father,[6] as John testifieth, "We have an advocate with God, Jesus Christ, who is just: and the same is the propitiation for our sins: and not for ours only, but also for the whole world."[7] That is now our comfort, hope and certainty, consoling us in all misery and tribulation, for we know that we have hope in Christ, not only in this world.[8]

FROM WHENCE HE WILL BE A JUDGE OF THE LIVING AND THE DEAD

We confess also that the Father hath committed judgment unto the Son,[9] who will come, and that right terribly, namely with flaming fire, to take vengeance upon all that is ungodly and all the wrong wrought by men,[10] and to render praise, honour and an intransient nature to them, who with patience seek in well doing the eternal, immortal life.[11]

32

But he to whom the Father hath given the power and might to judge[1] speaketh thus, "I judge no man;[2] but the word that I have spoken unto you will judge you in the last day."[3] And this word will justify none save him who hath surrendered with all his heart thereto, and now, in this life, allowed the same to judge, control and guide him. He, however, who hath not listened to the Word and hath been disobedient to it will be condemned.[4]

For this reason we say that when the last trumpets sound, when the Son of Man will come into his glory from heaven with his holy angels,[5] and those who are in their graves will arise[6] to meet him, the sentence of each is already passed,[7] as the word of Christ showeth when he saith, "He that believeth not is condemned already,"[8] and the place prepared, as we see when he speaketh of the last judgment with these words: "When the Son of Man will come in his glory and all the holy angels with him, then shall he sit upon the throne of his glory; and before him shall be gathered all nations; and he shall separate them one from another, as the shepherd divideth the sheep from the goats; and he shall set the sheep on his right hand, but the goats on the left."[9]

Thus we consider it to be clear enough that each one is already judged and sentenced: the devout to life, and the godless to death.[10] It remained only that Christ speak this sentence and show each his place as the words indicate: "Come ye blessed of my Father, inherit the Kingdom prepared for you from the beginning: for I was an hungred, thirsty, naked, a stranger, sick and in prison and ye ministered unto me," and to the others, "Depart from me, ye cursed, into eternal fire, prepared from the beginning for the devil and his angels, for I was in need of your help and ye ministered not unto me."[11]

As Daniel saith, "The judgment was set and the

books were opened,"[1] and after him John testifieth that the dead were judged out of those things which were written in the books, and received according to their works,[2] so we believe with our whole heart that all our words and works, be they good or evil, are preserved before God and his Son as though they were written in a book; and that when the time cometh God will open his secret casket, and will show to each all his doings;[3] as Paul saith, "The day of the Lord will make all things manifest, that each may know why he is or will be blessed or condemned."[4]

WE BELIEVE ALSO IN JESUS CHRIST, HIS ONLY SON, OUR LORD

We believe in Jesus Christ: that our whole salvation and redemption is in him, that he hath stilled the Father's wrath and that through him God is reconciled with the world,[5] as Paul saith, "God was in Christ and reconcileth the world with himself to himself, and imputeth not their sin to them."[6] Thus through him we are reconciled to God, and there is none other name whereby we can be blessed than the name of Jesus Christ of Nazareth.[7]

In the first place we believe that we have redemption in Christ, or that Christ hath redeemed us from the might and snare of the devil wherewith he held us captive; for he hath robbed the devil of his power, overwhelmed and overcome him.[8] And the snares of the devil, wherewith he held us captive, are the sins in which we lay bound, serving the devil by doing the same until Christ came to dwell in us by faith, and through his strength and working in us[9] weakened, quenched, killed and took away sin,[10] that we might be without sins and live unto righteousness.[11] This righteousness, however, he himself worketh and

34

bringeth forth in us, since without him we can do nothing.[1]

Now, since he, the Lord himself, worketh in us and taketh away the sins from which we could not otherwise become free but from which we are now through him so far freed[2] that the sins which we have long served no longer are able to rule over us as heretofore (though they do stir within our members)— he is in truth our redeemer.[3] He, however, who continueth in sins, who lieth therein and is held thereby captive, yet saith that Christ hath redeemed him, is even as a prisoner who lieth bound hand and foot, yet saith he is free. Who would not regard that as folly? For he that saith that he is free and yet is bound, seeketh and desireth all the less to become free. Likewise, also, he who saith that Christ hath redeemed him from sin and yet liveth therein, sheweth thereby that he desireth all the less to become free.[4] But, as we have said, through his coming to us he hath freed us from sin[5] that we might be servants of righteousness.[6]

Now, however, many say—especially the Lutherans —that Christ is their righteousness and goodness, although they still live in all abomination and lasciviousness, which thing is nought else than to draw near to God with the mouth while the heart is far from him;[7] therefore is this a seducing from Christ rather than a confessing of Christ. Why? For men are thereby hindered from seeking the true righteousness which is in Christ Jesus, so that Christ might be their true righteousness, and thus continue in their sins.

But we confess Christ to be our righteousness and goodness because he himself worketh in us the righteousness and goodness through which we become loved of God and pleasing to him;[8] for we have no goodness apart from that which he alone worketh

35

in us,[1] although many say of us that we seek to be good through our own works. To this we say, "No," for we know that all our work, in so far as it is *our* work, is naught but sin and unrighteousness;[2] but in so far as it is of Christ and done by Christ in us, so far is it truth[3]—just and good, loved of God and well-pleasing to him—which thing we are not ashamed to proclaim and declare, for the angel saith to Tobias, "It is good to keep close the secret of a king, but it is honourable to reveal and declare the works of God."[4]

For through this, his actual strength or working, he guideth us into his nature, essence and character.[5] Therefore is it a goodness that maketh blessed and leadeth to God.[6] Thus is Christ our righteousness and goodness, and also our life, for not we ourselves live but Christ liveth in us.[7] Thus is he also our resurrection and salvation and our all in all. We believe likewise that the incarnation of Christ[8] meaneth our transfiguration, and his suffering and death our salvation and life: that in him we have all things.[9]

WE ACKNOWLEDGE THE HOLY SPIRIT

Since the strength, power, nature, character and essence of the godhead are illustrated for us and to be recognized in the creation, the work of God's hand,[10] we say that just as, when one speaketh, one exhaleth and emitteth breath with the word, so that from both the speaker and the spoken word a living breath-wind bloweth and voice proceedeth and is uttered, even so doth the Holy Spirit come from the Father and the Son, or from the Truth and the Word. But as the Son or the Word proceedeth from the Father[11] and yet remaineth in him, the Holy Spirit proceedeth from them both and remaineth in them both for ever and ever.[12]

Thus we acknowledge him, with the Father and the Son, to be God. The names are three, but there is but one God,[1] rich above all who call to him, yea who call to him with trust. For even as fire, heat and light are three names and yet one substance, one nature and essence, even so are God, the Father, Son and Holy Spirit three names and yet but one being. And even as fire, heat and light do not separate or depart one from the other (for where one is, there are all three, and where one is lacking, none is present), even so the Father, Son and Holy Spirit: where one of them is, there they are, all three;[2] but whosoever hath one of them not, lacketh all three.[3] For just as little as one can take heat and light from fire and yet leave fire, even so and still less can one take the Son and Holy Spirit from the Father.

Just as the breath determineth the word and giveth it shape and sound, even so doth the breath, wind and spirit of God make the word living and active within us[4] and leadeth us into all truth.[5] This, yea even this, is the power of God that doeth, worketh and perfecteth all things, confirmeth all things, joineth, comforteth, teacheth and instructeth; and through this, his working in us, assureth us that we are children of God.[6]

WE BELIEVE IN THE HOLY SPIRIT

We believe that in the Holy Spirit we have all comfort, delight and fruitfulness and that he confirmeth, bringeth to pass, carrieth out and perfecteth all things; that he also teacheth, directeth and instructeth us,[7] assureth us that we are children of God,[8] and maketh us one with God, so that through his working we thus become incorporated into and partakers of the divine nature and character.[9] And this his work—God be praised!—we experience within ourselves in truth and power in the renewing of our heart.

In God we have absolute certainty that he hath drawn our heart to him and made it his dwelling place,[1] and removed and cut out from our heart[2] evil, sin and the lust to sin, so that he hath made our heart hang upon his word, to seek, love and with diligence to hear, and not only to hear but also to keep and with all diligence to follow, the same.[3] But all this doeth and worketh in us, we believe, the one Holy Spirit.[4]

THROUGH WHOM IS GATHERED TOGETHER ONE HOLY, CHRISTIAN CHURCH

We confess also that God hath, through Christ, chosen, accepted and sought a people for himself, not having spot, blemish, wrinkle, or any such thing, but pure and holy,[5] as he, himself, is holy.[6] Therefore is such a people, community, assembly or Church gathered and led together by the Holy Spirit, which from henceforth ruleth, controlleth and ordereth everything in her,[7] leading all her members to be of one mind and intention[8] (so that they want only to be like Christ, to partake of his nature, and diligently to do his will[9]), cleaving to him as a bride and spouse to her bridegroom, yea, as one body with him,[10] one plant, one tree, bearing and giving one kind of fruit,[11] as Paul saith, "As many as are led by the Spirit of God, they are the children of God," and again, "The same Spirit assureth us that we are children of God."[12]

Since, then the Church is an assembly of the children of God, as it is written, "Ye are the temple of the living God,"[13] as God hath said, "I will dwell in them and walk in them; and I will be their God and they shall be my people,"[14] "Wherefore come out

38

from among them, and be ye separate, saith the Lord, and touch no unclean thing; and I will receive you, and will be your father, and ye shall be my sons and daughters."[1] The children of God, however, become his children through the unifying Spirit.[2] Thus, it is evident that the Church is gathered together by the Holy Spirit: also that she hath being and is kept in being by him, and that there is no other Church apart from that which the Holy Spirit buildeth and gathereth.

Therefore is the assembly of the unjust and sinners, whores, adulterers, brawlers, drunkards, the covetous, selfish, vain and all those who lie in word and deed, no church of God, and they belong not to him;[3] as Paul saith, "If any man have not the Spirit of Christ he is none of his."[4] Thus is not only their assembly not a Church of Christ, but none of them can be or continue therein unless he repent of his sins, as David saith, "The sinner shall not stand in the congregation of the righteous."[5] After him John also saith, "There shall in no wise enter into it anything that defileth, neither that worketh abomination and lies; but they which are written in the living book of the Lamb.[6] But outside are dogs, sorcerers, and whoremongers, idolators, murderers, and whosoever loveth and maketh a lie."[7]

WHAT THE CHURCH IS

The Church of Christ is the basis and ground of truth, a lantern of righteousness,[8] in which the light of grace is borne and held before the whole world,[9] that its darkness, unbelief and blindness be thereby seen and made light, and that men may also learn to see and know the way of life.[10] Therefore is the Church of Christ in the first place completely filled with the light of Christ as a lantern is illuminated and made

39

bright by the light: that his light might shine through her to others.[1]

And as the lantern of Christ hath been made light, bright and clear, enlightened by the light of the knowledge of God, its brightness and light shineth out into the distance to give light to others still walking in darkness,[2] even as Christ himself hath commanded, "Let your light shine before men, that they may see your good works, and praise God, the Father in heaven."[3] Which thing, however, cannot be other than through the strength and working of the Spirit of Christ within us. As, however, the outward light sheddeth a ray and beam, in accordance with its nature, to give light thereby to men, even so doth the divine light, wherever it hath been lit in a man, give forth its divine ray and beam.[4] The nature of this light, however, is true, divine righteousness, brightness and truth, which is shed abroad by the lantern which is the Church of Christ, more brightly and clearly than by the sun, to give light to all men.[5]

Thus the Church of Christ is, and continueth to be, a pillar and ground of truth,[6] in that the truth itself sheweth and expresseth itself in her, which truth is confirmed, ratified, and brought to pass in her by the Holy Spirit. Thus, whosoever endureth and suffereth the working of the Spirit of Christ is a member of this Church;[7] but whosoever suffereth not this work but alloweth sin to have the rule over him belongeth not to the Church of Christ.[8]

HOW ONE IS LED THERETO

Now, since the Church of Christ is the foundation and ground of truth,[9] and the truth is built upon or entrusted to her, none can or may come thereto, still less dwell and continue therein,[10] except he live and walk in the truth, that is in God, and have the truth in him, and allow only the truth to rule over, guide and carry on its work within him;[1] that from him it may shine and stream out like a light.

As we have said, however, God gathereth together his Church through his Spirit—in no other way can she be gathered together—therefore those who are to gather men to her must have the same Spirit. Therefore Christ, when he desired to send his disciples to gather together his Church, commanded them that they depart not from Jerusalem until they be endued with power from on high, by means of which they should do this work.[2] He gave them an order and method, by means of which order or method they should gather the Church, namely, with word and sign.[3]

For as the covenant of God's grace is a covenant of the knowledge of God, as the word saith, "They shall all know me, from the least even unto the greatest,"[4] it is God's will to call men thereto by his word, and reveal and make himself known to them through the same. For as soon as one believeth his word with all his heart, it is God's will to seal the same in us with his Spirit,[5] who will lead us into all truth and reveal all things to us.[6]

Since, however, Christ would not send out his disciples before they had received the grace of the Holy Spirit,[7] it is clear and manifest that he will not have this order, that is his word and signs, treated lightly and carelessly, but that they should be observed as the Spirit of Christ inspireth, and not simply as the human spirit thinketh.[8] When, however, the word is spoken in the Spirit of Christ[9] and the man is moved thereby and believeth, the sign also should be given him in the same Spirit, but not without the Spirit.[10] Thus, it is the Spirit of Christ and not man that leadeth to the Church. What this

Spirit now buildeth hath also continuance through him, but what a man doeth, as a man, continueth not. Therefore is his work in vain, as David saith, "Except the Lord build the house, they labour in vain that build it."[1]

COMMUNITY OF SAINTS

Every good and perfect gift cometh down from above from the Father of lights, with whom is no variableness nor change to darkness.[2] He giveth and shareth all things with us who believe in him, as Paul saith, "If God be for us, who can be against us?"[3] He that spared not his only begotten Son, but gave him up unto death for us all, how shall he not, with him, also give us all things? Thus the Father desireth to pour out all good things upon those who believe his word and walk justly and faithfully before him; as his promise also showeth when he saith to Abraham, "I am God Shaddai," that is, one with authority and might, fullness to overflowing and sufficiency of all good things, "Walk before me and be steadfast, devout and faithful unto me, and I will make my covenant between me and thee, and will multiply thee exceedingly. And it shall be an eternal covenant, that I may be thy God and thy seed's God after thee eternally."[4] It is as though he saith, "If thou holdest to me and doest and keepest my will, thou shalt have all good things in me, yea, I shall give thee all that is useful and lovely."[5] Even as the Father is the fullness of all good things, hath he given it to the Son to be so likewise, as it is written, "For it pleased the Father that in him should all fullness dwell,"[6] and again, "The Word became flesh and dwelt among us, and we beheld his glory, the glory as of the only begotten of the Father, full of grace and truth,"[1] and again, "In him dwelleth all the fullness of the Godhead in essence, and ye are full of the same."[2]

We, however, become partakers of this grace of Christ through faith in the truth, as Paul saith, "And Christ dwelleth in your hearts through faith."[3] Such faith, however, cometh from the hearing of the preaching of the gospel.[4] Thus through attentive hearing and observing of the gospel we become partakers of the community of Christ, as may be recognized from the words of John, when he saith, "That which we have seen and heard declare we unto you, that ye also may have fellowship with us, and our fellowship is with God the Father and with his Son, Jesus Christ, our Lord,"[5] who hath given us all things that he hath heard and received of his Father.[6]

Community, however, is naught else than that those who have fellowship have all things in common together, none having aught for himself, but each having all things with the others,[7] even as the Father hath nothing for himself, but all that he hath he hath with the Son,[8] and again, the Son hath nothing for himself, but all that he hath, he hath with the Father and all who have fellowship with him.[9]

Thus all those who have fellowship with him likewise have nothing for themselves, but have all things with their Master and with all those who have fellowship with them,[10] that they might be one in the Son as the Son is in the Father.[11]

It is called the community of saints because they have fellowship in holy things, yea, in those things whereby they are sanctified, that is in the Father and the Son, who himself sanctifieth them with all that he hath given them.[12] Thus everything serveth to the betterment and building up of one's neighbour and to the praise and glory of God the Father.[13]

43

THE FORGIVENESS OF SINS

We acknowledge also that as Christ received from the Father might and power to forgive the sins of whom he will, he hath likewise committed power to his bride, spouse, consort and Church,[1] as he himself saith, "Receive ye the Holy Ghost: whose soever sins ye remit here on earth, they are remitted also in heaven; and whose soever sins ye retain here on earth, they are retained also in heaven."[2] Thus the words of Christ show that he giveth his Church power here on earth to forgive sins.

But that this power and key is given to the Church and not to individual persons is shown by the words of Christ when he saith, "If thy brother sin against thee, go and tell him his fault between thee and him alone: if he hear thee, thou hast won his soul. But if he will not hear thee, then take with thee one or two more, that in the mouth of two or three witnesses every word may be established. And if he neglect to hear them, tell it unto the Church, but if he neglect to hear the Church, regard him as a taxgatherer and sinner."[3]

Here it is, indeed, allowed the individual, if aught be done against him personally, to forgive his brother if he bettereth his way; but the full power of the key of Christ, that is to exclude and to accept, hath he not given to individuals, but to the whole Church.[4] Therefore whatsoever she excludeth is excluded, but whatsoever she forgiveth is forgiven here and in eternity, and apart from her there is no forgiveness, no goodness, no healing and salvation, no true comfort or hope.[5] For within her and not without her is and dwelleth the Father, Son and Holy Ghost who maketh all things good, and justifieth.[6]

44

WE ACKNOWLEDGE ALSO THE RESURRECTION
OF THE BODY

We acknowledge also that at the time of the last trumpets the Lord himself shall descend from heaven with a shout, with the voice of the archangel.[1] Then they that are in the graves shall rise and come forth; they that have done good to the resurrection of life, but the evil and sinners to the resurrection of judgment,[2] and with an incorruptible body,[3] shall appear before the countenance of the terrible Judge,[4] who will show and appoint to each his place, that he may receive the reward of the good or evil which he hath done now in his life.[5]

AND ETERNAL LIFE

"This," saith Christ, "is life eternal, that they might know thee, the only true God, and Jesus Christ whom thou hast sent."[6] Thus, in those who have the right and true faith, eternal life beginneth here and now and continueth until the time to come, when only it will be properly and fully revealed, as Paul testifieth saying, "Now we see truth reflected as in a mirror, in a word that is difficult to understand, but then we shall see from face to face; now we know partially; but then shall we know even as we are known."[7]

John agreeth likewise therewith when he saith, "Now we are the children of God, and it hath not yet appeared what we shall be. But we know that when he shall appear, we shall be like him; for we shall see him even as he is."[8] Now as it is really so that we shall see God from face to face,[9] and know God, who is eternal life and who maketh us eternal and to live eternally, we, who know him and see him from face to face, shall rejoice with him with eternal joy.[10]

Because, however, corruption cannot inherit incorruption, but corruption must put on incorruption and what is mortal immortality,[1] he who would rise again to life must here be born through faith in the truth to eternal life.[2] If we suffer this working of God here, then the Lord will there transfigure our insignificant body, so that it may become like his glorified body,[3] so that we may see his glorious brightness.[4] Thus we shall be where he is and all our joy shall be in him alone,[5] where suffering, sorrow and pain will touch us no more.[6]

Now we have told what we confess to be the essentials of true Christian faith, and we can also say freely with an upright and confident heart "To God alone be glory!" As we have now confessed with the mouth we believe with all our heart that through faith we may become righteous and blessed.[7]

WHAT FAITH IS

Faith is not the empty illusion that those men think who only bear it about with them in their mouths, and know no more about it; who think that Christianity is in words only, and therefore hold and regard each and all as Christians, no matter how they live, if they but confess Christ with the mouth.

True and well-founded faith, however, is not of men but a gift of God,[8] and is given only to those who fear God.[9] Therefore Paul saith, "Not every man hath faith."[10] For such faith seeketh that which doth not appear, and graspeth the invisible one and only mighty God, and maketh us at one and at home with him,[11] yea of his nature and character.[12] It dispelleth all wavering and doubt,[13] and maketh our heart hold surely, steadfastly and firmly to God, through all tribulation.[14]

Therefore it maketh us certain and well assured of

46

all God's promises, just as—to speak in parables—a man who taketh an object in his hand and holdeth it, as long as he doth hold it, is certain that he hath it. In the same way faith graspeth the promise of God which is invisible, and cleaveth and holdeth to the same as though it saw it.[1]

Therefore faith is a real divine power, which reneweth man and maketh him like God in nature, maketh him living in his righteousness, and ardent in love, and in keeping his commandments.

In order to make no one uneasy, we want to say why we give or ascribe such power to faith. This we do because faith is God's gift, and given to men that they might thereby seek and find God; who, when he hath been found, stirreth up and worketh all things in them through faith, so that in believers, in proportion to their faith, nought taketh place save what God worketh in men,[2] as Paul saith, "Not I, but the grace of God,"[3] and again, "Not I live now, but Christ liveth in me."[4]

Thus faith is also given victorious strength, as it is written, "And our faith is the victory that overcometh the world,"[5] as indeed God doth in us through faith. Thus faith doeth and worketh all things, and maketh man pleasing to and loved by God.

FROM WHENCE FAITH COMETH

According to the words of Paul, this faith cometh from a diligent hearing of the preaching of the word of God, which is proclaimed by the mouth of God by means of those whom he sendeth.[6] Here, however, we speak not of the literal, but of the living word that pierceth soul and spirit,[7] which God hath given and put in the mouth of his messengers.[8] The same word maketh wise unto salvation,[9] that is it teacheth to know God;[10] and from the knowledge of God faith springeth up, groweth and increaseth, and with faith knowledge.[1] These entwine and grow together and lead man to God, and plant the same in God,[2] so that he that hath such faith liveth and walketh in God, and God in him.[3]

The more zealously we hear and receive the word, the more doth knowledge grow. The more knowledge groweth, or the more we know God, the more do faith and trust in him grow. And the more we believe in him, the more doth he show himself to us, and giveth himself to us to know.[4] Where, however, such faith which doeth all this in man is not present, there is no faith but an empty delusion and darkness, by means of which men betray and deceive themselves. We have now made confession of our faith, and want next to give a faithful account, according to the grace God giveth us, of what we teach.

CONCERNING DOCTRINE

"Ye shall not add unto the word which I command you, neither shall ye diminish aught from it,[5] for I will be thy mouth, and teach thee what thou shalt do."[6] Therefore ought and must the teaching of Christ be guided only by the Holy Spirit, without any mixture of human understanding and desire;[7] as Peter saith, prophecy ariseth not from the will of man, but holy men of God spake at the urge of the Holy Spirit.[8] As it was in the days of old it must still be, that men speak not of themselves but let the Holy Spirit speak and teach in them or through them; as Christ saith, "It is not ye that speak, but my Father's Spirit will speak through you."[9] It must be so still if the word is to bring forth fruit.

Therefore was it that Christ did not want his disciples to go out until they had been endued with strength from on high and had received the Holy

Spirit;[1] therefore are all who await not this gift from God, but run of themselves before the time and without this grace, whether for the sake of worldly honour or possessions, even those of whom the Lord saith, "I have not sent these prophets, yet they ran: I have not spoken to them, yet they prophesied."[2] For this reason is their preaching fruitless, and their doctrine is not Christ's.

If it is to bring forth fruit, it must, as hath been said above, be done in the Holy Spirit and be placed by the same in the right order, that it may touch men in the right place,[3] hit the mark and pierce the heart like a two-edged sword;[4] for where the right order is not observed in doctrine it is not guided by the Spirit of Christ, but by human understanding and presumption. Therefore doth it bring forth neither fruit nor betterment, even though one trumpeteth the entire scriptures before men.

ORDER IN DOCTRINE

If one will preach in the right order the doctrine of Christ, which is given to man for his profit, betterment and edification,[5] one must first bring God in his omnipotence before the man, that he may recognize this and thereby learn to commit himself in trust to God; next, why man was created and made in God's likeness;[6] then how he forsook the same,[7] fell into sin and thereby was led to death.[8] Then when man, himself, is brought before his eyes, that he may know what he is and to what he hath come, and how deeply he hath sunk himself into death and eternal destruction through sin, one must once more bring before him the grace offered to all men by Christ, and show him how and in what way man can find it and be grafted into Christ. Then when the man hath partaken of this grace of Christ one must continue to

49

exhort him to stand firmly therein,[1] and to grow and become more complete daily.[2] Thus man is guided to the right way and made to cleave to God.

WHAT WE TEACH CONCERNING GOD

Firstly we teach that there is a God,[3] and that the same hath shown himself to be God by the works of his hands, by means of which he teacheth us still to-day and sheweth us his glory;[4] therefore do we with all zeal point out and bring the same before the eyes of men in all the creatures, the work of his hands, and then we testify with the power of his words that he only and alone is God,[5] a wellspring of all good things, who showeth kindness to all who seek him with all their heart,[6] and is found by the humble, contrite and broken heart.[7] He is not slow to do good through his beloved Christ to them who draw nigh to him, as hath been shown to some extent and recounted in the above confession, so for the sake of shortness we will not repeat it here.

CONCERNING IDOLATRY

Now, since there is one sole God from whom everything cometh,[8] man ought to set all his hope and comfort on him alone,[9] seek all healing and salvation in him through Christ,[10] follow him only, obey him and seek diligently to please him,[11] that is, cleave to God alone.[12] The opposite of this is idolatry.

Therefore is everything idolatry in which man seeketh salvation, comfort and help apart from God, whether it be in the saints or any other created thing, for thereby is God robbed of his honour. If man forgetteth to find refuge in God and fleeth to created things he maketh an idol of the same. For this reason Daniel refused to obey the counsel of the

50

Chaldeans to leave off seeking refuge in God and to seek and have it alone in the king.[1]

It is from this glorification and love of created things that images come, as the wise man showeth and saith, "It is as one who previously had had a son whom he loved, and when he died made a likeness of him and beginneth to worship as a god him who a short time before had lived as a man."[2] Thus have men followed error,[3] in that they have forgotten God and been led away from him,[4] therefore saith he: "The beginning of all fornication and forsaking of God is in the devising of shameful images;[5] therefore are all their makers cursed together with the work of their hands."[6]

But not in this alone, but in all that a man loveth more than God—whether wife, child, house, farm, money, goods or even himself—doth he practise idolatry, for he raiseth it above God and forsaketh for it the commandments and will of God, and giveth himself up to sin and taketh his heart from God[7] or turneth it away from him and setteth it upon created things.[8] This is the true forsaking of God and setting up of other gods.[9]

We say as well as this, that whosoever calleth upon the saints to help him, or to pray to God for his salvation, denieth thereby that Christ is his intermediary and advocate with God, and fleeth to what can neither speak for nor help him, for there is no other salvation and no other name given to men wherein they may be blessed, except in the name of Jesus Christ of Nazareth.[10]

WHY GOD CREATED MAN

Further, we teach that God made and created man solely for his honour,[11] and therefore gave him above all creatures reason, understanding and sense that he might know him and his will aright, and observe[1] and keep the same with diligence;[2] that he might cleave to God and seek, love and honour him alone.

For it is God's honour when the work of his hands remaineth in the condition in which he hath created and placed it and suffereth naught to move it therefrom. Thus God created man a heavenly being and placed in him what is divine, that he might set his mind upon what is heavenly and of God,[3] that he might seek and love, consort with and cleave to the heavenly and divine. For this purpose also hath he given him a heavenly body,[4] that is, the breath and spirit of God,[5] that it might lead the earthly body, that which was taken from the earth, to God.

The heavenly body should honour and glorify God through the earthly body in that it inspireth and urgeth it to abide in the state in which God hath placed it, that is in seeking and doing what is of God, as Paul also admonisheth us all, saying, "Set your affection on things above, and not on things on earth."[6] Even as it is to God's honour to abide in his condition or order, so is it to his dishonour to depart from and forsake the same.[7] And indeed the whole creation save man hath remained in its order, and waiteth for the word of its master, to fulfil the same. Only he to whom precedence and glory were given above all creatures hath forsaken his place and left the order in which he was set.[8] Well ought he therefore to turn again with all haste.[9]

THAT GOD CREATED MAN IN HIS LIKENESS

We teach that God, who is eternal truth, created and moulded man in his likeness, as he himself saith, "Let us make man, formed after our likeness."[10] That is a glorious likeness, one truly that we should all rejoice over and desire. Let none, however, be so foolish as to think that the Godhead is like flesh and blood or that flesh and blood is a likeness or similitude of the Godhead, for that hath been taken from the earth and is of the earth.[1] The likeness of God, however, is from heaven and is heavenly. Thus the whole of a man's life should show forth God's likeness.

WHAT GOD'S LIKENESS IS

"God," saith Christ, "is a Spirit"[2]—not, however, a spirit of lying, but of truth,[3] for which reason, as hath been said, the likeness of God is not flesh and blood but spirit. Now since man hath been created after this likeness and should bear this likeness,[4] it is therefore God's will that he should not be carnally minded but spiritually minded.[5] For this reason God breathed upon him the breath of his mouth, gave him the spirit of his truth and likeness of his glory to rule over the earthly body, to prove and show forth his nature through it, and in so doing glorify the Creator.[6]

For God the Lord breathed upon man and he received a living soul. This wind and breath of God, which came from God and was given to man, is the true likeness, the similitude of God, of his character and nature.[7] Now since man was given of the spirit of truth, he was created and given his place in truth that he might live and walk therein, which truth is God himself, whose likeness he should bear and show forth. So long therefore as man liveth and walketh in truth and in obedience to God, suffering the Spirit to rule, lead and control him, so long hath he and so long doth he bear God's likeness.[8] As soon, however, as he forsaketh the same and suffereth the flesh to control and drive him, he casteth from him God's likeness. Then he cannot please God, as Paul saith, "They that are in the flesh cannot please God."[9]

53

OF THE LIKENESS OF THE DEVIL

Now as God is the Spirit of truth, the devil is contrariwise the spirit of lying and father of the same. Wherefore lying, sin and injustice, or the spirit of lies is a similitude of the devil wherewith he adorneth his children, even as God adorneth his with truth, that one might distinguish one from the other,[1] as John declareth, "In this we recognize who are the children of God and who are the children of the devil."[2] Now he that chooseth sin taketh upon himself the likeness of the devil and forsaketh the likeness of God.[3]

HOW ADAM FORSOOK THE LIKENESS OF GOD AND FELL INTO SIN

Adam bore and had the true likeness of God, therefore was he made by God a lord and ruler of all other things created, which God made subject to his will,[4] save the tree of knowledge and of the recognition of evil and good,[5] through which God the Lord desired to prove man, to see if he wanted to abide in his obedience and will. For through this command or prohibition God desired to show man and to impress upon his inner being that even as he was made by God lord over all things created,[6] even so was God Lord over him, one to whom he should cleave, one whom he should serve and obey as his Lord, Father and Creator.[7]

Man, however, deceived and beguiled by the counsel of the serpent, forsook such obedience and so cast from him the likeness of God,[8] that is God's righteousness, purity and holiness; and spotted himself with sin,[9] the similitude of the devil whom he obeyed. Here some say, indeed, that the serpent is the presumption and will of the flesh; we, however, desire not to say so for at that time there was naught of evil in man. Therefore we teach that the devil himself in the form of a serpent deceived and beguiled man,[1] and that the presumption of the flesh grew out of the serpent's counsel and raised itself up in man, as is then clearly seen. When Eve heard the words of the serpent she beheld the fruit. As soon, however, as she perceived that it made one clever and wise, presumption was roused and grew in the woman,[2] for she desired to be more clever than she had been made, and so through her beholding came a lust for the forbidden fruit, which when it was achieved and carried out in deed brought forth sin in her,[3] as James showeth, "When lust hath conceived, it bringeth forth sin: and sin, when it is finished, bringeth forth death."[4]

Now because she and her husband, urged on by her, transgressed the command, sin was brought into the world, and death by sin, and passed upon all men.[5] As soon, however, as the transgression took place their eyes were opened and they saw that they were naked,[6] that is, stripped and emptied by the serpent's counsel of all God's grace. Thus they knew evil and good, that is they knew how wrong, wicked and evil it was to transgress the command and forsake the word of the Creator,[7] and how holy, how good and profitable it was to keep the same.[8] Now because they perceived and saw that they had made the Creator wroth, shame and dread, fear and trembling came upon them,[9] and because they had been deceived and overcome by the devil, sin planted the devil's likeness in them and clove for ever to them.[10] Therefore the wrath of the Creator came upon them and all their seed, nor could it be removed save through the promised seed, Christ.

WHAT SIN IS

Sin is, in essence, the forsaking of obedience to God, or disobedience,[1] and from this all else that is wrong hath come, as branches grow from a tree.[2] Evil hath now taken the upper hand in the world[3] and still increaseth daily, so that men proceed from iniquity to iniquity,[4] because they have yielded and committed their members to serve sin.[5]

Now all unrighteousness is sin,[6] as John saith, but disobedience is the mother of all sin. For as, through obedience, all the righteousness of God cometh through Christ, so also cometh all sin and unrighteousness from disobedience to, and the forsaking of, God's command.[7]

CONCERNING ORIGINAL SIN

Just here there ariseth oft very much quarrelling and strife, for the one wanteth this and the other that; from which strife cometh more destruction than betterment, for since God is not a God of quarrelling but a God of peace and of love,[8] he hath no pleasure in strife, neither hath he aught to do with the same, hence there is naught therein save destruction.

Now, therefore, we confess and teach that all men[9] save Christ only have a sinful nature which they inherit from Adam,[10] as it is written, "The imagination and desire of man's heart is evil from his youth."[11] David saith likewise, "Behold I was shapen in iniquity; and in sin did my mother conceive me."[12] Paul speaketh clearly, and saith, "By one man sin entered into the world and passed upon all men."[13] Because then it hath come upon us all from him, it is thereby clear that we have inherited it from him.

WHAT ORIGINAL SIN IS

But the inheritance that we all have from our father, Adam, is the inclination to sin: that all of us have by nature a tendency toward evil and to have pleasure in sin.[1] This inheritance manifesteth and showeth itself in all the children of Adam—all who are born after and according to Adam—and removeth, devoureth and consumeth all that is good and of God in man; so that none may attain it again except he be born again.[2]

This inheritance Paul nameth the messenger of Satan, who striketh him on the head or buffeteth him with fists,[3] and speaketh thereby of the movement of the sinful inclination which stirreth in him, as in all men. Therefore saith John also, "He who saith he hath no sin, deceiveth himself, and the truth is not in him,"[4] and speaketh thereby of the inheritance which we all have from Adam, which he calleth sin;[5] as also David saith in the Book of Psalms: "In sin was I conceived and born."[6] Thus through Adam we have all become sinful and must be justified once more through Christ, if we would have life with him.[7]

THE HARM WROUGHT BY ORIGINAL SIN

Original sin, we say, is firstly the cause of physical death for men, for originally they were created and placed in life, so that there was naught corrupt in them. For God did not make death.[8] Since, however, we have all inherited sin, all, both young and old, must taste of death. In truth if Christ were not sent and come into the world, there would be no more hope of life.

Because, however, it was planned from the beginning by the Father, and because Christ hath come into the world and become the reconciliation[9] not only for us but also for the whole world,[1] we believe that he hath brought it about that original sin, before it stirreth within man leading to further sin, now causeth physical death only and not eternal, that the word might be fulfilled: The children shall not bear the iniquity of the fathers, but he who sinneth shall himself die.[2] Accordingly, we say that God also accepteth little children, as such, for indeed Christ is also their reconciler.[3]

Secondly, we say that original sin is also the cause of eternal death to man, in that it leadeth, guideth and bringeth man into all sins, and through it we do much sin; for this is the sin that stirreth up, rouseth and bringeth to pass all other sins within us, as Paul declareth when he saith, "Sin, that it might appear sin, worketh death in me by that which is good, that it might become exceedingly sinful by the commandment."[4]

Thus, therefore, all men have died in Adam,[5] fallen away from God and forsaken him,[6] as it is written, "There is none righteous, no, not one. There is none that understandeth, there is none that asketh after God. They have all gone out of the way, and are become good for nothing; there is none that doeth good, no, not one. Their throat is an open sepulchre; with their tongues have they used deceit; the poison of asps is under their lips; whose mouth is full of cursing and bitterness; their feet are swift to shed blood; destruction and misery are in their ways: and the way of peace have they not known; there is no fear of God before their eyes."[7] Thus we show men how far they have estranged themselves from God and submerged themselves in their sin.

We show them also that all sin hath its source and origin in wrong taking,[8] that man taketh what he should not and what is not his and leaveth what he ought to take,[9] loveth what he ought to hate and hateth what he ought to love.[1] Thus man is turned aside and led away from God by that which should point and lead him to God, teach him to know God and show him God.[2] Thus, if one would come to God he must leave and deny what he hath previously wrongly taken, that is, all that is temporal and transitory, to cleave to God alone. This is the true repentance that the Lord demandeth and desireth.[3]

NOW FOLLOWETH HOW MAN MAY AGAIN FIND GOD AND HIS GRACE

CONCERNING REMORSE

Now those who seek further counsel as to how to free their souls from the eternal destruction and death into which they are led by sin;[4] desiring to free themselves from their sins, which are the snares of the devil,[5] and partake of the grace of Christ—such we teach, together with John, the preacher of repentance, Peter and the apostles, that they must repent. But he who would truly repent with all his heart must first feel real remorse for his sin.[6] But if he is to feel remorse for his sins he must first recognize how wrong, evil, harmful and destructive they are.[7] Without this, remorse and repentance cannot endure —still less can he receive grace. For true remorse followeth the recognition of sin.[8] The man feeleth real repugnance, hatred and horror of his sin,[9] yea, real loathing of himself for having so long obeyed it, for having suffered himself to be guided and controlled by it[10] and led away from the God for whose sake he hath being.[11]

Now he who is sorry for his sin and regretteth having obeyed it ought and must from henceforth all the more diligently and earnestly guard himself against it, and flee from it as from a serpent.[12] For true remorse effecteth diligent care, attention and watchfulness lest sin creep in again upon him and once more have dominion over him.[1] Even as one saith, "A burnt child dreadeth the fire." And in truth it is so that he who once burneth himself doth not again lightly touch fire. So, and much more so, will he who hath once recognized sin guard and watch himself against it, for it burneth to eternal death, and destroyeth.[2] He who fleeth not from it, however, who hateth it not with all his heart, showeth thereby that he hath not yet really recognized it aright, and knoweth not what harm it doeth him; for were this so he would take it more in earnest.[3] For the man who hath once recognized it aright would henceforth sooner die than willingly and with his heart consent to sin in word, let alone in deed; on the contrary all the days of his life he would regret the sin already committed,[4] whereby he roused the wrath of God, his Creator.[5]

CONCERNING REPENTANCE

Thus remorse leadeth to true repentance, that is real humiliation and abasement before God because of the transgression. For repentance meaneth to humble and abase oneself before God, and to be ashamed before him because of one's vice;[6] which shame bringeth a real turning point, so that the man runneth with haste, calleth, crieth and prayeth to God for forgiveness and grace,[7] and beginneth at the same time to bring the flesh into subjection, to slay and kill it, to break it in, bridle it and feed it with hyssop.[8] For recognized sin filleth the conscience with fear and leaveth it no peace. But the uneasy conscience seeketh, searcheth and asketh where help, counsel and healing may be found, as David saith, "I lifted up mine eyes unto the hills to see from whence help would come to me, even so cometh my help from the Lord who hath made heaven and earth."[1] Every anxious, troubled, fearful, broken and contrite heart, if it flee to him, will find with him peace and comfort. As it is written, "Upon whom shall I look but upon him who is of a broken and contrite spirit."[2]

We point out also thereby that no such death-bed remorse and repentance as the world hath, which saith to-day, "I am sorry for my sin" and yet doeth the same again to-morrow, can stand before God and receive grace; but only that which proceedeth from a sincere heart. To such an one will God draw nigh, and will both begin and bring to perfection his work in him.[3]

MAN IS GRAFTED INTO CHRIST

To such a fearful and anxious heart, that is sorry for its sin and knoweth not where to turn in its distress, so that the world itself is too strait for it and it lifteth up its heart to God alone[4]—to such an one will God show himself, and will comfort him in his sorrow, showing him his Son who saith, "Come unto me all ye that are heavy laden, and I will refresh you. Take my yoke upon you for it is easy and light."[5] He calleth to us in this way, however, through the servants whom he hath chosen from the world[6] to be his witnesses.[7] Those who hear his voice and come to him he will in no wise cast out.[8]

We teach further, that Christ came into the world to make sinners blessed,[9] as it is written, "This is the Father's will, that every one which seeth the Son and believeth in him should not be lost but have everlasting life";[10] and that man through faith might be planted and grafted into Christ. This, however, taketh place as follows: as soon as the man heareth

61

the gospel of Christ and believeth the same from his heart, he is sealed with the Holy Spirit, as also Paul saith, "After that ye believed, ye were sealed with the Spirit of the promise, that is with the Holy Spirit, which is the pledge of our inheritance, the pledge of the redemption of us, who are his property, for the praise of his glory."[1] This Spirit of Christ which is promised and given to all believers maketh them free from the law or power of sin, and planteth them into Christ,[2] maketh them of his mind, yea, of his character and nature, so that they become one plant and one organism together with him:[3] he the root or stem, we the branches, as he himself saith, "I am the true vine, ye, however, are the branches."[4] Thus we are one substance, matter, essence, yea, one bread and body with him[5]—he the head, but we all members one of the other.[6] Now, because Christ is the root and the vine and we are grafted into him through faith, even as the sap riseth from the root and maketh the branches fruitful, even so the Spirit of Christ riseth from the root, Christ, into the branches or twigs to make them all fruitful. Hence the twigs are of the same character as the root, and bear only corresponding fruit,[7] as Christ himself saith in the parable, "No man gathereth figs from thistles, or grapes from thorns. No good tree can bring forth evil fruit, neither can a corrupt tree bring forth good fruit, but each tree bringeth forth fruit of its own kind."[8] Now since Christ is a good tree and vine, naught but what is good can or may grow, flourish and be fruitful in him.[9]

Thus doth man become one with God, and God with him, even as a father with his son, and is gathered and brought into the Church and community of Christ, that he with her might serve and cleave to God in one Spirit,[10] and be the child of the covenant of grace, which is confirmed by Christ.[11]

62

CONCERNING GOD'S COVENANT

God's covenant is an eternal covenant, which is from the beginning, continueth in eternity and ceaseth not. It implieth that it is his will to be our God and Father, and that we should be his people and loved children, and that he desireth through Christ to fill us at all times with every divine blessing and with all that is good.[1]

That such a covenant of God was from the beginning is shown in God's creating man in his own likeness,[2] so that all was well with him and there was none of the poison of destruction in him.[3] Even when man was deceived and robbed of this likeness by the counsel of the serpent,[4] the purpose of God endured none the less,[5] and the covenant which he had previously made—that he should be our God and that we should be his people[6]— expresseth this clearly with a promise, in that it threateneth to take away the devil's power through the woman's seed.[7] From this it can well be seen and known that it was God's intention to redeem us from this power and restore us and accept us as his children.[8]

Thus hath God made his covenant firstly with Adam[9] and then also with Abraham and his seed, the latter with more definite words than the former;[10] and now hath he made it with us through Christ and established and confirmed it through his death.[11] For as a testament is not valid except through the death of him who maketh it, even so did God give his Son into death,[12] that we, redeemed from death through him, might be the children of his covenant and that the same might be ours eternally.[13]

CONCERNING THE OLD COVENANT

The old covenant, in so far as it is called old, is that which was given to Israel without the pouring out of the Spirit of grace, for which reason also their obstinate heart was not circumcised and sin not taken from them[1] as the apostle showeth, "It is not possible that the blood of bulls and goats should take away sins."[2] With this Esdras also agreeth saying, "When thou leddest the seed of Israel out of Egypt, thou broughtest them up to the Mount Sinai, and bowing the heavens, thou didst set fast the earth, and madest the earth to quake and the depths to tremble, and terrifiedst the men of that age. And thy glory went through four gates, of fire, of earthquake, of wind and of cold; that thou mightest give the law unto the seed of Jacob and diligence unto the generation of Israel. And yet tookest thou not away from them a wicked heart, that thy law might bring forth fruit in them."[3]

Now because the heart was not changed by all this, and the people remained the same old people, it was no testament of sonship, but one of servitude, as indeed Paul doth term it, when he speaketh of the two covenants in the terms of two women saying, The covenant from the Mount Sinai gendereth to bondage and is in bondage with her children.[4]

Although it gendereth to bondage, yet is it the bringing in of something better and more perfect. Now, because something better is come, that is, the covenant of God is more clearly and perfectly revealed and come fully to the light, that which is dark and imperfect must cease and come to an end.[5]

"Wherefore also Moses," saith Paul, "put a veil over his face that the children of Israel could not look to the end of that which ceaseth."[6]

But that it ceaseth is testified by the apostle in

that he saith, "In that God promiseth a new covenant, he maketh the first old. Now that which decayeth and waxeth old is near its end."[1] Not that God's covenant is finished and done with, but the imperfect revelation and darkness of the same is ended and ceaseth that the covenant itself might be revealed in its strength and clarity and brought to light, as hath been done in Christ. Thus the apostle nameth the new better,[2] because of the overflowing clarity of its revelation.[3] Of which more later.

CONCERNING THE LAW

The law is the testimony or word which beareth witness to the old covenant, that is the covenant of bondage,[4] and is therefore called a yoke of bondage,[5] doing naught but driving, commanding and demanding, and yet on account of its weakness not able to give but only to demand and to require.[6] For where the Spirit doth not accompany the word, it is impossible to attain the righteousness that standeth before God.[7]

Nevertheless, it showeth, pointeth out and maketh men conscious of sin; striketh, breaketh and terrifieth the conscience, that by so doing men might be moved to seek and ask for something better.[8] Wherefore is the law our schoolmaster until we are in Christ,[9] through whom the promise of the Father is poured out on all who believe in his name,[10] which promise is the Spirit of grace through whom, if we suffer him to rule and lead us, we are set free from the law,[11] as Paul saith, "If ye walk in the Spirit, ye are no more under the law."[12] Thus is Christ the end of the law; whoever believeth in him is righteous.[13]

Christ is not the end of the law, however, in that sense that God's law is done with and ceaseth, for Paul saith, "Do we then make void the law through faith? God forbid, yea, we establish the law."[1] There-fore the law, in so far as it is spiritual, is not made void, but its true spiritual nature is established and ordained and it is led to true fulfilment and perfec-tion in accordance with God's will by the Spirit of Christ.[2] Therefore it is only the law in so far as it is summed up in writing, in the letter, which is done away with by Christ,[3] because the letter killeth; for Christ hath given us his Spirit, who performeth with-in us all that God willeth with joy, and not from the coercion and force of the commandment.[4] Thus we are no more under the law, and yet we are not with-out God's law.[5] Now all that is expressed in words, in so far as it is of the letter, whether it was written by Paul, Peter or any other from among the apostles, we call law and command, for so it is. For that letter, likewise, doeth naught but kill, like the letter of the law of Moses. In so far as it is spiritual, however, and treated and accepted spiritually, it is a word of grace, even though written by Moses.[6] Therefore those who have not the Spirit of Christ cannot be servants of the gospel, but only of the letter of the law.[7]

CONCERNING THE GOSPEL

The gospel, however, is glad tidings from God and Christ, which is proclaimed, treated and accepted through the Holy Spirit.[8] Therefore it is a word of liberty, that setteth free and maketh devout and blessed,[9] as Paul saith, "It is the power of God, making all those blessed who believe therein."[10] And again, "That is the true grace of God wherein ye stand, by which also ye will be blessed if ye retain it as ye have received it."[11]

This word showeth us that God hath given and restored his promised grace through Christ;[12] it maketh

66

us heirs of the same grace and sharers in its fellowship.[1] Thereby doth it raise up again the conscience that hath been beaten down by the law, and accomplisheth that which the law demandeth but is unable to achieve; it maketh man at one with God,[2] begetteth us as sons,[3] so that man becometh a new creature[4] and of divine nature.[5]

This, however, is not moulded and imprinted in stone or on paper, but in the fleshy tables of the heart; not with pen and ink, but with the finger of God, with his Holy Spirit,[6] as God hath promised, saying, "I will write my law in their hearts and put it in their inward members, that none need say to his brother, 'Know the Lord,' for they shall all know me from the least of them unto the greatest."[7] That is the living word, piercing soul and spirit,[8] of whom all who would inherit the promise must be born.

CONCERNING THE NEW COVENANT

Since the old covenant cometh to an end on account of its darkness and imperfection,[9] God hath established, revealed and brought to light a covenant that is perfect, that abideth unchanged throughout eternity,[10] as he hath promised aforetime, "Behold, the days come, saith the Lord, that I will make a new covenant with the house of Israel, but not according to the covenant I made with their fathers in the day that I took them by the hand to bring them out of the land of Egypt, because they continued not therein."[11]

This covenant is a covenant of the grace, the revelation and the knowledge of God, as the word signifieth, "They shall all know me, from the least unto the greatest."[12] This knowledge, however, cometh alone from the receiving of the Holy Spirit.[13] Thus

67

the covenant of God is confirmed by Christ, sealed and established by the Holy Spirit,[1] as is promised, "And it shall come to pass in the last days, saith the Lord, that I will pour out my Spirit upon all flesh; and your sons and your daughters shall prophesy, and upon my servants and upon my handmaids in those days I will pour out my Spirit."[2]

This is the covenant of child-like freedom; of which we also are the children if we let ourselves be sealed by this covenant and submit and surrender ourselves to its working.[3] As Paul also saith, "The law of the Spirit hath made me free from the law of sin and death."[4] Now whom Christ thus maketh free, is free indeed.[5] Therefore saith Paul, "Stand fast therefore in the liberty wherewith Christ hath made us free, and let not yourselves be entangled again with the yoke of bondage."[6] For if ye again let yourselves be led into the yoke of bondage, then are ye led from the Spirit to the letter and Christ profiteth you nothing. For which reason those who have not the Spirit are not the children of this covenant.[7]

CONCERNING THE BAPTISM OF CHILDREN

Since children are not born of God after the Christian manner, that is through the preaching of the word, faith and the Holy Spirit,[8] they cannot be baptized in the right way. For baptism is acceptance into the Church of Christ. Now, since all who are born of Adam partake of his fellowship, should they desire to be embodied in the Church of Christ, they must be born of Christ in the Christian way;[9] that they may be accepted in the right way, which was committed to his Church by him.[10]

The birth of Christ, however, took place as is said

68

eth truth; regarding which we want to speak later. Thus, their most striking reasons are practically all mentioned, and from them one can well see that there is naught in them, that they do not at all reach that which they desire. Thus, they twist the word of God[1] to their own hurt for the sake of their pleasure and their bellies.

CONCERNING THE BAPTISM OF CHRIST AND OF HIS CHURCH

Now because it is a testament of the recognition, knowledge and grace of God,[2] baptism is also, according to the words of Peter, the bond of a good conscience with God, that is, of those who have recognized God.[3] The recognition of God, however, cometh, as hath been said, from hearing the word of the gospel. Therefore we teach that those who have heard the word, believed the same, and have recognized God, should be baptized—and not children.[4]

For since all who are born in the human way inherit from Adam his nature and partake of his fellowship, that is, of sin,[5] therefore Christ, who was to take away sin and destroy its strength and power,[6] had a quite different beginning of his birth,[7] as is said above. Thus, those who are to inherit his nature,[8] share his fellowship and become members of his body[9] must also be born of him, not in the human way but in the Christian way, which birth cometh about through the word, faith and the Holy Spirit.[10] For whosoever receiveth the word in faith, becometh God's child,[11] as also John declareth, "As many as received him, to them gave he power to become the sons of God, even to them that believe on his name; which are born, not of blood, nor of the will of the flesh, nor of the will of man, but of God."[12] Therefore, also, Paul saith, "They are not the children of God

77

who are children according to the flesh, but the children of the promise are counted for seed."[1]

Since then we must be born of God, and are children of Christ and not of Adam, we must consider carefully how the birth of Christ came to pass, which, as we have said above, took place in faith through the working of the Holy Spirit.[2] Now, whosoever is to be born of his nature and character must also be born of God[3] that he may be his child, together with Christ,[4] as also Peter saith, "Being born again, not of corruptible, but of incorruptible seed, namely of the word of truth."[5]

This birth, however, taketh place in this wise. If the word is heard and the same believed, then faith is sealed with the power of God, the Holy Spirit,[6] who immediately reneweth the man and maketh him live[7] (after he had been dead in sin[8]) in the righteousness that standeth before God, so that the man is formed a new creature,[9] a new man after God's likeness,[10] or is renewed therein.[11] Thus, whosoever is born in this wise, to him belongeth baptism as a bath of re-birth,[12] signifying that he hath entered into the covenant of the grace and knowledge of God.[13]

Therefore we teach that as Abraham was commanded to circumcise in his house,[14] even so was Christ to baptize in his house, as the words that he spoke to John indicate, "Suffer it to be so, for thus it becometh us to fulfil all God's righteousness."[15] Now, just as Abraham could not circumcise in his house before the child was born to him, nor all his seed after him, neither can anyone be baptized in the house of Christ[16] unless he be first born of Christ through the word and faith.[17] But he who is born in this manner, is baptized after he hath confessed his faith.[18] History hath proved, likewise, that all the apostles also did this, and we follow them.

78

THE MANNER OF BAPTIZING, OR HOW ONE BAPTIZETH

If one is to baptize, it is necessary that there be at least two persons, namely, he that baptizeth, and he that is baptized. He that baptizeth, however, first calleth and crieth out that one must repent, pointeth out to the man his sin, how he may come to God and find grace with him,[1] and how baptism is a bond with God;[2] in this way he showeth him the benefit of baptism, through which the man is moved to desire baptism.[3] Thus, he who is to be baptized must first request, ask for, and desire it.

Then, when he desireth baptism, he who baptizeth asketh him if he believeth in God the Father, Son and Holy Spirit.[4] Thus, he who is to be baptized must confess his faith. He that baptizeth asketh him further who desireth baptism if he reject the world, sin and the devil. These he must reject.[5] Further, he that baptizeth asketh if he desireth to yield himself to God with all his heart and all his soul and all his members,[6] henceforth to live no more to himself but to God and his Church and to suffer God, only, to rule over, and use all his members.[7] If this is his desire, the baptizer asketh further whether he be well assured of all this and certain in his heart that this is the truth, and that there is no other way to life than is shown him in Christ. And if he likewise confess this, the baptizer asketh if he desireth to bind himself to God and be baptized.[8] If he so desireth, the baptizer telleth him to humble himself with bent knees before God and his Church and kneel down, and he taketh pure water and poureth it upon him and saith, "I baptize thee in the name of the Father and of the Son and of the Holy Spirit,[9] who, in accordance with thy faith, hath forgiven thy sins and drawn and received thee into his kingdom,[10] wherefore sin henceforth no more, lest a worse thing befall thee."[11]

Now, since in baptism the man's sins are left behind and forgiven,[1] and the Church hath the key, this should take place before the Church,[2] who, together with him who baptizeth and him who desireth baptism, kneeleth down and asketh God to forgive his sins before baptism taketh place. Where, however, this cannot be and the Church cannot be reached, the baptizer may do it apart, or alone.[3]

WHO CAN SO BAPTIZE AND TEACH

It is not for all and sundry to take upon themselves such an office, namely that of teaching and baptizing; as James declareth, saying, "Dear brothers, let not each strive to be a teacher, for we all sin much, and shall then receive all the greater condemnation."[4] For which reason none must take upon himself or accept such power, unless he be chosen properly and rightly by God in his Church and community,[5] as the apostle showeth the Hebrews, saying, "Let no man take this honour unto himself, but he that is chosen of God as was Aaron. For also Christ glorified not himself to be made an high priest."[6] Thus, his ministers likewise must not press themselves forward and come to the fore, but wait until God draweth them out and chooseth them.

CONCERNING ELECTION

If the Church needeth one or, indeed, more ministers, she must not elect them as pleaseth herself, but wait upon the Lord to see whom he chooseth and showeth them.[7] Therefore they should continue in earnest prayer and petition to God that he might care for them, answer their need and show them whom he hath chosen for his ministry. After continuing thus earnestly in prayer, those who have

been recognized through God's counsel to be suitable are presented to all. If there be many of them we wait to see which the Lord showeth us by lot;[1] if, however, there be only one or just as many as are needed, then we need no lot, for the Lord hath shown us him, therefore we accept him or them in the fear of God as a gift and present from God. His appointment to the office is then confirmed before the Church through the laying on of the elders' hands.[2]

None, however, is confirmed in his office except he be first proved and revealed to the Church, and have the testimony of a good life and walk,[3] lest he fall into the snare of the wicked. Now, however, many say, "Who then chose the first one?" To which we say, "God." For in the Old Testament when Israel had turned away from him, God showed his grace again and again and gave them a saviour out of their midst, who set them once more in the right way; that he might prove that he was Israel's God.[4]

Thus also hath he done anew, since the people had fallen away and estranged themselves from him or had departed and forsaken him. Nevertheless, for the sake of those remaining, he turned not away his mercy, but, when the time had come when he desired to have compassion upon us once more, that the wicked might have less cause to rejoice,[5] he clothed with the power of his Spirit one who had held the office of preacher among those who with their mouth professed to be Christians but denied this in power, that he might bring them back.[6] For this reason also he laid his word in his mouth, and himself gave witness to the same in the power of his working;[7] and hath opened for us the hearing ear to heed it, and also, himself, made it fruitful in us to his praise.

DIFFERENCES OF MINISTRIES

Paul saith that God set first apostles in the Church.[1] These are they who are sent out by God and his Church in accordance with the command of the gospel to go through the country and establish through the word and baptism[2] the obedience of faith in his name.[3]

Secondly, there are bishops and shepherds,[4] who have the same office of teaching and baptizing as the apostles, except that they remain in one place and care for the Church of Christ. There are also helpers, who serve along with the shepherds, exhorting and calling the people to remain true to the teaching they have received.[5] Then there are rulers, who order and arrange the house or the Church, putting each in his place that everything may go properly and well.[6] They also see that the Church is cared for in temporal distribution and are also called ministers of temporal need.[7]

Lastly, there are elders, who are used wherever need requireth in the Church, and who with all diligence consider the good of the Church community together with the minister, seek its well-being and thus help the ministers to bear the burden, so that the whole Church need not be burdened with each and every matter.[8]

CONCERNING THE MISUSE OF THE LORD'S SUPPER

All things have been appointed by God through Christ in a right order for the benefit, betterment, comfort, salvation and blessedness of man, but have been twisted and contorted by the enemy for man's harm and destruction;[9] even so hath he harmfully distorted the Lord's Supper,[10] which was given us to comfort and remind us of God's grace, that he might thereby bring death. For what is greater harm than to forsake the right use and to turn to idolatry, which is truly the greatest abomination;[1] as Israel also did, in that they forsook the right use of their silver and gold, which was given them to use for their benefit, adornment and honour,[2] and made of it a calf to their great dishonour and shame, of which they said, "These are our gods who have led us up out of Egypt." Thus, they stole the honour from God and gave it to an image that was cast, that their own hands had made.[3]

Even so doeth this people with bread. It forsaketh the right usage of it, which was given and appointed them by Christ,[4] and inventeth therefrom idolatry, an abomination to our God. For it is idolatry, to honour as God what is not God and to seek him where he is not.[5] And that he is not in bread is shown by the words, "God dwelleth not in temples made by human hands."[6] Bread, however, is always made by human hands. Therefore he is not therein.

Some, however, reply, "That is said of the Father—he will not dwell in temples that are made with human hands—but not of the Son, who during his sojourn in this world was therein;[7] and it is of the Son we are here speaking."[8] We say, it is of God that ye speak, who never dwelt therein, nor ever will dwell therein. But in that Christ after he became man was therein proveth, as doth his whole life, that he was a real human being,[9] who also, in so far as he was a man, cannot be found at one time in more than one place.[10] His whole life showeth that he was not everywhere, as also the apostle testifieth, "He was found in form and habit as a man,[11] except that he was without sin."[12] But men are not present everywhere. Now, since naught save sin was excepted, universal existence was not excepted.

Then they say, "It is true that during the time of his life he was not present everywhere. But now he is glorified; therefore he is present everywhere." Answer: But he was truly not yet glorified when he held the supper with his disciples.[1] Because, therefore, he was not everywhere before he was glorified,[2] even so he was not in every little piece of bread. Since then he was not in it, for he himself saith the words, "This is my body,"[3] whence doth one now desire with the same words to bewitch him into bread and thus imagine and invent a god?

But that the human form which Christ took upon himself is even so little present everywhere after as it was before he was glorified, and that he leaveth not his place beside the Father is proved by Christ's words in that he saith, "The poor ye have always with you; but me ye have not always."[4] Herein is it truly clear enough that the humanity of Christ is in no more than one place. Even though, however, the divinity of Christ is universal and everywhere, it doth not follow therefrom that he desireth to be enjoyed and received in bread as a god.

But we do truly confess that God, or the deity, extendeth into all things created, into each as such: into wood as wood, into bread as bread, into man, whom he hath especially made a dwelling for himself,[5] as man. Why, then, should one come to seek him, other than in the way mentioned, in bread; or in this bread other than in any other bread? Therefore it is naught but deception, leading away from God.

Secondly, if they have made an idol, or as they say a Christ, out of it, they want to sacrifice him again to the Father in opposition to the word that Christ with one sacrifice hath accomplished everything;[6] and are thus worse than the Jews, who crucified him once, whereby he sacrificed himself to the Father.[7] For they sacrifice him often and must sacrifice him often, yea, never cease to crucify him—for which they

84

ought truly to be ashamed, since they presume to call themselves by his name.

Thirdly, Judas sold him once,[1] but they sell him oft and so treat him worse than Judas. Thus, they have done naught but make a money-making concern therefrom, whereby they trap money as a fowler birds with a net, until they draw and have drawn land and people to themselves. Let us now leave the many other misuses on one side, and consider the right use.

CONCERNING THE SUPPER OF CHRIST

The Lord Christ, the salvation of the world,[2] was sent by the Father that those who believe on his name might have eternal life[3] and be renewed into the divine likeness[4] and grafted into his nature;[5] which access to the Father and his grace he won through his death for us, who bear the likeness of his death.[6] Therefore when he desired to go again to the Father from whom he had come,[7] he wanted to show this to the disciples whom he had chosen from the world and to impress it on their inner being, so that after he had gone from them they might remember his grace and know for what purpose they had been chosen and accepted by God,[8] that they might not be without hope like the rest, who know naught of God.[9]

Therefore he took a loaf of bread, thanked his Father, broke it and gave it to his disciples and said, "Take, eat: this is my body, which is broken for you: this do, as oft as ye do it, in remembrance of me." He took the cup in the same way and said, "Drink ye all of it.[10] This is the new covenant in my blood, which is shed for you for the forgiveness of sins: this do in remembrance of me."[11]

Now, in taking the bread and giving it to his

disciples, Christ desireth to show and explain the community of his body to his disciples, that they had become one body, one plant, one living organism and one nature with him,[1] as Paul interpreteth it, "We who are many, are one bread and one body; we, who all partake of one bread."[2] He, however, in saying this, doth not give them his body, his flesh and blood, to eat,[3] as it hath been twisted by the deceiver and made into idolatry; but, as we have said, he teacheth them that they are members of his body, and as the bread is made a loaf by the bringing together of many grains,[4] even so we, many human beings, who were scattered and divided, of many minds and purposes are led by faith into one, and have become one plant,[5] one living organism and body of Christ,[6] cleaving to him in one Spirit,[7] as the Lord pictureth more clearly for them in still another parable, when he saith, "I am the vine. Ye are the branches."[8] Here he showeth once more distinctly and clearly that they are one plant, organism, matter, substance and body with him. Therefore it is sufficiently clear that naught other than this alone is Christ's meaning.

In that he breaketh the loaf for them, however, and commandeth them to eat,[9] he showeth that they must bear the likeness of his death: be ready to die like him, if they would partake of his grace and become heirs of God. As Paul also saith, "We are heirs of God and joint-heirs with Christ, if so be that we suffer with him, that we may be raised to glory with him."[10]

That it hath the above-mentioned meaning, and that this is truly what Christ meaneth, is proved by his own words, in that he saith, "This is the new covenant in my blood that is shed for you."[11] Here he doth not say, "This is my blood. Drink ye all of it," but, "This is the new covenant." What is then the new covenant? Is it to eat the body of Christ and drink his blood? On the contrary, show where that is anywhere promised! O, what great folly—that one doth not want to see and know! We find indeed that God hath promised a new covenant, not of the body or of eating flesh and blood, but of the knowledge of God, as the word saith, "This shall be the covenant that I will make with them: I will give my law into their mind and write it in their inner members, that they shall all know me."[1] Through this knowledge, however, man is led to God,[2] is grafted into and becometh a fellow-member of his nature and character,[3] whereby we are also all led into the one mind and will of Christ.[4] For this reason he giveth them wine, since many grapes have become one drink, and saith, "This is the new covenant in my blood,"[5] as though he meaneth to say, That is ratified or made strong and confirmed by my blood. For I have led you into such a covenant of grace and made you partakers of it,[6] that ye now have become one bread and one body with me through faith;[7] that from henceforth, led by one Spirit, ye be of one mind and purpose[8] to prove that ye are my disciples.[9]

Thus, the meal, or the partaking of the bread and wine of the Lord, is a sign of the community of his body, in that each and every member thereby declareth himself to be of the one mind, heart and spirit of Christ.[10] Therefore saith Paul, "Let a man truly examine himself before he eateth of this bread and drinketh of this cup, for he that eateth and drinketh unworthily thereof, eateth and drinketh judgment to himself,"[11] as though he would say, Let the man consider, examine and search himself well to see if he is partaking of this grace of Christ[12] and is a true member of Christ, as he declareth himself to be. For where this is not so he bringeth judgment upon himself in that he eateth and drinketh.[13]

CONCERNING COMMUNITY OF GOODS

Now, since all the saints have fellowship in holy things, that is in God,[1] who also hath given to them all things in his Son Christ Jesus[2]—which gift none should have for himself, but each for the other; as Christ also hath naught for himself, but hath everything for us, even so all the members of his body have naught for themselves, but for the whole body, for all the members.[3] For his gifts are not sanctified and given to one member alone, or for one member's sake, but for the whole body with its members.[4]

Now, since all God's gifts—not only spiritual, but also material things—are given to man, not that he should have them for himself or alone but with all his fellows, therefore the communion of saints itself must show itself not only in spiritual but also in temporal things;[5] that as Paul saith, one might not have abundance and another suffer want, but that there may be equality.[6] This he showeth from the law touching manna, in that he who gathered much had nothing over, whereas he who gathered little had no less, since each was given what he needed according to the measure.[7]

Furthermore, one seeth in all things created, which testify to us still to-day, that God from the beginning ordained naught private for man, but all things to be common.[8] But through wrong taking, since man took what he should not and forsook what he should take,[9] he drew such things to himself and made them his property, and so grew and became hardened therein. Through such wrong taking and collecting of created things he hath been led so far from God that he hath even forgotten the Creator,[10] and hath even raised up and honoured as God the created things which had been put under and made subject to him.[11] And such is still the case if one steppeth out of God's order and forsaketh the same.

Now, however, as hath been said, created things which are too high for man to draw within his grasp and collect, such as the sun with the whole course of the heavens, day, air and such like, show that not they alone, but all other created things are likewise made common to man.[1] That they have thus remained and are not possessed by man is due to their being too high for him to bring under his power, otherwise— so evil had he become through wrong taking—he would have drawn them to himself as well as the rest and made them his property.[2]

That this is so, however, and that the rest is just as little made by God for man's private possession, is shown in that man must forsake all other created things as well as this when he dies, and can carry nothing with him to use as his own.[3] For which reason Christ also called temporal all things foreign to man's essential nature, and saith, "If ye are not faithful in what is not your own, who will entrust to you what is your own?"[4]

Now, because what is temporal doth not belong to us, but is foreign to our true nature, the law commandeth that none covet strange possessions,[5] that is, set his heart upon and cleave to what is temporal and alien.[6] Therefore whosoever will cleave to Christ and follow him must forsake such taking of created things and property,[7] as he himself also saith, "Whosoever forsaketh not all that he hath cannot be my disciple."[8] For if a man is to be renewed again into the likeness of God, he must put off all that leadeth him from him—that is the grasping and drawing to himself of created things—for he cannot otherwise attain God's likeness.[9] Therefore Christ saith, "Whosoever shall not receive the kingdom of God as a little child shall not enter therein,"[10] or, "Except ye overcome yourselves and become as little children, ye shall not enter into the kingdom of heaven."[11]

Now, he who thus becometh free from created things can then grasp what is true and divine; and when he graspeth it and it becometh his treasure, he turneth his heart towards it, emptieth himself of all else[1] and taketh naught as his, and regardeth it no longer as his but as of all God's children.[2] Therefore we say that as all the saints have community in spiritual gifts,[3] still much more should they show this in material things, and not ascribe the same to and covet them for themselves, for they are not their own; but regard them as of all God's children,[4] that they may thereby show that they are partakers in the community of Christ[5] and are renewed into God's likeness.[6] For the more man yet cleaveth to created things, appropriateth and ascribeth such to himself, the further doth he show himself to be from the likeness of God and the community of Christ.[7]

For this reason the Holy Spirit also at the beginning of the Church began such community right gloriously again, so that none said that aught of the things that he possessed was his own, but they had all things in common;[8] and it is his will that this might still be kept, as Paul saith, "Let none seek his own profit but the profit of another," or, "Let none seek what benefiteth himself but what benefiteth many."[9] Where this is not the case it is a blemish upon the Church which ought verily to be corrected. If one should say, it was so nowhere except in Jerusalem, therefore it is now not necessary, we say, Even if it were nowhere but in Jerusalem, it followeth not that it ought not to be so now. For neither apostles nor churches were lacking, but rather the opportunity, manner and time.[10]

Therefore this should be no cause for us to hesitate, but rather should it move us to more and better zeal and diligence, for the Lord now giveth us both time and cause so to do. That there was no lack of

90

either apostles or churches is shown by the zeal of both. For the apostles have pointed the people thereto with all diligence and most faithfully prescribed true surrender, as all their epistles still prove to-day.[1] And the people obeyed with zeal, as Paul beareth witness—especially of those of Macedonia— saying, "I tell you of the grace that is given to the churches in Macedonia. For their joy was the most rapturous since they had been tried by much affliction, and their poverty, though it was indeed deep, overflowed as riches in all simplicity. For I bear witness that with all their power, yea, and beyond their power, they were themselves willing, and besought us earnestly with much admonition to receive the benefit and community of help which is given to the saints; and not as we had hoped, but first gave themselves to the Lord, and then to us also, by the will of God."[2]

Here one can well see with what inclined and willing hearts the churches were ready to keep community not only in spiritual but also in material things, for they desired to follow the master Christ, and become like him and one with him,[3] who himself went before us in such a way, and commanded us to follow him.[4]

CONCERNING SEPARATION

Firstly, we say that God hath taken and chosen a people for himself through his Christ to be his property,[5] wherefore also he hath bestowed on it his Spirit that they might be of his nature and character, and no longer carnal but spiritual,[6] as Paul saith, "Ye are not in the flesh, but in the Spirit, if so be that the Spirit of God dwell in you. But if any man have not the Spirit of Christ, he is none of his."[7] Therefore the Church of Christ is not carnal but spiritual, and there is no Church of Christ save that which the Holy Spirit gathereth, ruleth, teacheth and directeth. Now those who surrender themselves to the Spirit that the same might rule over them, yield themselves to the Church of Christ,[1] in which the Holy Spirit worketh.[2] But those who yield themselves to sin, to serve it and let the same rule over them, these separate themselves from the Church of Christ and estrange themselves from her, and if so be that they leave her, they go even farther into destruction.[3]

For this reason we by no means admit that we have separated ourselves from such a Church of Christ, on the contrary we have drawn near to her, yielded ourselves to her, that he who worketh in her might also work in us, and that we through his working might be assured that we are God's children.[4] Thus, we are in the community of the Church of Christ or of the children of God, where there are no more servants,[5] but all are children through faith in Jesus Christ.[6]

Thus, we say and must say and confess, that not we but all baptizers of children have forsaken the Church and community of Christ and separated themselves from the same. They have fallen away, and are become so corrupt that they neither know nor recognize what the true Church of Christ is and in what way she proveth herself the Church of Christ. To which thing, if one ask them and tell them, they give the answer, "The saints did that, who had the Holy Spirit. But we are not able to do so."[7] They know not that the Church of Christ is a house of the Holy Spirit, and that none is therein unless he hath the same,[8] as also Paul saith, "If any man have not the Spirit of Christ, he is none of his."[9]

Since then God hath chosen this Church for himself and separated her from all nations that she might serve him[10] with one mind and heart[11] through the one child-like Spirit, there is, as hath been said, no more a servant therein but only children.[1] Nor have they separated themselves, but God hath separated them from all other peoples,[2] and hath therefore also given them a sign of the covenant, that is baptism, whereby they receive all who surrender themselves to God into the Church.[3]

Since, however, God allowed us all to fall away because of our many sins, in that we had all turned from good to evil[4] and had twisted the usage and order of the Church into what was evil, and misused it, so that we all now walked in darkness until God, who desireth not the death of the sinner,[5] had mercy upon us and once more let the true light of his grace shine and brought his truth to light, we—as the wise man teacheth, "My child, neglect not to turn back to the Lord, and put it not off from one day to the next"[6]— have with haste turned again to the Lord, to keep his ordinances, which we had forsaken and from which we had fallen, and to thank God who hath accepted us.

Thus, we have not turned away from the Church of Christ, but to it; but we have left the soiled and impure assembly, and would wish that all men did so too.[7] Therefore we call to repentance[8] and tell whoever is willing to hear to harden not his heart[9] and so bring the wrath of God upon him.[10] Whosoever will not repent, however, and cleave to the true ordinances of God, but remaineth in his sins, we must let go his way and leave him to God.

CONCERNING THE TEMPLE AND THAT WE GO NOT THEREIN

God the Lord hath built a temple for himself. That is his Church wherein he desireth to be honoured, and apart from it he desireth to plant the memory of his name neither here nor there—for the ceremonial semblance hath been brought to an end, and in Christ Jesus the real and true service of God hath begun, which must take place through the one sole Spirit.[1] Therefore all else that taketh place through human choice is no service of God, however much it may deceptively seem to be, since there is no other divine service than in the Church of Christ, which he himself hath sanctified so that there is neither spot nor blemish in her.[2] The assembly in the temple, however, is a rabble and gathering of whores and adulterers and of all unclean spirits, whom God hateth; wherefore there is no divine service there,[3] but on the contrary blasphemy and contempt of the Almighty,[4] and this hath moved us to flee from and avoid their assembly.[5]

With regard to the buildings of stone and wood—these originated, as the history of several showeth, when this country was forced by the sword to make a verbal confession of the Christian faith. Further, men dedicated temples to their gods, and then made them "Churches," as they are wrongly named, of the Christians. Thus, they originated through the instigation of the devil and are built up through sacrifice to devils, since as Paul saith, "The things that the heathen sacrifice, they sacrifice to devils and not to God: and I would not that ye should be in the fellowship of devils."[6] For that is also not God's will, for Christ hath no fellowship with Belial.[7] Therefore, also, hath he commanded in the Old Testament that they should utterly destroy and break down such places, that they might not share in that fellowship. Nowhere doth he say, change it and use it aright; but saith break it down utterly.[8]

Now, because the people did this not, but left the root in the earth,[9] they not only brought not the heathen practices to the right usage, but they themselves forsook the right usage and surrendered them-

94

selves to all manner of idolatry, and they have now changed so much that they call "saints" what those called "gods." And for the same reason—because the root is left in the earth—they have gone farther and have built one house after another for their gods (or "saints," as they call them), and filled them with their gods and idols,[1] and thereby show that they are the children of their fathers, and have not left their fellowship.[2]

But because we know that God hated such places from the beginning,[3] and still hateth them, we likewise avoid and flee from them (as those who know most surely that therein is no true service of God, but on the contrary that he is continually dishonoured and despised)[4] that we might not share their fellowship and again fall away from the truth we have recognized; since God might because of this turn from us as from Israel.[5] We know well, however, that if a path goeth through such a temple, if one goeth straight through he maketh himself not unclean before God. But to go in to partake of such fellowship, to hear aught therein, to learn or receive aught, of that Paul saith, "I would not that ye have fellowship with devils."[6]

CONCERNING PRIESTS AND WHY WE HAVE NAUGHT TO DO WITH THEM

Now, since the priests have presumed to take upon themselves the proclaiming of the gospel, yet teach only the literal word, law and doctrine, for they have not the strength of God, the Holy Spirit, which glorifieth and maketh worthy of such an office,[7] we cannot hear their voice, for it is that of strangers, and not of those sent by God,[8] and the Lord saith, "My sheep hear not the voice of strangers."[9] Now all words that are but words are strange, for the word of the gospel hath come. For Paul saith, "The Lord is the Spirit, and where the Spirit of the Lord is there is freedom. And now the glory of the Lord is reflected in us all from our uncovered faces and we are transformed into the same likeness, from one glory to the next, and all this through the Lord who is the Spirit."[1]

That they have not the Spirit of the Lord is shown by their own works, such as drunkenness, greed, vanity, pride, swearing and all manner of lust,[2] for the wise man saith, "The Holy Spirit disliketh and fleeth from those who only have the outer appearance of wisdom and righteousness, and departeth from thoughts that are without understanding and fleeth away when evil taketh the upper hand."[3] Since therefore these things are found in them they cannot proclaim the word of the gospel, which is proclaimed in the strength of the Spirit,[4] as it is written, "The Spirit of the Lord is upon me, wherewith he hath anointed me and sent me to preach the gospel."[5]

That they preach not the gospel but only the literal word is shown by their own deeds, in that they drive and press men to hear their teaching by means of the stocks, the dungeon and keep, torture, banishment and death. For were they children or servants of the Spirit, they would have the strength and working of the same within themselves,[6] and would thereby know that such action engendereth not sonship but only slavery. Therefore do they plant nothing but a slavish people that hath no part in Christ, as Paul saith, "There are no more slaves, but all are children."[7] It is the free Spirit that leadeth to sonship— through his own working and inspiration in man[8] and not through the bullying of the priests and their following. Because in the teaching of Christ they have not the nature and order of the Spirit, they show that they are not servants of the Spirit, but of the letter.

But the service of the new covenant is not a service of the letter, but a spiritual service, performed in the strength of the Spirit of Christ, as Paul saith, "Our ability and sufficiency is of God who hath sent us and made us capable of being servants of the new covenant—not of the letter but of the Spirit. For the letter killeth, but the Spirit giveth life."[1] All who dare to preach the gospel other than in the strength of the Spirit of Christ come and run before Christ hath sent them, therefore they are thieves and murderers, as Christ saith, "All who come before me are thieves and murderers, who come only to slay, to steal and to destroy."[2] Therefore Christ's sheep rightly hear them not.

Now, since the teaching of Christ is not of the letter but of the Spirit[3] it cannot be taught by the carnally minded man, therefore doth John say, "If there come any unto you and bring not the doctrine of Christ with him, receive him not into your house, nor even greet him, that ye may not become partakers of his evil deeds. For he that greeteth him becometh a partaker of his sins."[4] For this reason we receive not priests into our house; that is, we have naught to do with them, buy naught from them and likewise sell naught to them, neither food nor drink when they demand it. Neither in work nor in any business connection have we aught to do with them, that we may not be partakers of their sins.[5]

CONCERNING MARRIAGE

Marriage is a union of two, in which one taketh the other to care for and the second submitteth to obey the first, and thus through their agreement two become one, and are no longer two but one. But if this is to be done in a godly way they must come together not through their own action and choice, but in accordance with God's will and order, and therefore neither leave nor forsake the other but suffer both ill and good together all their days.[1]

Marriage is, however, in three grades or steps. First is that of God with the soul or spirit,[2] then that of the spirit with the body,[3] and thirdly that of one body with another, that is, the marriage of man with woman;[4] which is not the first but the last and lowest grade, and is therefore visible, recognizable and to be understood by all. Now because it is visible, recognizable and to be understood it is a picture, an instruction and indication of what is invisible, that is of the middle and highest grades.[5] For as man is head of the woman,[6] so is the spirit the head of the body, and God is the head of the spirit.

Thus, we see marriage instructeth and leadeth men to God, for if one regardeth and observeth it aright it teacheth us to know God and to cleave to him. Where, however, it is not regarded and observed rightly it leadeth men away from God and bringeth them to death. And since they are few who regard it rightly and many who regard it not aright (still less observe it aright) Paul saith, it is good for a man not to touch a woman lest in their ignorance they lapse and destroy themselves.[7] Therefore we want to speak of marriage in so far as is given us from God to speak.

We say, first, that since woman was taken from man, and not man from woman,[8] man hath lordship but woman weakness, humility and submission,[9] therefore she should be under the yoke of man and obedient to him,[10] even as the woman was commanded by God when he said to her, "The man shall be thy lord."[11] Now, since this is so she should heed her husband, inquire of him, ask him and do all things with and naught without his counsel. For where she doeth this not, she forsaketh the place in the order in which she hath been set by God, encroacheth upon the lordship of the man and forsaketh the command of her Creator as well as the submission that she promised her husband in the union of marriage: to honour him as a wife her husband.[1]

The man, on the other hand, as the one in whom something of God's glory is seen, should have compassion on the woman as the weaker instrument,[2] and in love and kindness go before her and care for her, not only in temporal but also and still more in spiritual things; and faithfully share with her all that he hath been given by God. He should go before her in honesty, courage and all the Christian virtues, that in him she may have a mirror of righteousness, an instigation to blessedness and a leader to God.[3] Where, however, the husband doeth this not or is careless and superficial therein, he forsaketh the glory which was given him by God, as well as God's order.[4]

Thus to both man and woman is ordained and commanded what is severally theirs, for he willeth thereby to lead us into deeper knowledge, namely, that even as the man should love the woman, care for her and bear rule over her, even so doth the spirit desire to care for, control and rule over the body, and God the spirit.[5] And, on the other hand, as the woman should obey the man,[6] even so should the earthly the heavenly body, that is the spirit; and from now on one should enter upon, do and undertake naught from the carnal or earthly will, but in all things seek, ask and look to the heavenly body and let oneself be ruled thereby.[7] The heavenly body, however, should heed and look to him from whom it hath come[8] and allow itself to be ruled and led by the same alone.[9] When this hath taken place, then is marriage rightly observed in all its three grades and one is kept close to God.

Marriage must not come about through the will of the flesh, whether for the sake of beauty, youth, money, possessions or any other thing that the flesh desireth. For that is not of God, but cometh from the devil; as the angel saith to Tobias, "Hear what I say to thee and I shall show thee who they be over whom the devil hath dominion, namely, those who marry without regard to God in their heart, but only to satisfy the wantonness of the body, even as a mule or horse that knoweth no better; yea, over such hath the devil dominion."[1] Thus, marriage serveth for destruction to all who enter upon it from carnal desire.

Therefore such a thing should not take place, and one should in no case choose from the flesh but await such a gift from God, and with all diligence pray that God in accordance with his divine will might send what he from the beginning hath provided, serving to one's salvation and life.[2] Then after such a prayer one should ask not his flesh but the elders that God might show him through them what he hath appointed for him. This, then, one should take with real gratitude as a gift from God, whether young or old, poor or rich, even as God hath shown through their counsel.[3] What, therefore, God hath joined together, man should not sever.[4] They should, however, be married openly in the presence of the Church, by an ordained minister of the Word.

The man should also be the husband of only one wife,[5] even as Christ is the head of the one Church.[6] For, since marriage is a picture of the same, the likeness and indication must resemble what it indicateth. Therefore must a man have no more than one wife.

CONCERNING ADULTERY

Marriage is a union of two, in which one taketh the other to care for and the second submitteth to obey the first, and thus through the agreement of both the marriage is confirmed. Contrariwise, where this agreement is broken and transgressed, it mattereth not by whom, the marriage is broken.[1] If the husband preserve not his honour as the glory of God and go before his wife and guide her to blessedness, he hath already broken the marriage with his wife,[2] and if he breaketh it thus with his wife, he soon sinneth in the next grade, namely against his spirit, for he alloweth himself not to be ruled by it but by the flesh, and becometh superficial and forsaketh his lordship;[3] if, however, his spirit is overcome and weakened by the flesh, he falleth in the third grade and breaketh his union with the Creator by whom he is led.[4]

Likewise, if the woman forsake obedience to her husband who faithfully goeth before her, she hath broken and transgressed against the marriage with her husband, that is the union made with him.[5] If she thus sinneth against her husband, she, likewise, goeth on to sin as is said above in all three grades; except where her husband through carelessness hath first broken the marriage with her, become superficial and wanted also to draw her after him. In this case she should let the broken marriage go and hold to that which is unbroken, that is obedience to the Spirit and to God, otherwise she falleth into death, together with her husband.[6]

Where, however, the man doeth his part, but his wife acteth not with but without his counsel, she transgresseth her marriage and union in small things as well as in great things, and taketh from her husband his honour and lordship.[7] If the man permit her to do this he sinneth with her as Adam did with Eve,[8] in that he consented to eat of the forbidden fruit, and both fell to death. For they broke marriage with their Creator and transgressed his order.[1]

The Lord Christ saith concerning adultery, "Whosoever looketh on a woman to lust after her hath committed adultery with her already in his heart."[2] Thirdly, there cometh adultery with the work of the flesh, if one or the other of the partners in marriage go to another man or woman. Where this taketh place, where one committeth adultery in this way, the other should put him or her away and have no more in common with him or her before he or she hath shown real fruits of repentance. For where one mixeth with the transgressor before he or she hath repented, one committeth adultery with the other, even though they were husband or wife before. For it is no longer a marriage, because it is broken until through repentance it is healed, therefore this should be punished by separation as much as the other.[3]

CONCERNING GOVERNMENTAL AUTHORITY

Governmental authority is appointed and ordained by God as a rod of his anger for the discipline and punishment of the evil and profligate nation.[4] Therefore doth Paul name it a servant of God's vengeance,[5] by means of which God will avenge himself on their sins and bring the evil they have done upon their own head, that their wickedness might not continue to spread and that the whole earth might not on their account become blemished and unclean.[6] Therefore one should be obedient and subject to rulers as ordained by God for the purpose of protection,[7] in so far as they do not attack the conscience or command what is against God. As Peter exhorteth us saying, "Submit yourselves to every ordinance of man for the Lord's sake: whether it be to the king, as supreme; or unto the governors, as unto them that are sent by him."[1] And Paul saith, "Remind them to be subject to the principalities and powers, to obey magistrates, to be ready to every good work."[2]

Therefore is one rightly obedient and subject to them, and the more diligent one is therein, the better is it and the more pleasing to God. For whosoever resisteth this, resisteth the ordinance of God.[3] Where, however, the rulers command and act against God, there one must leave their command undone, and obey God rather than man.[4] For the conscience hath been set free and is reserved for God alone, that he and no human being may be Lord of the same and rule over, teach and direct it whithersoever it pleaseth him. Therefore wherever the government presumeth to lay hands upon the conscience and to control the faith of man, there it is robbing God of what is his. Therefore it is wrong to obey it in this.[5] Now, since the office of government is an ordinance and establishment of God and because it hath been appointed and ordained by God, within its own limits it is right and good, but where it is abused, this same misuse is wrong. The office, nevertheless, remaineth as it was ordained. Therefore is the office to be honoured. For, even though godless men fill it, the office is not thereby annulled.[6] And God permitteth this to the godless for the greater punishment of the people.[7] But just as a godless government is given to the nation by God as a punishment, even so is a disobedient nation given to the godless government, that they might tear and devour one another and at last be consumed together.[8]

WHY GOVERNMENTAL AUTHORITY
HATH BEEN ORDAINED

Governmental authority hath been ordained by God because of the turning aside of the people, in that they turned away from him and walked according to the flesh. For God saith, "My Spirit shall not always strive with men, for they are flesh."[1] For this reason, after the flood, he ordained governmental authority for them to be a rod of the anger and vengeance of God,[2] to shed the blood of those who have shed blood.[3]

And again, when Israel had once more turned away from the Lord who was their King, had forsaken him and desired a king, God spake to Samuel, "They have not rejected thee, but they have rejected me, that I should not reign over them. They do to thee as they have always done. Since the day that I led them up out of Egypt they have forsaken me and served other gods, therefore hearken unto their voice and give them a king."[4]

From these words we see how governmental authority grew and from whence it came, namely, from the wrath of God; even as it is written, "Thou didst say, Give us a king. I gave thee a king in mine anger and took him away again in my wrath."[5] Thus, it is evident that governmental authority is not of grace but is given in disfavour and anger, and that after the turning away of the people. Since they forsook God and followed the flesh, flesh had to have dominion over them.

Therefore the government is a picture, sign and reminder of man's departure from God,[6] and ought well to be to all men an urge to retire within themselves and to consider to what they have come and to what they have fallen, that they might with all the more haste turn back to God to receive again the grace they had lost. There are few, however, who consider thus, therefore do they remain in their sins.

Over and above all this, because governmental authority is a servant of God's anger and vengeance, as long as it hath being it indicateth that God's anger and wrath is still over sinners and is not at an end.[1]

WHETHER RULERS CAN ALSO BE CHRISTIANS

Here beginneth a quite other kingdom and reign, therefore that which is old must stop and come to an end, as also the symbol of the Jewish royal house signifieth, which was there until Christ came, as the scriptures declare, "The sceptre shall not depart from Judah until the hero, Christ, shall come."[2] Therefore it is ended, stopped and broken in Christ. He now sitteth upon the throne of his father, David,[3] and hath become a king of all true Israelites. He also hath now begun a new regime that is not like the old one and is not supported by the temporal sword.[4]

Now, since the regime of the Jews, who until then were God's people, came to an end in Christ, ceased and was taken from them, it is clear that it should be no more in Christ, but it is his desire to rule over Christians with his spiritual sword alone.[5] That the power of the temporal sword was taken from the Jews and hath passed to the heathen signifieth that from henceforth the people of God ought no longer to use the temporal sword and rule therewith; but ought to be ruled and led by the one Spirit of Christ alone.[6] And that it hath gone to the heathen signifieth that those who do not submit themselves to the Spirit of Christ—that is, all heathen and unbelievers—should be disciplined and punished therewith. Therefore hath governmental authority its place outside Christ, but not in Christ.[7]

Thus God in Christ, alone, is king and commander of his people, as it is written, "God hath set a ruler over every people, but over Israel he alone is Lord." [1] Even as he is a spiritual king hath he also spiritual servants and wieldeth a spiritual sword—both he and all his servants—that pierceth soul and spirit. [2]

Now because the Son was appointed by the Father, [3] as it is written, "I have set my king upon my holy hill of Zion," [4] and given not in anger like the other but in blessing, [5] and hath become a source of blessing to us all (as, indeed, it had been promised that in him all peoples should be blessed), [6] therefore, even as the other was ordained to shed the blood of him who sheddeth a man's blood, [7] this king hath been ordained to preserve the souls of men; [8] as the other to take vengeance on evil, [9] this to recompense it with good; as the other to hate the enemy, this is ordained to love. [10] Thus is Christ King of all kings, and at the same time the opposite of all the rulers of this world; therefore doth he say, "My kingdom is not of this world: if my kingdom were of this world then would my servants fight for me." [11]

Thus, he setteth up quite a different kingdom and rule [12] and desireth that his servants submit themselves to it and become like him; [13] therefore doth he say to them, "The princes of the world are called gracious lords, and the powerful exercise dominion over the people, but it shall not be so among you: but let him who is the greatest among you be your minister." [14] Thus the glory of Christ and of his servants consisteth in the putting off of all worldly glory. And the more one putteth this aside, the more glorious doth he become in Christ's kingdom, as the word showeth, "Whosoever exalteth himself shall be abased, and whosoever humbleth himself shall be exalted." [15]

Now because in Christ our King is the full blessing

of God[1]—yea, he is himself the blessing[2]—all that was given in wrath must come to an end and cease in him, and hath no part in him. But governmental authority was given in wrath,[3] and so it can neither fit itself into nor belong to Christ. Thus no Christian is a ruler and no ruler is a Christian, for the child of blessing cannot be the servant of wrath.[4] Thus, in Christ not the temporal, but the spiritual sword doth rule over men, and so ruleth that they deserve not the temporal sword, therefore also have no need of it.[5]

If one were to say, however, "It is necessary because of evil men," this we have already answered in saying that the power of the sword hath passed to the heathen, that they may therewith punish their evildoers. But that is no concern of ours; as Paul saith, "What have I to do to judge them that are without?"[6] Thus no Christian can rule over the world.

To this someone might say, "Then according to this view, the way to life is closed to those in governmental authority!" We say, "No," for Christ saith, "Come unto me all ye that are weary and heavy-laden. I will refresh you and give rest unto your souls."[7] Therefore is this free to all—to rulers as well as to subjects. Whosoever cometh to him will he in no wise cast out.[8]

Therefore if rulers divest themselves of their glory as Christ did, and humble themselves with him[9] and allow Christ, only, to use them, then the way to life would be as open to them as to others.[10] But when Christ beginneth to work in men, he doth naught other than what he himself did—and he fled when men sought to make him a king.[11]

If, however, their spirits remain unbroken and they remain in their glory, Christ himself saith, "Whosoever divesteth not himself of all that he hath—yea, of his own life also—cannot be my disciple."[12] From this it is clear that not only governmental authorities but all who still cleave to created things, and forsake them not for Christ's sake, are not Christians.[1]

CONCERNING WARFARE

Now since Christ, the Prince of Peace, hath prepared and won for himself a kingdom, that is a Church, through his own blood;[2] in this same kingdom all worldly warfare hath an end, as was promised aforetime, "Out of Zion shall go forth the law, and the word of the Lord from Jerusalem, and shall judge among the heathen and shall draw many peoples, so that they shall beat their swords into ploughshares and their lances or spears into pruning hooks, sickles and scythes, for from thenceforth nation shall not lift up sword against nation, nor shall they learn war any more."[3]

Therefore a Christian neither wages war nor wields the worldly sword to practise vengeance, as Paul also exhorteth us saying, "Dear brothers, avenge not yourselves, but rather give place unto the wrath of God, for the Lord saith, Vengeance is mine; I will repay it."[4] Now if vengeance is God's and not ours, it ought to be left to him and not practised or exercised by ourselves. For, since we are Christ's disciples, we must show forth the nature of him who, though he could, indeed, have done so, repaid not evil with evil.[5] For he could, indeed, have protected himself against his enemies, the Jews, by striking down with a single word all who wanted to take him captive.[6]

But though he might well have done this, he did not himself and would not permit others to do so. Therefore he said to Peter, "Put up again thy sword into his place."[7] Here one can see how our King setteth out with a powerful host against his enemy; how he defeateth the enemy and how he taketh vengeance: in that he taketh Malchus' ear, that had been struck off, and putteth it on again.[1] And he who did this saith, "Whosoever will be my disciple, let him take his cross upon him and follow me."[2]

Now, therefore, Christ desireth that we should act even as he did, so he commandeth us, saying, "It hath been said to the men of old, 'An eye for an eye, and a tooth for a tooth,' but I say unto you, that ye resist not evil: but whosoever shall smite thee on thy right cheek, turn and offer to him the other also."[3] Here it is clearly to be seen that one ought neither to avenge oneself nor to go to war, but rather offer his back to the strikers and his cheeks to them that pluck off the hair[4]—that is, suffer with patience and wait upon God, who is righteous, and who will repay it.[5]

If one should say that David, who was loved by God, and other saints, went to war,[6] and therefore one should still do so when one hath right and justification thereto, we say, "No." That David and other saints did this, but that we ought not so to do, can be seen by all from the words quoted above, "To them of old is said, 'An eye for an eye and a tooth for a tooth,' but I say unto you, that ye resist not evil!"[7] Here Christ maketh the distinction himself. There is therefore no need for many words, for it is clear that Christians can neither go to war nor practise vengeance.[8] Whosoever doeth this hath forsaken and denied Christ and Christ's nature.

CONCERNING TAXATION

Since governmental authority is ordained by God and hath its office from him, the payment of taxes for this purpose is likewise ordained and commanded, as Paul saith, "Thus ye must also pay tribute."[9] For this reason we, likewise, willingly pay taxes, tribute or whatever men may term it, and in no way oppose it, for we have learned this from our master, Christ, who not only paid it himself,[1] but also commanded others to do so, saying, "Render unto Caesar what is Caesar's, and to God what is God's."[2] Therefore we, as his disciples, desire with all diligence to follow and perform his command, and not to oppose the government in this.

But where taxes are demanded for the special purpose of going to war, massacring and shedding blood, we give nothing. This we do neither out of malice nor obstinacy but in the fear of God, that we make not ourselves partakers of other men's sins.[3] If one should say, "But ye ought to pay tribute to whom tribute is due, therefore ye do wrong to refuse it,"[4] we answer: We do not at all refuse to render tribute to whom it is due, and in the way in which it is due. For God, as is said above, hath ordained that rulers receive taxes, which they have to collect and raise yearly.[5] Therefore we do not refuse to pay the same. But that it followeth from the words of Paul that one should submit to every whim of the ruler is not the case. That this is true is shown by the words of Paul in the same passage, when he saith, "Render therefore to all their dues: tribute to whom tribute is due." He doth not say, "Render whatsoever and however much they want," but, "Render their dues."[6] That is, the yearly taxes which are ordained by God.[7] But what God hath not ordained, what is not regular taxation—that is given, not as a duty and as the ruler's due, but is given because one doth so willingly and because one agreeth thereto, or, in most cases, because one is pressed and coerced to do so.

Therefore the paying of such taxes followeth neither from this word nor from the word of Christ commanding to render to Caesar what is Caesar's.[8] For Christ, likewise, was speaking of the yearly taxation, which was first imposed when Augustus was emperor and then continued;[1] and at this time there was neither war nor rumours of war. Therefore money was neither gathered nor given for this purpose. It was rather as if the count were now to put a tax on the wood on his land: for example, that whosoever taketh wood away in a cart should pay one gulden a year; whosoever taketh it in a barrow half a gulden; and whosoever carrieth it home himself a quarter gulden. It was of such taxation that the Lord spoke when he said one should not refuse to pay, but give willingly: he spoke not of taxation for the shedding of blood. For this reason we also have no objection, but willingly pay such. Where, however, our conscience is violated, there we both must and desire to obey God rather than man.[2]

CONCERNING THE MAKING OF SWORDS

Since, as hath been said above, Christians should beat their swords into ploughshares and take up arms no more[3]—still less can they make the same, for they serve for naught else than to slay, harm and destroy men—and Christ hath not come to destroy men[4]— therefore his disciples, also, refuse to do so; for he saith, "Know ye not of what Spirit ye are the children?" as though he would say, "Doth the Spirit of grace teach you to destroy, or will ye walk according to the flesh and forsake the Spirit, whose children ye have become? Know ye not that I am not come to destroy men? If ye will be my disciples, ye must let my Spirit rule over you and not walk after the flesh.[5] For he who obeyeth the flesh cannot please God."[6]

Now, since Christians must not use and practise such vengeance,[7] neither can they make the weapons by which such vengeance and destruction may be practised by others, that they be not partakers of other men's sins.[8] Therefore we make neither swords, spears, muskets nor any such weapons. What, however, is made for the benefit and daily use of man, such as bread knives, axes, hoes and the like, we both can and do make. Even if one were to say, "But one could therewith harm and slay others," still they are not made for the purpose of slaying and harming, so there is naught to prevent our making them. If they should ever be used to harm another, we do not share the harmer's guilt, so let him bear the judgment himself.[1]

CONCERNING THE MAKING OF CLOTHES

We both ought and desire to serve our neighbour with all diligence in our work, making all manner of things to meet his needs, that in this way God be praised, and our diligence and conscientiousness felt, that men may recognize that the work is honestly done.[2] What, however, serveth but pride, magnificence and vanity, such as elaborate braiding, floral and embroidery work, we make for no man, that we may keep our conscience unspotted before God.[3]

For we have been chosen by God, not only not to make and use such, but also to testify against it and to make men aware of sin.[4] Now, if we must testify against such things, we cannot help to establish and make the same. Therefore James saith, "Pure and undefiled service of God is to keep oneself unspotted from the world."[5] That, with God's help, we want to do with all our power and to strive for this end as long as we live.

WHETHER A CHRISTIAN CAN GO TO LAW OR SIT IN JUDGMENT

Since, as is said above, all temporal things are foreign to us and naught is our own, a Christian can neither strive, quarrel nor go to law on their account;[6]

on the contrary, as one whose heart is turned from the world and set upon what is divine, he should suffer wrong; as Paul saith, "Now therefore there is utterly a fault among you because ye go to law one with another. Why do ye not rather take wrong? Why do ye not rather suffer yourselves to be defrauded?"[1] Thus, since Christians must not sue one another at law, going to law and sitting in judgment are completely done away with among Christians.[2]

It followeth from this that no Christians can sit upon or call a court. For Christians do not go to law in this way. Paul saith, "For what have I to do to judge them that are without?"[3] Thus, as hath been said, judging and bringing to law have ceased and come to an end in the Church of Christ. The reason why the Christian must not judge those who are without is that they have not subjected themselves to the Spirit of God, so should not be judged by means of the same; since the Lord saith, "My Spirit shall not always strive with them, for they are flesh."[4] For the Church of God is not concerned about temporal things, for the sake of which those that are without are in the habit of quarrelling; therefore hath he not given his Spirit to be a judge of such things.

For the same reason Christ said to the young man who desired him to speak to his brother that he divide the inheritance with him, "Who made me a judge or divider over you?"[5] as though he would say, "What is your quarrel to me—the quarrel that ye have between yourselves over what is temporal? For I have not been sent by God to judge such matters, but I am come to plant what is of God,[6] that he who desireth it may receive and find it in me.[7] But since thou desirest not what is divine but what is earthly and worldly, go thy way and let those who are appointed thereover decide."[8] For he who seeketh temporal things, seeketh not what is in Christ, therefore can he receive no decision from him. And those who are his, like him, have not been appointed to judge over temporal things.

That Christians must not go to law is shown by Christ in the words, "If any man will sue thee at the law, and take away thy coat, let him have thy cloak also,"[1] as though he would say, "Sooner let him take all, than quarrel with him over it and on its behalf go to a court that is foreign to thy nature." All this is Christ's will, that we may thereby show that we seek not what is temporal and foreign to us,[2] but what is divine and our own.[3] Thus it is evident that a Christian can neither go to law nor be a judge.

CONCERNING SWEARING

Even as the law was an introduction to the greater grace and knowledge of God, likewise also are the commandments. For this reason God, the Lord, desired naught else by swearing in the old covenant than to direct and bring men to his name;[4] that they might learn to know him aright, to cleave to him[5] and give him alone the honour.[6] For God, who is the truth, by commanding his people Israel to swear by his name,[7] meaneth to teach them to speak the truth and cleave to the same; therefore also forbade he them to speak his name vainly or lightly[8]—as though he would say that they be careful in all that they say to be found servants of truth, that is of God. For this reason doth he also threaten not to hold him guiltless who speaketh his name vainly and lightly, that is, who is careless about the truth. That it is true, however, that through the command to swear in the old covenant God hath chosen in the new (since the will of God is fully revealed[9]) the speaking of truth and walking therein, or the knowing of God aright and cleaving to him, may be seen from David's words

114

when he saith, "The man that sweareth by God is praised; but the mouth of them that speak lies must be stopped."[1] Who, then, can say aught else than that here "swearing" meaneth speaking the truth and cleaving to the same?

But that by means of the command to swear in the old covenant, we in the new are to understand to know God aright and cleave to him, is shown by the words, "Unto me every knee shall bow and by me every tongue shall swear saying: Surely in the Lord is my righteousness and strength."[2] This word is thus treated and explained by Paul, "Every knee shall bow to me, and every tongue shall confess to God."[3] Here it is evident that swearing in the old covenant meaneth in the new knowing God and cleaving to him alone.[4] Thus, the law is now a guide to a better knowledge and hope; by the which we draw nigh to God.[5]

Now, since the light of divine grace hath appeared and been revealed more brightly in Christ, the servants of the new covenant lay no longer upon us the shade but the glory of the light of truth in its clarity.[6] Therefore Paul saith plainly, as one who hath no veil before his face, "Put away lying and speak every man truth with his neighbour; for ye are members one of another."[7]

If one should say, "But Israel was also commanded to speak the truth, and hate lies,[8] so this is not the meaning." We say, it is true that Israel was also commanded to speak the truth, but since at that time sonship had not been distinguished from the state of bondage, and the spirit of bondage cannot attain the real truth,[9] God desired to show them by means of swearing by his name that there is no other truth,[10] and that he who would walk in the truth must enter through the name of God and be established therein.[11] That is what God desireth to teach us by means of swearing in the old covenant.

Since, however, at that time sonship was not distinguished from the state of bondage, those who had the child-like Spirit were then held under the ceremonial semblance of the law,[1] as Paul saith, "The heir, as long as he is a child, differeth nothing from a servant, though he be lord of all; but is under tutors and governors until the time appointed of the father. Even so we, when we were children, were in bondage to outward regulations until the time was fulfilled when God sent his Son, who redeemed us from the law, that we might receive sonship."[2]

Now, however, hath the shadow ceased, the light is arisen,[3] sonship is separated from bondage[4] and the covenant of sonship ratified, so that henceforth there are no more servants but all are children,[5] that is, those who have received the child-like Spirit and have been brought by the same into the covenant of the knowledge of God, who now himself testifieth, speaketh and doeth everything in them,[6] of which swearing had hitherto been a figure. For swearing by God's name[7] meant naught else than to prove that God must testify, confirm and bring to pass everything in his people. Now, however, since the truth is revealed,[8] the shadow, the outward appearance—swearing—must give way and cease and let the Spirit of truth himself testify in us with power and give proof of his working.

For this reason Christ saith, "It was said to them of old, Thou shalt not forswear thyself, but I say unto you, Swear not at all; neither by heaven; for it is God's throne: nor by the earth; for it is his footstool: neither by Jerusalem; for it is the city of the great King. Neither shalt thou swear by thy head, because thou canst not make one hair white or black. But let your yea be yea; and your nay be nay: for whatsoever is more than these cometh of evil."[9] The evil one, however, is the devil, who worketh in men everything whereby God is reviled.[10]

Now it cannot be denied, for it is clear to all men, that God desireth from us Christians a true worship performed in spirit and truth and more perfect than the service of the old covenant.[1] Therefore we are not only not to forswear ourselves, but we are not to swear at all.[2] Christ thereby teacheth us to give and ascribe honour to God alone, and to humble ourselves before him, as those who of themselves can do nothing; for we can do nothing,[3] not even promise to do something of ourselves—let alone swear to do it.[4] Thus, it is evident that on account of our weakness and unprofitableness we swear not, for we will not rob God of his honour.

They say further, "We ought to swear by no created thing, but we may, indeed, swear to the truth by the Creator, for he hath sworn by himself.[5] Therefore we are here not forbidden to swear by him, but by created things." To this we say, God hath sworn by himself,[6] but we ought not so to do, for what God promiseth he both can and will do of himself,[7] therefore hath he the right to swear; but we have not, for of ourselves we can do nothing. Moreover, that Christ forbiddeth us to swear, not only by the creation but also by the Creator is shown by the words, "Swear not at all."[8]

Also if one is not to swear by the creation which is, indeed, less than God, verily one must not swear by God, who is much higher and greater. For who shall presume in regard to what is greatest when he may not seize upon what is less? That this should in no wise be the case, indeed, even less by the greatest than by the least, is shown by Christ when he saith, "Woe unto you ye blind guides, which say, Whosoever shall swear by the temple, it is nothing; but whosoever shall swear by the gold of the temple, he is bound thereby. Ye fools and blind: for whether is greater, the gold, or the temple that sanctifieth the gold? and, Whosoever shall swear by the altar it is nothing; but whosoever sweareth by the sacrifice that is upon it, he is guilty. Ye fools and blind: for whether is greater, the sacrifice or the altar that sanctifieth the sacrifice? Whoso therefore shall swear by the altar, sweareth by it, and by all things thereon. And whoso shall swear by the temple, sweareth by it, and by him that dwelleth therein. And he that shall swear by heaven, sweareth by the throne of God, and by him that sitteth thereon."[1]

Here it is made evident that Christ desireth even less swearing by the greatest than by the least, therefore doth he rebuke the Jews because they find fault with little things and not with the greatest; for the temple is more than the gold within it, and the altar more than the sacrifice upon it. Therefore he who sweareth by the temple and altar doth sin more than he who sweareth by the gold in the temple and the sacrifice on the altar, since he sweareth not only by the temple, but also by him who dwelleth therein, that is, he sweareth by God. Likewise he who sweareth by heaven sweareth by God's throne and by him who sitteth thereon. For this reason he calleth them blind guides, who strain at a gnat and swallow a camel,[2] that is, observe the smallest in the law and pass over the greatest.

Thus it is clear that one ought not to swear at all. As James saith, "Above all things, dear brothers, swear not, neither by heaven, neither by the earth, neither by any other oath: but let your yea be yea; and your nay be nay."[3] And that solely as hath been said, that we encroach not upon God's honour and glory; but, since we can do nothing without him,[4] give him the honour, who must do everything in us, and say, Yea, if the Lord will, I will do it,[5] as James teacheth us, For whoso knoweth to do good, and doeth it not, to him it is sin.

118

CONCERNING GREETING

Greeting in itself is wishing what is good.[1] Therefore one ought to wish good to all who desire good. Thus, when one member of the Church meeteth another, he should greet him with the good wish, that is, offer him the blessed gift, the peace of Christ, which he gave us and left with us.[2] For so he teacheth his disciples, "Into whatsoever house ye enter, say, Peace be unto thee. If there be one like-minded therein, then your peace shall rest upon him: if not, your peace shall turn to you again."[3]

From these words we learn that both he that greeteth and he that is greeted must be children of peace, if God is to give the blessing. For the peace of Christ cannot rest upon one who is not like-minded with the gospel, or who desireth not with his whole heart so to be. But the Lord's greeting shall not be given with the lips only, or from a thoughtless heart; but with the whole heart, in firm faith, and confident that God most certainly will grant this good wish; yea, even is it as though God himself speaketh it through him.[4] The other, likewise, should accept it with the same confidence and wholehearted desire. Then God, the Lord, will give the blessing and grant the greeting wishing that the Lord be with them,[5] and will abide with them at all times[6]—so that this greeting, like Mary's to Elizabeth,[7] will bring forth joy. Where, however, it is given carelessly, with a thoughtless heart, there it is sin, for God's name is taken in vain,[8] therefore is this an abomination to him, and God will not hold him guiltless who doeth it: he shall not remain unpunished. Even as he sinneth who giveth the greeting lightly, so likewise doth he who accepteth it carelessly and not reverently before God. He also taketh God's name in vain, who giveth it to those whom he knoweth desire it not, such as gamblers, drunkards and the like. Therefore let each who feareth God be circumspect in this and preserve his soul from evil.

CONCERNING THE GIVING OF THE HAND AND EMBRACING

To give the hand and embrace is a sign of peace, love and unanimity in God, a sign by which those who are in the Church show that they are of one mind, heart and soul,[1] as may be learnt from Paul's words, "When Peter, James and John saw the grace of God that was given to me, how the gospel was entrusted to me as it was to them, they gave to me and Barnabas the right hand and became one with us."[2] Thus, it is a sign of unanimity, peace and love.

For even as the hands are clasped within each other, one showeth thereby that the hearts are likewise interwoven and clasped. The same is true of embracing: that as men embrace one another, and put their arms around one another, even so have they embraced and enclosed one another in their hearts.[3] Since, however, these two signs are signs of peace, they should be observed in the Church strictly, firmly and in their true nature with the fear of God, and one member of the Church should receive another with this reverence.[4] But where one showeth himself thus to another, while his heart is not turned in the same direction, then is the same an hypocrite and the truth is not in him.[5] In the world, however, it is a sign of friendliness, therefore a Christian may use it as such with those who are of the world. But when it is a sign of an oath or of swearing, he must not use it or do so.[6]

Since, however, both these signs should signify one thing, in order to avoid offence and also to give no occasion to the flesh or instigation to sin,[7] let a brother take and embrace a brother in love and a sister a sister that, as is said above, they may thereby show what is in their heart. But brothers and sisters should express this by giving hands and not by embracing, that the teaching of Christ be not thereby brought into disrepute and dishonour.

CONCERNING PRAYER

Prayer must and ought to be from a right heart, that is, in spirit and in truth,[1] if it is to be pleasing to God. Therefore he who would so pray must prepare his heart, firstly,[2] through the laying aside of all that is wrong, since God heareth not sinners;[3] and must strive, as far as it is at all possible, to be at peace with all men, above all with the believers;[4] as Christ saith, "If thou comest before the altar to lay thy sacrifice thereon, and rememberest at the same moment that thy brother hath something against thee, then go and first be reconciled to him, and then come and sacrifice thy gift."[5] Therefore each one who would offer the fruit of his lips to God—that is, praise and prayer—must first be reconciled to all, so that none of the believers have aught against him.

Further, he also must have forgiven if he have aught in his heart against any, as Christ teacheth, saying, "When ye stand and pray, forgive, if ye have aught against any: that your Father also which is in heaven may forgive you your trespasses."[6] And when the heart is thus purified it must then be adorned with true faith and real confidence.[7] Yea, the man must have such trust in God that he surely, firmly and certainly believeth that God, as a father who seeketh always the best for his children, will hear him and grant his prayer;[8] as the words of Christ show and indicate, "If ye, who are evil, can yet give your children good gifts, how much more will your

Father in heaven give the Holy Spirit to them that ask him?"[1]

Thus, they who pray in faith will receive. And he who prayeth thus in faith ceaseth not to make his request to God, and alloweth no other concern to hinder or delay him; and if there should be delay and it seem as though God will not grant it, he waiteth with all patience in the firm confidence that God will certainly give without delay.

He, however, who after he hath prayed turneth his heart to something else and so is drawn away from his request, and ceaseth to pray, and becometh weary of his request and leaveth it, can receive nothing, since he hath not continued in faith;[2] as James saith, "If one would ask aught of God, let him ask in faith, nothing wavering. For he that then doubteth or ceaseth to make his request is an unstable man. Let not that man think that he shall receive anything of God."[3]

If, however, we, who are children of Christ's Spirit, know not by reason of our weakness how to come before God so that our desire and request may stand before him,[4] then, saith Paul, "The Spirit upholdeth our weakness; for we know not what we should pray for as we ought: but the Spirit itself intercedeth for us mightily, with unspeakable groaning; and he that searcheth the hearts knoweth what is the mind of the Spirit, because he maketh intercession for the saints according to the will of God."[5]

Now, it is in this one Spirit that God desireth to be honoured and worshipped,[6] and therefore one ought to await his instigation and learn of him. Then what he teacheth and inspireth in us will be heard by God and will be pleasing unto him, and since he heareth us we shall have the petition that we have asked of him.[7]

CONCERNING SINGING

Paul saith, "Sing and make melody in your heart to the Lord, with psalms and hymns and spiritual songs."[1] For this reason we say that to sing spiritual songs is good and pleasing to God if we sing in the right way, that is, attentively, in the fear of God and as inspired by the Spirit of Christ.

For it is for this reason that they are called spiritual songs: namely, that they are inspired and made and composed by the urge of the Spirit,[2] and also attract and move men to blessedness. Therefore, since they are composed and made by the inspiration and urge of the Spirit of Christ, they must also be sung as inspired by the same Spirit, if they are to be sung aright and to be of service to men.

Where this is not the case, and one singeth only for carnal joy or for the sweet sound or for some such reason, one misuseth them, changing them into what is carnal and worldly, and singeth not songs of the Spirit, but of the letter. Likewise also, he who enjoyeth listening for the music's sake—he heareth in the letter and not in the Spirit, so with him also is it without fruit; and because they are not used, sung and heard aright, he that so doeth sinneth greatly against God; for he useth his word, which was given for his salvation and as an urge to blessedness, as leading to the lust of the flesh and to sin.[3] Thus, it is changed by him into harm, for though the song in itself is spiritual, yet is it to that man no longer a spiritual song. It is a worldly song, for it is not sung in the Spirit.

He, however, who singeth in the Spirit, considereth diligently every word, how far and whither it goeth, why it hath been used and how it may serve to his betterment.[4] He who doeth this singeth to the Lord's praise, to the betterment of both himself and others and as an instigation to a godly life. This is to sing well; to sing in any other way is in vain. Thus, we allow it not among us that other than spiritual songs are sung.

CONCERNING FASTING

To fast is to chasten and subdue the body, that the flesh may be humbled and the more easily controlled, mastered and overcome. Fasting hath arisen among the devout that they may crucify their flesh and overthrow its lusts; and thereby cleave the more freely and joyfully to God. By the ungodly, however, it was soon subverted and made unclean,[1] since they fasted for the sake of gain, thinking thereby to get something from God; therefore it is in vain, as can be seen from the words of Isaiah, when he saith, "They say to God, Wherefore do we fast and thou seest not? We afflict our soul and thou takest no notice!"

To which the Lord saith, "For ye fast not aright. For though ye fast, your desires remain and ye press your debtors no less than before. Behold, ye fast for strife and debate and to strike him whom ye address with the fist. Ye fast not so that your voice may be heard on high. Think ye that I find pleasure in the fast in which a man afflicteth his soul for a day: and bendeth his neck about like a hook, and lieth in a hair-shirt on the earth? Is that fasting, and a day in which the Lord delighteth?"[2]

From this it is evident how the ungodly have subverted and misused it, that is those including the Papists, who think thereby to wipe out their sins and to reconcile themselves to God, though they have not left off their sins; as the words show, "Though ye fast your desires remain,"[3] as though he would say: What then is the good of your fasting, since ye chasten yourselves only with the denial of the needs of

124

the body, while leaving the flesh all the obstinacy of its desires and lusts? Is that a fast or a day that pleaseth God? It is, indeed, far from the mark. For so fasted not your fathers, who drew nigh unto me.

But that fasting is right, good and pleasing to God when done aright, is proved by the words, "Ye fast not in such a way that your voice is heard on high."[1] Here one seeth the true fasting that was done by the saints: they chastened the obstinacy and desires of the flesh and broke off the same in that they forsook and refused what is wrong, concerned themselves with God alone, and clove to and served him in true faith, through which their voice rose up to heaven.

Such fasting is held up to us by the Lord as pleasing to him, when he saith, "Is not this the fast that I have chosen? that thou loose the bond of him that is entangled by thee, that is, that thou forgive him his debt, that thou exact not usury, but turn away therefrom, letting the oppressed go free and breaking every yoke; giving thy bread to the hungry, bringing the orphan to thy house and feeding him, clothing the naked and turning not thy face from the needy?[2] Then shall thy light break forth as the morning, and thy health shall blossom speedily; and thy righteousness shall go before thee; and the glory of the Lord shall surround thee."[3] That is the fasting which is pleasing to the Lord, the fasting which all the saints practised diligently. Therefore were they called friends of God. And he who would be pleasing to God with his fasting must still fast in like manner.

CONCERNING CELEBRATIONS

To keep a festival or holy day is likewise not for the sake of the outward appearance, for the outward celebration is no more than a shadow and picture of that which is to come; but the essential reality itself is Christ.[1] Since, then, the essential is Christ, the shadow must give way to him, that is, the outward to the real and true celebration in which the Lord delighteth, which celebration is, namely, to seek diligently to obey God, to do his will, to please him,[2] to meditate upon his word day and night[3] and do what is good and blessed, and, as one saith, to leave off and stop working or revelling in evil, and to work in good, that is to say, to live and walk in the Spirit.[4] That is the true celebration that God demandeth, as it is written, "Blessed is the man that doeth this, and the son of man that observeth this; that keepeth the sabbath from polluting it, that is, that keepeth his hand from doing any evil."[5]

That is the festival that God commandeth,[6] which we should now diligently observe and keep. But celebrating as it is practised in the world is an abomination to God.[7] For the evil and shameful things that men are unable to do during the week because of their work, they do on the holy day, using it thereby for the very opposite, and it were, indeed, better that they had no holy days.

Yet we, also, have a day of quiet in which we read the Lord's word and listen to it,[8] and thereby revive our heart to continue in the grace of God. Since, however, it is usual for all men to observe Sunday, we, in order to do offence to none (for which day is kept is a matter of indifference), keep the same day; but not because of the law, which is done away with in Christ,[9] but, as we have said, to exercise ourselves in the word of God.

CONCERNING TRADERS

We allow none of our number to do the work of a trader or merchant, since this is a sinful business;

as the wise man saith, "It is almost impossible for a merchant and trader to keep himself from sin.[1] And as a nail sticketh fast between door and hinge; so doth sin stick close between buying and selling."[2] Therefore do we allow no one to buy to sell again, as merchants and traders do. But to buy what is necessary for the needs of one's house or craft, to use it and then to sell what one by means of his craft hath made therefrom, we consider to be right and not wrong.

This only we regard as wrong: when one buyeth a ware and selleth the same again even as he bought it, taking to himself profit,[3] making the ware dearer thereby for the poor, taking bread from their very mouths and thus making the poor man nothing but the bondman of the rich. Paul saith likewise, "Let him who defrauded, defraud no more."[4] They say, however, "But the poor also profit in that one bringeth goods from one hand to another!" There they use poverty as a pretext, seeking all the time their own profit first, and thinking only of the poor as having an occasional penny in their purse. Therefore we permit this not amongst us, but say with Paul that they should labor, working with their hands what is honest, that they may have to give to him that needeth.[5]

CONCERNING INNKEEPERS

Neither do we allow any of our number to be a public innkeeper serving wine or beer, since this goeth with all that is unchaste, ungodly and decadent, and drunken and good-for-nothing fellows gather there together to carry out their headstrong wills. This they must permit, and listen to their blasphemy. For this reason we believe not that this is something that one who feareth God may do; namely, for the sake of money listen to such blasphemy, allow it and make themselves partakers of their sins.[1] For the wise man saith also, that it is nearly impossible for an innkeeper to keep himself from sin.[2]

But this we do, and regard it as doing right: if one cometh over the pasture land and can go no farther, and cometh upon one of our brothers, he receiveth him and lodgeth him, serveth him and doeth him all the good he can; but not for money, but freely, for nothing. For we find that thus also did the saints, and that they were given to hospitality.[3]

CONCERNING STANDING DRINKS

Standing drinks is a cause of evil and transgression of the commandments of God. For from standing drinks followeth and cometh drunkenness, through which a man squandereth and destroyeth both soul and body,[4] therefore we allow it not among us. If one saith, "A drink taken in friendship, just as much as one liketh and desireth—that is not wrong," we say: Be that as it may, it is truly used—or misused— other than as God hath appointed for his creatures, for thereby is the man moved and lured on to drink, when he otherwise would not do so. Therefore is it against nature, and is sin and evil.

By means of such instigation, in which the one would please the other and taketh drink to himself without the urge and call of nature, doth one transgress God's order,[5] forgetteth the Creator and oneself as well, and each desireth to be cock of the roost and bear off the prize at tippling, and beginneth to drink full and half tankards, not thinking that it is written, "Woe unto them that are mighty to drink wine, and great at producing drunkenness. But the Lord's work they perceive not, nor consider why God made it. Therefore do they come into captivity, for

128

they know nothing, and hell openeth its jaws exceeding wide to receive all proud magnificence and foolhardiness, together with them who find pleasure therein."[1]

Therefore is the standing of drinks evil at the root, no matter how it is done. It is an invention of the devil to catch men, draw them into his net, make them cleave to him and forsake God, and lead them into all sin. Therefore, one should flee from it as from the face of a serpent.[2]

CONCERNING COMING TOGETHER

When we come together, we do so with the desire to encourage and awaken our hearts in the grace of God, to walk in the Lord's sight with greater diligence and attention.[3] Therefore, the people are first encouraged to mark diligently and to consider why we have met and come together, that they may prepare their hearts for prayer, so that they may come worthily before the Lord and pray[4] for what concerneth the Church and all her members.[5]

After this we give thanks to God for all the good that he hath given us through Christ,[6] and for accepting us into his grace[7] and revealing to us his truth. This is followed by an earnest prayer that he keep us faithful and devout therein to the end, and supply all our desires and needs, and open our hearts that we may use his word with profit, hear, accept and keep it.[8] When this is done, one proceedeth to proclaim the Lord's word faithfully, according to the grace given by God, encouraging the heart to fear the Lord and to remain in his fear.[9] When all this is completed the minister commendeth the Church to God the Lord and letteth them depart one from another, each to his place. When, however, we come together to keep the Lord's Memory or Supper the people are encouraged and taught for one, two or three days and told vividly what the Lord's Supper is, what happeneth there and what one doeth thereby, and how one should prepare himself worthily to receive the same.[1] Every day, however, hath also its thanksgiving and prayer. When all this hath taken place, and the Lord's Supper hath been kept, a hymn of praise is sung to the Lord. Then the people are admonished to walk in accordance with what they have shown to be in their hearts, and then they are commended to the Lord and allowed to separate.

CONCERNING THE EDUCATION OF CHILDREN

"Ye parents," saith Paul, "provoke not your children to wrath: but bring them up in the nurture and admonition of the Lord."[2] For this reason is our education of children such that we permit them not to carry out their headstrong will and carnal practice. Therefore in such places as in the country of Moravia, where we have many households we have schools in which we bring up our children in the divine discipline, and teach them from the beginning to know God.[3] But we permit them not to go to other schools, since there they teach but the wisdom, art and practices of the world, and are silent about divine things.

Our practice is as follows: as soon as the mother hath weaned the child she giveth it to the school. Here there are sisters, appointed by the Church to care for them, who have been recognized to be competent and diligent therein; and, as soon as they can speak, they lay the word of God's testimony in their mouths and teach them to speak with or from the same,[4] tell them of prayer and such things as children can understand. With them children remain until their fifth or sixth year, that is, until they are able to learn to read and write.

When they are thus far they are entrusted to the schoolmaster, who teacheth them the same and thereby instructeth them more and more in the knowledge of God, that they learn to know God and his will and strive to keep the same. He observeth the following order with them: when they all come together in the morning to school he teacheth them to thank the Lord together, and to pray to him. Then he preacheth to them as children for the space of half an hour, telling them how they ought to obey, be subject to and honour their parents, teachers and those set over them,[1] and illustrateth from the Old and New Testaments both the promise to godly and the punishment of disobedient and obstinate children.[2]

From such obedience to parents he teacheth them obedience to God and the keeping of his will;[3] that they should reverence him as their almighty Father, and love, honour and worship him above all things; and serve and cleave to him alone, as him from whom they have all that is good.[4] Thus we teach our children from babyhood to seek not what is temporal but what is eternal.[5]

They remain with the schoolmaster until they reach the stage when they can be taught to work. Then each is set to the work for which he is recognized to be gifted and capable. When they have thus been educated and have learnt to know and believe in God,[6] they are baptized upon confession of their faith.[7]

CONCERNING EXCLUSION

Paul saith, "Put away from among yourselves what is evil."[8] Therefore in the fear of God we observe and watch over one another, since the one would protect and keep the other from all wrong and from such evil as deserveth exclusion. Therefore do we watch over one another, telling each his faults, warning and rebuking with all diligence. But where one will not accept the rebuke, but disregardeth it, the matter is brought before the Church, and if he hear not the Church, then he is excluded and put out.[1]

If, however, one be discovered in the gross and deadly sins of which Paul saith, "If any man that is called a brother be a fornicator, or covetous, or an idolater, or a railer, or a drunkard, or a thief or a robber, with such an one ye must not even eat."[2] Such an one is put out and excluded or separated from the Church without admonition, since the judgment of Paul is already spoken.

And if one is so excluded, we have naught to do with him: have no company with him, that he may be ashamed.[3] Yet is he called to repentance, that perchance he may be moved thereby and return the more quickly to God;[4] and where not, that the Church may remain pure and innocent of his sin, and bear not guilt and rebuke from God on his behalf.[5]

In all such cases, however, is a distinction made, that he who sinneth wilfully be punished according to the weight of his sin; and the more wilful the sin, the sharper the punishment. If, however, he sin in the haste of the flesh and not wilfully or recklessly, but through the weakness of the flesh, he is punished, but not completely separated from the Church or excluded from all fellowship; but he is not permitted to use the Lord's greeting,[6] to give or accept "Peace,"[7] that he may humble himself before God for his sin, and thereafter watch all the more carefully against it.

CONCERNING READMISSION

Now when one is excluded we have no fellowship with him until he hath truly repented: though he may run with entreaty and desire, he is not accepted until he hath received from the Church the good report of a truly repentant life; yea, he is not accepted until one senseth that the Lord hath again drawn nigh to him, been gracious to and accepted him. When, however, this is recognized, the Church likewise offereth him the hand, that is, she doeth what she hath been commanded by God, so that he is accepted by her and is counted once more a member of the Church.[1] But as in the beginning one is received into the Church by means of a sign (that is baptism),[2] so also after he fell and was separated from the Church he must likewise be received by a sign, that is through the laying on of hands, which must be done by a servant of the gospel. This indicateth that he once more hath part and is rooted in the grace of God.[3] When this hath taken place he is accepted again in full love;[4] all suspicion, complaint and disinclination are swept away and cut off—lest Satan should get the advantage of us—and one hath a right and completely trusting heart toward him as toward all the other members of the Church. Therefore it is so long postponed until, as hath been said, the grace of God is once more felt to be at work in him, drawing the confidence of the Church once more toward him.

CONCERNING THE WHOLE LIFE, WALK, DRESS AND ADORNMENT OF CHRISTIANS

Firstly, we say with Peter that the dress of Christians consisteth not in outward magnificence and ornament such as the wearing of gold chains and

133

fine clothing and such like trappings, but that the hidden man of the heart be adorned with the incorruptibility of a gentle and quiet spirit, which is glorious and greatly prized in the eyes of God; wherewith also the saints who set their hope on God adorned themselves.[1]

Therefore Christians should not strive to please the world by means of outward decoration as the world doeth,[2] in that one lureth another with such outward show or seeketh his own pleasure therein, thereby forgetting God, forsaking the divine adornment and jewel and concerning himself with vanity, until Satan hath them firmly and utterly within his power.[3]

Therefore saith Paul, "Be not conformed to this world, but let yourselves be changed by the renewing of your mind, that ye may prove and know what is the will of God, what is pleasing to God and perfect."[4] It is evident from these words that each one who would know what is right in the eyes of God, must lay aside all that maketh like the world and conformeth thereto or showeth itself to be worldly and carnal minded; and give himself wholly to the practice of what is blessed.[5]

Thus is such decoration and zeal for the same not only not an adornment of Christians, but, on the contrary, a proof of the non-Christian; therefore all godly hearts rightly lay it aside, fight shy of, flee from and avoid it, and concern themselves with and use only the true decoration, jewel and adornment of Christians, which, as is said above, is of the inner man.[6] For, since their citizenship is in heaven,[7] they ought to put on heavenly jewels, and learn diligence from the children of the world, who, in whatsoever land they live, strive to dress and adorn themselves to the very uttermost in accordance with the custom of the same land, in order to please him who dwelleth in the world. How much more should Christians give heed to and regard the ways of their land, into which they are led by Christ: that is the divine nature and character;[1] and in accordance with the custom of the same land also adorn themselves to the uttermost to please him who dwelleth in heaven.[2]

Thus, all their desire and effort, all their care and consideration, as well as their prayer and petition, both day and night,[3] should be that they may receive from God this heavenly adornment; and this they should seek with such diligence and constancy that they forget thereby all other adornment and have in mind only the jewel of the godly, which is true blessedness; then, it will be given them in abundance.

But such diligence cometh only from love to him for whose pleasure one adorneth oneself. Therefore the greater our love to him who dwelleth in heaven, the more greatly will we strive for the jewel in which he delighteth, that we may adorn ourselves therewith to please him.[4]

He, however, who seeketh not this jewel with diligence showeth that he hath no great reverence for him for whose sake one should so adorn oneself.

But he who desireth such a jewel with all his heart will be adorned by the Lord himself with holy adornments, that is with all manner of Christian virtues,[5] which he putteth on and weareth as a garment which adorneth him better than a necklace of gold.[6] Now, he who recognizeth this will from henceforth forget all pearls and necklaces of silk and gold and such-like jewels in seeking to lay hands upon the one jewel of blessedness which remaineth in all eternity. On this one jewel he hath set his heart, and in striving for it he showeth his faith.[7]

But we do say also that he, who previously made such clothing in the world before he came to the true recognition of the truth, doth not sin thereby when he weareth it out, if he layeth aside its misuse and permitteth not such outward adornment to be an hindrance to him in striving for the divine adornment. For if it should hinder him it were better that he threw it into the fire than that he put it on; but to make and order such things after the recognition of truth we permit not among us; that Satan may not thereby find cause to betray the man again.

Now through the grace of God we have shown forth and rendered an account of our faith, teaching and whole life (all praise and honour be to the almighty God!), in which we believe every man who desireth not to fight wilfully against the truth can well see, sense and recognize that we have done nothing without or apart from the truth, or chosen anything for ourselves; but have set before us what God himself hath ordained, commanded and inspired, to cleave faithfully to the same. May he, the Lord our God, perfect the work that he hath begun in us all to his praise, and establish us in his truth, and keep us true and devout in his Son until the end, that we may become worthy to receive the promise with all the saints; and may he enlighten those who still walk in darkness that they may see and know the light of life. Amen,

Yea, Amen

Sit laus Deo.

Ecclesiasticus IV.28.

"Strive for the truth unto death, and
the Lord shall fight for thee."

THE SECOND PART

HOW GOD DESIRETH TO HAVE A PEOPLE, WHOM HE HIMSELF HATH SEPARATED FROM THE WORLD AND CHOSEN TO BE HIS BRIDE

God the Almighty, that he might be known and praised and his holy name honoured, made man in his own likeness.[1] Now, since he is truth, it is clear that he desireth naught else from man than that he should show forth this likeness of truth and live and walk therein,[2] that he may appear what he is, namely the glory of God,[3] and no poison of destruction be found in him.[4] But deceived by the counsel of the serpent, man left this glory,[5] fell into sin, the likeness of the devil, to whom he surrendered himself.[6] And because he surrendered himself to the service of unrighteousness the wrath of his Creator came upon him, and he fell into his disfavour,[7] for which reason he was driven out of the Garden of Eden.[8]

Thus was transgression introduced,[9] which thereafter continued to increase more and more in the children of men, so that the indignation of the Lord grew against them, and he desired to forsake them and said, "My Spirit shall not always be judge among men, since they are flesh. I shall take it from them."[10] This can be seen in Saul[11] and many others who rejected the word of God, as the wise man telleth us in the words, "The Holy Spirit, who teacheth aright, fleeth from them who turn away from God and departeth from them who are malicious."[12]

Here it is evident that God at the beginning separated and sundered the devout from the godless. Of these he saith that the Holy Spirit will not dwell in them who are subject to sin;[1] with the others, however, he promiseth to be at all times[2] and to be their God[3] if they zealously keep his commandments, teaching and ways,[4] as we see especially in the case of Abraham,[5] who was called the father of all believers.[6] The Lord appeared to him and said, "I am God, Shaddai, that is one with authority, overflowing fullness and sufficiency of all good. Walk before me and be steadfast and faithful to me, and I will make a covenant between me and thee."[7]

Moses saith the same also to Israel, "If ye hearken to these judgments and keep and do them, that the Lord thy God shall also keep unto thee the covenant and mercy which he sware unto thy fathers: and he will love thee, and bless thee."[8] Now, as God hath at all times distinguished between the devout and the godless, as is said above—loved the devout and hated the godless,[9] as he still doeth and finally will do —he desired that this separation and distinction should not be before his eyes only but also before men;[10] which separation hath begun in Christ,[11] in whom also the restoration of salvation was promised from the beginning.[12]

When, however, God the Almighty in his grace desired to show and reveal that he had pleasure in the devout and not in the godless,[13] he separated for himself from all nations a nation,[14] in whom he had pleasure,[15] and strengthened his covenant with them[16] and gave them circumcision as a token, that they should circumcise the flesh of the foreskin of every man child born to them or bought by them; which thing was a distinction between them and the heathen.[17]

To the same doth God promise to be their God and to have them as his people,[18] when he speaketh to Abraham saying, "I will be thy God and thy seed's God after thee."[19] He made, moreover, yet another distinction among them, saying, "As for Ishmael,

I have heard thee, but with Isaac will I establish my covenant,"[1] as though he would say, "Not with the bondwoman's son, who was born after the flesh, but with the free son, who was born after the promise, will I establish my covenant. In him will I keep the promise to thee and give the blessing, for of him shall they be who are called thy seed."

Therefore doth Paul treat and interpret this word thus, "They which are the children of the flesh these are not the children of God: but the children of the promise are counted for the seed."[2] From this it is evident that God at the beginning chose not all the seed of Abraham, as Paul declareth clearly, saying, "For they are not all Israelites, which are of Israel: neither, because they are the seed of Abraham, are they all children."[3]

Thus, if this is the case, it cannot be denied that the figure, in that the Scripture saith, "Cast out the bondwoman and her son: for the son of the bondwoman shall not be heir with the son of the freewoman,"[4] implieth the separation of the state of sonship from that of slavery, which latter cannot remain in the house. But children remain for ever therein.[5] Therefore is the promise for them alone: that God will be their God and will have them for his people,[6] yea that he will be their father and they shall be his children.[7] For this reason doth he richly bless the same with all manner of good things,[8] as it is written, "The Lord shall command the blessing upon thee in thy storehouses, and in all that thou settest thine hand unto; and he shall bless thee in the land which the Lord thy God shall give thee."[9]

With this outward blessing, however, the Lord desired to show the unfathomable riches of his grace which will hereafter be given us in Christ,[10] from whom we have received grace for grace.[11] Therefore saith Moses, "The Lord shall establish thee an holy people unto himself, as he hath sworn unto thee, if thou shalt keep the commandments of the Lord thy God, and walk in his ways. And all people of the earth shall see that thou art called by the name of the Lord."[1] Of this promise Esau was by birth also an heir, since he was born of Isaac,[2] in whom Abraham received the promise.[3] But he made himself unworthy of this promise in that he sold his birthright to Jacob for a paltry meal.[4] And he found no place of repentance, though he sought it with tears; therefore he was not reckoned as a son, but was appointed to bondage[5] and was separated from Jacob.[6]

But in Jacob, who is also called Israel,[7] the promise came to pass[8] for the tribe increaseth according to the measure of the number of his children.[9] For the same also doth he care as for his people,[10] though not for the sake of their devoutness but for his faithful promise's sake[11] that he might not forget but hold firmly to the covenant[12] promised to the fathers.[13]

Therefore for their sake did he punish Egypt and separate them from their plagues,[14] that it might be known how the Lord doth part Egypt and Israel one from the other.[15] Thus did Israel go out[16] with joy and delight, in hope, to receive the promised land,[17] although they soon departed from this hope[18] and became disobedient to his Spirit,[19] so that he thought to destroy them in the wilderness.[20] But for his name's sake and for the sake of the prayer of Moses, his servant, he refrained from doing so.[21]

Thus, they were spared, but as we have said, not for the sake of their devoutness,[22] but through the grace and mercy of the Almighty,[23] that the promise which he gave the fathers[24] might stand and the promised grace[25] of the coming Christ be given in his time;[26] for he, as was promised, was to be born of them.[27] Therefore did he give them his law,[28] statutes and judgment[29] that they might keep them diligently, observe them and walk therein,[1] and with all diligence teach and instruct their children[2] that they might observe the same for their children:[3] that they learn to fear the Lord their God as long as they live[4] and depart from his commands neither to right nor left,[5] that the curse that was foretold come not upon them.[6]

And these are the commands that God the Lord gave Israel with others through Moses, "Take heed that ye make not a covenant with the inhabitants of the land whither thou goest that they become not a stumbling block to you. Ye shall not make friends with them. Ye shall not give your daughters to their sons and ye shall not take their daughters for your sons, for they seek to turn your sons away from me, to make them serve strange gods;[7] but thus shall ye do to them: Ye shall destroy their altars, break their pillars, cut down their groves and burn their gods with fire.[8] But ye shall not do so unto the Lord your God,[9] but in the place which the Lord your God shall choose[10] shall ye serve[11] and unto it ye shall come[12] and bring your sacrifices and tithes."[13]

Here it is clear that God desireth not that his people mingle with the heathen in their disorderly conduct[14] and take part in their ceremonies, nor that they come to the places where they practise idolatry, for the heathen seek something other than the faithful seek.[15]

God speaketh through the prophets saying, "Can two go together except they be agreed?"[16] But because believers and unbelievers are not one,[17] the Lord hath forsaken and rejected the one[18] and chosen the other, as he himself testifieth,[19] "I have accepted thee alone out of all the peoples on the earth."[20] Therefore also doth Esdras say of Israel, when he speaketh to God, "Of every tree of the earth thou hast chosen thee the vine, of all the fowls the dove, of all cattle the sheep and of all the peoples thou hast chosen one people, namely, thy people Israel, to be the people of thine inheritance."[1]

For even as God the Lord, who is God over all gods, is separate from all idols,[2] as he himself saith, "To whom then will ye liken me or what likeness will ye compare unto me, for I declare beforehand things that have not yet come to pass."[3] And of Christ, Paul saith, "What concord hath Christ with Belial?"[4] In the same way will he have his people separate, because the believer hath no part with the unbeliever,[5] as he himself saith, "If thou holdest to me, then will I also hold to thee, and if thou teachest the devout to separate themselves from evil men, then thou shalt be my mouth, and before thou fallest to them they must fall to thee, for I have made thee to a strong brazen wall against this people. Though they fight against thee they shall not prevail against thee: for I am with thee to help thee and to save thee."[6]

And further, he saith, "Depart ye, depart ye, go ye out from thence, touch no unclean thing; go ye out of the midst of her; purify yourselves, ye that bear the vessels of the Lord."[7] And further, "Come out from among them, my people, and be ye separate," saith the Lord, "and touch no unclean thing; and I will receive you and will be a Father unto you and ye shall be my children."[8] And again, "Come out of her, my people, that ye be not partakers of her sins, and that ye receive not of her plagues."[9]

For as he is holy[10] and, as is said above, apart from all abomination,[11] even so will he have his people sundered from the assembly of godless men,[12] that they may be to him an holy people,[13] as it is written, "Ye shall be holy; for I the Lord your God am holy."[14]

Here all who have eyes to see may know the reason why God commandeth his people to sunder themselves from such ceremonies—namely, that they may not be defiled and made unclean thereby or even think that in so doing they are serving God, as the heathen do abominations to idols and devils.[1] Therefore also did Moses say to Pharaoh, "It is not meet that we sacrifice in the land for we might sacrifice to the abomination of the Egyptians and not to our God."[2] Mark well, here will Moses not only not go to the place where they serve their abominations, but he will not even sacrifice in the land.

Though some may say this took place for another reason, yet the word remaineth clearly and distinctly expressed, so no one can doubt or deny that God did not desire them to serve any longer in Egypt, for the command to go had been given.[3] The same is shown also by the Lord after the command had been carried out, namely that they should destroy and tear down the places where the heathen had served their gods.[4] For this reason also did Moses seek an opportunity to lead the people out with haste,[5] according to the Lord's command.[6] Not only so, but the Lord forced also the haughty king to let his people go,[7] which king he later slew in the sea as he hurried after them.[8]

Likewise also he commanded them later that when they should come into the land into which he would lead them, they should destroy the inhabitants thereof, that they might not be enticed and moved by the daily sight of their ceremonies to subject and surrender themselves to their idols; likewise also they should destroy all places where they served their gods[9]—not that they should change or use them aright, but that they should utterly destroy them.[10] Besides all this he warned them earnestly, showing them the harm that would come upon them if they should transgress this command and not observe it, saying: "But if ye will not drive out the inhabitants of the land from before you; then it shall come to pass, that those which ye let remain of them shall be pricks in your eyes, and thorns in your sides, and shall vex you in the land wherein ye dwell. Moreover it shall come to pass, that I shall do unto you, as I thought to do unto them."[1]

Now as long as they remained in these commands and held them firmly, the Lord cared for them as for his children, shielded and protected them and suffered no man to harm them.[2] As soon, however, as they forgot these and other commands and no longer observed them faithfully, the Lord gave them into the hands of them that hated them,[3] as he had told them beforehand through his servant Moses[4] and the song of witnesses pictureth the same clearly for them;[5] of which thing Joshua, when he was old and full of days and soon to fall asleep, warneth them saying, "Ye have seen the great things that the Lord your God hath done[6] unto your enemies and himself fought for you.[7] Be ye therefore very courageous to keep all his commands given you through Moses[8] and turn not aside from them to the right hand or to the left,[9] then the Lord your God will be with you[10] and fight for you,[11] so that one man of you shall chase a thousand.[12] But if ye go back and cleave unto the remnant of these nations and make friends with them so that ye go among them and they among you, then they will be snares and traps unto you and thorns in your sides and pricks in your eyes[13] until the Lord shall drive you out of the good land and overthrow you."[14]

Furthermore, Joshua saith, "Not one thing is lacking of all the good that the Lord hath promised you, but all hath come to pass. Now just as all the good hath come to pass, even so will he bring upon you all the evil[15] that he hath promised, and not one thing will be lacking, if ye transgress his commandments."[16]

146

Now, since all this—their land, glory, rule and later kingdom—is a sign and figure of the kingdom of Christ and of Christ, the king, which was promised beforehand[1] and then later established,[2] this driving out is nothing other than the separation of the believing from the unbelieving,[3] who can neither be nor stand in the Church of God;[4] for God desireth to have an holy bride, who is without wrinkle, spot or blemish,[5] holy, as he is holy.[6] Therefore just as little as the Lord, the almighty God, had pleasure therein when Israel left the heathen to dwell in the land and drove them not out (For the angel of the Lord spake to them, saying, "I have led you out of Egypt,[7] as I swore to your fathers: I will never break my covenant with you.[8] And ye shall make no league with the inhabitants of this land; ye shall throw down their altars. But ye have not obeyed my voice. Why have ye done this? Wherefore I also said, I will not drive them out from before you; but they shall become traps unto you and their gods, snares"), even less hath he pleasure therein today if one setteth up a church with the world, or taketh it into the Church of the saints, since, as is said above, David saith that the sinner cannot remain or stand in the congregation of the upright.[9] Thus, if one should say, "We also set up no church with unbelievers, but with those who confess Christ. Though they have fallen into many sins and have gone as far as to depart completely, because they propose betterment again, it is meet for us to help them thereto and not to withdraw completely from them; even as in the Old Testament the prophets did not separate themselves from Israel, though they had, indeed, done evil, but remained with them and led the whole people with earnest admonitions back to God.[10] Thus, this is meet for us now."

To this we say: In that the prophets did not

147

separate themselves from Israel, though they had, indeed, done evil, they acted rightly and not foolishly, since at that time servitude had not been distinguished from sonship.[1] Therefore although they were truly sons and the others slaves, yet they were held under the outward law until Christ.[2] Now, however, the time appointed by the Father hath come that the slaves are separated from the children, that the latter might receive their inheritance and freedom,[3] so now there are no longer slaves here, but all are children through faith in Christ.[4] Then, if some one saith: "They also believe in Christ, only they have fallen into certain errors—therefore we must help to raise up everyone who hath fallen." Then we say, to help to raise a fallen man we do not regard as wrong, if he is ready to let himself be raised. But no one is raised up by a dead faith,[5] nor is anyone helped who continueth in sins any more than was Pharaoh,[6] whom for this purpose God awakened, namely to show his power in him.[7] Therefore is no one helped but by proper preaching, followed by faith which is sealed with the Holy Spirit.[8] For Paul saith, "For as many as are led by the Spirit of God, they are the sons of God."[9] Now, since this work of God alone maketh children and leadeth the children here and now into their freedom through Christ,[10] who hath made the distinction between servants and children,[11] this distinction stands and no one will be accepted into the covenant of sonship and reckoned to the Church of the saints who is not urged by the Spirit of God.[12]

Therefore do we also say that we also desire the betterment of every man and to draw him to love and to all blessedness. But not in such a way, for we can clearly see through the grace of God that this is not pleasing to God, and also that it cannot be attained and accomplished in this way, for God is not himself urging the work. But we desire it in the right way, in accordance with our Master's instructions[1] and the inspiration of his Holy Spirit,[2] first to call every man to repentance through the Lord's word.[3] Now, all who respond to this and sacrifice themselves completely to God[4] and allow him, that is the Holy Spirit, to work in them and drive them into a new life, all such will we with joy also number in the Church of the children of God, as those who have received Christ;[5] the others, however, who continue in their sins[6] we allow to go and remain in their ways, as Christ and the apostles also did.

If one should say of their falling away,[7] as ye say, that they have been seduced by papistry, we answer: Yes, so seduced, darkened and blinded that they know neither of God nor of Christ[8] but only bear him about in their mouths and deny him with their whole lives;[9] hence also have they sought salvation in created things and have served the creature more than the Creator himself.[10] Of this, eternal Wisdom speaketh, saying, "This people praiseth me with the lips, but their heart is far from me, therefore do they serve me in vain, and I will not hear their prayer."[11]

Now, as the men of old were so completely deceived, seduced and corrupted by papistry that they even honoured the creatures more than the Creator himself,[12] it is certain that this is a heavy sin and a deep falling away from God.[13] For it is to leave the community and fellowship of the saints[14] and to surrender to the abominations of the heathen[15]—this none can deny. Now, if one will be reconciled with God and come back to God, he must separate himself from such godless company,[16] turn completely to the word of truth[17] and allow himself to be renewed by the same,[18] then will God be gracious to him[19] again and accept him.[20]

The same is shown also in the allegory of the strange wives,[21] whom they had to put away from them if they were to be reconciled again with God.[1] Thus, it cannot be otherwise than that whosoever hath entangled himself in a strange bond must break the same and join Christ if he is to be accepted. Otherwise will he drive him before him as Nehemiah drove the other before him. If one were to leave the Church or be excluded, he would not be accepted until he had first truly repented.[2] And while one is unfaithful to the Church he is also without God and Christ, as John saith, "Whosoever transgresseth, and abideth not in the doctrine of Christ, hath not God."[3] If therefore they have for so long been transgressing and have not God, then their preaching, baptizing and all that they do must be impure. For unto them that are defiled is everything defiled.[4] Because everything is impure to them, it is an abomination before God, yea, it is naught. For, since they have departed from the word, which is God,[5] they have no word. Therefore saith the Lord, "Hear the word of the Lord, for the Lord hath cause to rebuke the inhabitants of the land. For there is no faithfulness, no faith, no love and no word of God in the land, but blasphemy, lying, murder, stealing and adultery have taken the upper hand and blood-guilt followeth blood-guilt."[6] Therefore have they neither word nor baptism. From whence then are the people baptized to-day? If I must say it, they preached to them though they were not sent, and baptized when they were not commanded.[7] Now, since they were not commanded, their baptism is naught, for every plant which my heavenly Father hath not planted, saith Christ, shall be rooted up.[8]

Therefore I say of this people that they neither know Christ[9] nor have received[10] and accepted him.[11] They have but heard from their fathers from generation to generation a verbal confession and have learnt to say it after them.[12] That this is true is shown

150

by their own education—they teach blessedness so well that as soon as a child beginneth to speak he learneth to curse, and in this the parents praise him and say, "That will be a fine boy!" And this is most common among the nobles, who ought rather to oppose it.

Thus, the spirit of the parents is known in their children,[1] and such a verbal confession is naught to me. For the devil can also use God's name and confess him with the mouth.[2] Therefore I know also that it is an abomination to God.[3] Therefore, to say the whole truth, I consider that they have conquered and accepted Christianity even as the Philistines took the ark of God from Israel,[4] when they slew Israel and brought the ark with them into their land, and had it in their land to their own hurt and to the hurt of their god,[5] and growing wiser by misfortune had to send it home again;[6] or at least even as the heathen whom the Assyrian king led into the land of Israel and planted in the cities, among whom the Lord sent lions which slew them until they received a priest from Israel, who taught them the manner and practice of the law. Thus, they learned to serve the God of heaven but left not their abominations, therefore had God no pleasure in their service. Even so did their children.[7] The like is also to be seen in the supposed Christians of to-day, especially the Lutherans, who continually profess to love and serve God, and yet will not leave abominations of sin and vice with all the service of the devil, but continue from generation to generation therein; as their fathers did, do they and still worse. Therefore doth John say how finely they walk in the truth![8]

What took place later, however, when God the Lord had mercy upon Israel in accordance with his promise[9] and led them again into their land to build again through Cyrus, the king, the temple which

Nebuchadnezzar had broken down?[1] For Cyrus saith, "The Lord God of heaven hath given me all the kingdoms of the earth; and he hath charged me to build him an house at Jerusalem, which is in Judah. Who is there among you of all his people? His God be with him, and let him go up to Jerusalem, which is in Judah, and build the house of the Lord God of Israel, he is the God which is in Jerusalem. And whosoever remaineth in any place where he sojourneth, let the men of his place help him with silver, and with gold, and with goods and with beasts with a free will for the house of God at Jerusalem."[2] Thus, they whose hearts were touched by the Lord their God went up to build his house. Now, as they were building and the work progressing, came the heathen, or the chief among them who used to live in the country, and spake, "Let us build with you: for we seek your God, as ye do; and we do sacrifice unto him[3] since the days of Esarhaddon, king of Assur, which brought us up hither."[4] Then answered them Zerubbabel, Joshua and the chief of the fathers of Israel, "It is not meet that we and you build an house unto our God, but we will build alone unto the Lord, the God of Israel,[5] as the king hath commanded us."[6] Thus did the heathen hinder Israel and deterred them in the work, and sought by letters power from Artaxerxes, the king, to cause the work to cease; which thing they also achieved[7] until the time of Haggai and Zechariah, the prophets, who urged the people to continue the work of the Lord.[8]

Thus do we see before our eyes how things go with us at the hands of so-called Christians to-day, for they likewise seek to build with us and to undertake the Lord's work, and they also, when they hear the answer of the devout Zerubbabel, Joshua and all the chiefs of Israel—"It is not meet that we and you build an house unto our God, but we will build alone"[1]—seek with much cunning and tyranny, more cruel than Pharaoh,[2] Antiochus[3] or Nero, to deter us from such work and from building the Lord's house. But in all this we set our hope upon our God that they succeed even less than those; for the work went forward most gloriously through the perseverance of the prophets, and they were not allowed to build with them.[4]

Thus we hope, in spite of what they do, that their raging and tyranny will not hinder us in the work that the Lord our God hath begun in us through Christ, but that he accomplish the good work that he hath begun in us to his praise, and give us richly of his manifold divine grace; for we strive with earnestness and all our power to be pleasing to his will, to observe the same, as he promised us,[5] saying, "I will turn unto you and make you fruitful and multiply you, and will keep my covenant with you. And ye shall eat old store, and bring forth the old because of the new.[6] And I shall dwell among you: and my soul shall not abhor you. And I will walk among you, and will be your God, and ye shall be my people."[7]

Thus we wish with all our heart that all men might build themselves up with us into an holy house.[8] But as this is not the case, we pray to God day and night that he might keep all whose heart he hath touched, pierced and moved to come and build themselves up into such an house that they be not deterred by cunning, by threats or in any other way;[9] and also that he might move those who are not yet so moved that they may come to the building of the Lord's house,[10] that the building may go forward, as it began in Christ, to the praise of God the Father through Jesus Christ eternally.[11]
Amen.

NOW HOW THE HOUSE OF THE LORD IS BUILT UP IN CHRIST IN WHICH HOUSE THE SEPARATION IS COMPLETED

Now, since much hath been said of the building of the former temple, which was at Jerusalem and which, as a picture, is an indication of the Church of God,[1] it is necessary that we consider the matter, which now doth touch and concern us, to learn the truth. Thus one findeth, when one beholdeth the truth and desireth to hold the matter up to the light, that God at the beginning made and created man as a dwelling for himself, since he made him in his likeness,[2] and also, as the wise man saith, it was well with them, and there was no poison of destruction in them.[3]

It followeth from this, since there was to be nothing of destruction in them, that all good, which is God himself,[4] was to dwell in them; which thing is shown by the likeness of God in which he was created.[5] Because, however, this temple was laid waste, desecrated and broken down through the counsel of the serpent,[6] it hath become, on the contrary, a dwelling-place of idols and of all unclean spirits, as Christ showeth in the words which he saith concerning Satan, that, when he findeth no rest he speaketh to himself, saying, "I will return into my house from whence I came out."[7] Thereupon, saith Paul, he hath and doth carry on his work in the children of unbelief,[8] to bring forth all manner of unrighteousness, that the Spirit of the Lord may depart far from them.[9]

Although all this hath happened and taken place, which hath justly aroused and brought the wrath of the Almighty[10] over the human race, nevertheless, God, as a wellspring of mercy whose streams never run dry,[11] remembering his holy name, desired not to give up his plan to have in man his temple,[12] but thought to restore and to make good this fall and hurt; which thing he also promised soon after the transgression had taken place, in that he spake to the serpent, saying, "The woman's seed shall bruise thy head."[1] This he hath also shown, after the promise, in manifold ways in those who were pleasing to him, namely, from the beginning, in the devout, with whom he was and to whom he showed himself,[2] until the promise was strengthened in Christ[3] and the time of grace[4] came again when he built and established once more a temple for himself,[5] which was separate from all abominations,[6] with him, Christ, as the first stone[7] and foundation,[8] upon whom we must all be built;[9] who also was delivered up for us,[10] and was raised from the dead on the third day,[11] that we, also, might walk in a new life.[12]

Therefore saith Paul, "He hath given himself for us, that he might sanctify for himself a church, and cleanse it with the washing of water by the word, that he might present it to himself a glorious church, not having spot or wrinkle, or any such thing;[13] but that it should be holy and without blemish."[14]

Now, since this building is not earthly and of man, but heavenly and of God,[15] it is the duty of the builders to learn their art not from earthly men, whether they be termed doctor or master, but to learn it in heaven from the Father of all grace,[16] from whom come all good gifts;[17] as Christ himself saith, "They must all be taught of the Lord.[18] Every man, therefore, that hath heard, and hath learned of the Father, cometh unto me."[19] Therefore we must first of all go to this school and climb with Moses into the mount[20] to see the tabernacle aright, to see its form with all its adornment and observe the same well, as well as the command given to Moses, "Now look, observe and take care, saith the Lord, that thou make them after the pattern that I shewed thee in the mount."[21]

Woe, indeed, to the foolish workers, who have

never come into the mount,[1] still less have seen the likeness of the tabernacle![2] What kind of work shall they perform who have remained all the time in the valley and in the camp, and have not gone out to Christ and know naught[3] of the form and fashion of the tabernacle?[4] How can they work, when they know neither how nor what is necessary thereto,[5] and bring rather thorns than firs, rather dross than silver and gold to the work? What kind of a house will that then be? Or who will have pleasure to dwell therein?[6]

See to it that that tabernacle will be as the tabernacle of Shiloh,[7] which the Lord forsook together with her priests, who were slain according to the word of the Lord[8] which he had told to Eli.[9] O look and at last become wise! Moses, a servant of the Lord, who spake with him mouth to mouth,[10] knew naught of the tabernacle.[11] He had to learn and receive from the Lord its fashion and form in the mount,[12] which thing was yet but a picture of holy things.[13] Now what will they do, who should build the holy tabernacle? From whence shall they take the picture[14] who have never been up into the mount, and yet presume to do this work?[15] Truly, they must be those of whom the Lord, the Almighty God, hath said, "I have not sent these prophets, yet they ran: I have not spoken to them, yet they prophesied. But if they had stood in my counsel, and had heard my word, then they should have turned my people from the evil of their doings and from their evil ways."[16]

Therefore saith the Lord to such prophets, "Ye have scattered my flock, and driven them away and have not cared for them, so I will visit upon you the evil of your doings, and I will gather the remnant of my flock out of all countries whither I have driven them, and will bring them again to their folds; and

156

they shall be fruitful and increase. And I will set up shepherds over them which shall feed them."[1] Therefore Christ, the minister of the sanctuary,[2] who was fore-ordained by the Father before the foundation of the world was laid,[3] to reveal to us the eternal will of the Father[4] and to build and raise once more[5] the tabernacle that had fallen,[6] cometh not from Mount Sinai like Moses,[7] but from heaven itself.[8] At the Father's bidding, however, he climbeth the mount as he appointed him. As David saith, "I have set my king upon my holy hill of Zion, that he may preach my law, as I have informed and sent him for this purpose,"[9] as Isaiah testifieth of him, saying, "The Spirit of the Lord is with me, therefore hath he sent me to preach good tidings to the poor."[10] Therefore doth he cry to us and call us to come to him, as our Captain,[11] saying, "Come unto me, all ye that labour and are heavy laden, and I will refresh you. Take my yoke upon you, and learn of me; for I am meek and lowly in heart."[12] Since, however, no one can come to him, except the Father draw him,[13] it is evident that only they whose heart God the Lord doth touch and whose spirit he doth awaken to go up to build the Lord's house,[14] hear and attend to the voice of Christ calling, come to him that they may come to the Father,[15] since no one can come to the Father except by him,[16] that he may show them the form and fashion of the tabernacle or house, with all the glory with which they should prepare it according to his will.[17]

What, however, saith the Lord? "No man shall see me, and live!"[18] Therefore there cometh first a dying, when the inspiration of God beginneth[19] and one must hear,[20] see,[21] taste[22] and prove or feel the Lord God in the countenance of Jesus Christ,[23] all of which must precede such building, as is clear from the words of Peter, "If so be ye have tasted that the

Lord is gracious, to whom ye have come as to a living stone, build yourselves up to a spiritual house!"[1]

If, however, God is to draw nigh to man and begin to work, he must hear what the Lord speaketh in him, that is, must mark, heed and pay attention to that which the Lord rouseth, moveth, worketh and doeth in him, and allow himself to be ruled and led by the same. Therefore it is no work of flesh and blood,[2] nor aught undertaken at one's own choice,[3] nor, as is said above, may it be undertaken by man. Because this is so, the herald of Christ cometh and crieth with a loud voice, "Repent ye: and be converted, for the kingdom of heaven is at hand."[4] He saith, furthermore, "The axe is already laid unto the root of the trees. Every tree which bringeth not forth good fruit will be hewn down and cast into the fire."[5] And Paul saith, "Mortify therefore your members which are upon the earth, that sin may no longer rule over us,"[6] as it is written, "Let not sin therefore reign in your mortal body, that ye should obey it in the lusts thereof. Neither yield ye your members as instruments of unrighteousness."[7]

Where this dying is not, or before it taketh place, the man cannot come unto the mountain[8] and draw nigh unto the Lord,[9] can neither hear,[10] see,[11] feel[12] nor perceive,[13] much less learn from him the fashion of the tabernacle.[14] Hence, I conclude that all they who still remain in the plain, and have not come up unto the hill of the Lord, have not been sent by him at all;[15] much less can they speak his word, as Paul saith, "How shall they preach, except they be sent?"[16] Therefore Christ also saith, "He whom God hath sent speaketh the words of God."[17] Now, how can any be sent by him before he heareth his voice?[18] But who can hear it and live?[19] Therefore the dying[20] and laying aside of the old man must first take place,[21] as Paul also teacheth, "So put off now the old

158

man with his deeds in accordance with your former life which was corrupt through the lust of sin."[1]

Now, he who is broken and killed in the old man through hearing the divine answer in his heart cometh to Christ. As he himself saith, "Every man that hath heard, and hath learned of the Father, cometh unto me."[2] Therefore saith Moses also, "All thy saints are in thy hand. They shall sit down at thy feet and learn of thy words."[3] He who learneth thus from him is revived to a new life through faith in Jesus Christ;[4] as he himself also testifieth, saying, "The hour is coming, and now is, when the dead shall hear the voice of the Son of God: and they that hear shall live."[5] Now, we should walk not in the sins to which we have died, but as he is risen, we also should walk in newness of life.[6]

Therefore those who have been upon the mount with Christ, who have seen the tabernacle with all its adornments, together with all that pertaineth thereto, even they and none other are able to know how to do the work to please him,[7] who shall dwell therein;[8] since this temple must be right exquisitely adorned with many precious stones and beautiful jewels, as the scripture saith, "Behold, I will lay thy stones with fair colours, and lay thy foundations with sapphires. And I will make thy windows of agates and thy gates of rubies and all thy borders of choice stones, and all thy children shall be taught of the Lord; and great shall be the peace of thy children. In righteousness shalt thou be established."[9]

Therefore Peter as a wise master-builder, who will not build hay and straw on the foundation that hath been laid—for other foundation can no man lay than that is laid[10]—telleth everyone first of all to repent, for he holdeth to the word and command of his master,[11] who himself first called the people to repentance[12] and also commanded his disciples to do so.[13]

And they who have repented and laid aside sin,[1] he further admonisheth to build themselves up to the house of the Lord, when he saith, "If ye have now laid aside all malice, desire reasonable, sincere milk, the word of truth, that ye may grow therein as new-born babes, if so be ye have tasted that the Lord is gracious. To whom ye have come as to a living stone, rejected of the builders, but chosen of God and precious. Therefore ye also build yourselves up to a spiritual house and priesthood."[2]

Paul glorieth likewise that he hath laid the foundation, as a wise master-builder.[3] Each, however, who would build thereupon should take heed how he buildeth, for fire will try every man's work. Thus, if any should work at this building and set one stone upon another, he must first have learned from the true master-builder, Christ,[4] the way of the other fellow-workers, such as Peter, Paul and the rest, that he use not stones for lime and lime for stones and the building remain unfinished, like the tower of Babel.[5] For God the Almighty hath sent his Christ into the world[6] that he should lead the human race again to God,[7] and that we might receive sonship,[8] which he hath also shared and given to all who receive him,[9] for not physical birth leadeth thereto, but birth from God, which taketh place through the word.[10]

Hence, it becometh clear who they are who have accepted him—namely, they who believe in his name or in his word. To the same saith he also, "If a man love me, unto him will we come, I and the Father, and make our abode with him."[11] Note here, how or by what means the tabernacle or dwelling of God is built. Even so will every faithful builder go about his building. For that is the true pattern of all stones belonging to this house. Now, in those from whom all that is rough, that is sin, is cut away[12] and who

160

are measured in accordance with the plumbline and level of Christ, who have brought their hearts to him, to love him[1]—in them will he dwell.[2] He who doeth other than this buildeth naught but hay and straw.[3]

Thus is this building gloriously built to please him who should dwell therein,[4] namely, so that naught but pure love, which love he is himself,[5] is therein; by means of which also all God's commandments are fulfilled.[6] Therefore doth he himself say, "He that loveth me, keepeth my commandments."[7] But this power and fulfilment he himself, who is love,[8] worketh in us. From this it is evident that they who transgress his command and walk in sins belong not to his temple, since John also saith, "Whosoever transgresseth and abideth not in the doctrine of Christ, hath no God, but he that abideth therein hath both,"[9] and again, "He that saith he loveth God, and keepeth not his commandments, is a liar, and the truth is not in him."[10] Hence it is incontestable that they who walk in sin belong not to the house of God. David also saith that the ungodly shall not stand in the judgment, nor sinners in the congregation of the righteous.[11] Above all, no man can serve two masters: God and the devil.[12]

Therefore the wise man also saith, the Holy Spirit hath an horror of those whose discipline and wisdom is deceit, and removeth from thoughts that are without understanding; and where sin taketh the upper hand he departeth.[13] Now, if he departeth from the same, how can they then be the dwelling of him who hath departed from them and also desireth not to be with them?[14] Therefore Paul saith bluntly, "If any man have not the Spirit of Christ, he is none of his."[15]

Thus the stones for this building are discerned as to whether they serve thereto or not. If any should do other he will find his judge.[16] Now, since this tabernacle must be built up as a dwelling for God[1] and founded on the foundation that hath been laid, namely Christ,[2] each must take care what he bringeth thereto and will build thereon. Since we see how God nameth exactly what one should take to build the first tabernacle, which was yet but a picture,[3] such as gold, silver, brass, yellow silk, purple, scarlet, goat's hair, rams' skins dyed red, badgers' skins, shittim wood, oil for the lamps, spices for anointing oil and sweet incense, onyx stones and other stones to be set, and, as well as this, commanded them that they should follow his instructions[4]—Christ hath also instructed us how and what we should bring to his house. Therefore it is necessary that the builders who would build on this foundation[5] must first be planted and rooted in him,[6] have grasped his full nature,[7] mind and character;[8] which thing cannot be without the drawing of the Father.[9] Therefore it is not of the human will or running, but of God who worketh.[10] For, though the man who runneth of himself so crieth and calleth that the veins swell in his throat, yet doth his word bring forth no fruit. Reason: It is a dead letter and no life-giving word and hath no power. But he who is sent by God and hath his word in his mouth[11] which pierceth soul and spirit[12]—his word shall not pass away void. Just as little as the rain which falleth from heaven returneth without fruit, just as little and even less will the word of the Lord.[13] Therefore he who will build this house must take the tools, by means of which the stones and wood are prepared, from the Lord in heaven, as the scriptures say, "They will sit down at thy feet and learn of thy words."[14] When they have been forged they will hew, to God's praise. For God himself will be the tool[15] that prepareth all in all.[16]

Wherefore in whomsoever God speaketh not, the same hath no word of God,[17] even though he speaketh with the tongues of angels,[1] for God, himself, is the word.[2] But in whomsoever God himself speaketh and desireth to build his temple, he first cutteth away what is coarse and wild, which befitteth not his house, through the preaching of repentance.[3] Now they who receive the word and repent he placeth on the foundation, which is Christ,[4] if in him they die unto sin, and become like him in death. They will then be revived again through faith and made alive in a new life,[5] which is not human strength[6] but the grace and working of God.[7]

Now as it is not the working of men, but the working of God,[8] Paul exhorteth us as follows, "Yield your members to God as instruments of righteousness, that they may be holy."[9] For if God is to do aught good in man, he must surrender himself to him;[10] otherwise good will remain undone in him. For as little as a man can do anything good of himself, just as little doth God desire to do aught in man, except he give himself with all his heart to be his instrument. But when the surrendered will of man hath confined and interwoven itself into the will of God, so that God's will and the man's will become one, so that from henceforth the man desireth naught, but God desireth, chooseth and doeth everything in him, while the man, as an instrument, suffereth the same,[11] then he may say with the dear apostle Paul, "I live no more, but Christ liveth in me."[12] For so doth God work in man.

Where, however, the man yet reserveth aught for himself, chooseth, desireth or undertaketh aught of himself and not God in him, the work of God is hindered and can make no progress; then the man remaineth unprepared for this building and will not fit himself to it. But God worketh in surrendered men,[13] proveth his power[14] through the renewal of the man,[15] whom he, through his work, maketh of his

Son's[1] nature and character[2]—also in part omnipotent, as it is written, "All things are possible to him that believeth."[3]

Since, however, the world itself saith that it cannot keep what God hath commanded, it is certain that they are not believing but unbelieving; who desire not to suffer the Lord's working, that he may take away what displeaseth him and plant his good pleasure in them,[4] that they may strive diligently to be precious and living stones in this building.[5]

Therefore it is, indeed, unfitting to set up this building with the unbelieving. That, then, is the reason that we set up no church with the world: for to him that believeth all things, which God hath promised, are possible,[6] yea, light and easy. Therefore we recognize that they have no faith but an empty delusion[7] which is dead before God.[8] For faith worketh righteousness through the hand of God,[9] but unbelief, sin through the hand of the devil.[10] What concord hath then Christ with Belial,[11] that their children should work together and build the Lord an house or dwelling?[12] For John saith, "He that doeth right is of God. Whosoever committeth sin is of the devil."[13] Therefore saith Paul, "Go out from among them, and be ye separate; and I will receive you and will be your Father, and ye shall be my sons and daughters, saith the Lord Almighty."[14] Hence, Christ, himself, who bringeth to the Father a people out of all peoples,[15] commandeth in the new covenant as a greater security, that there should be a distinction between his people and the other peoples.[16]

For as circumcision separated them from the heathen,[17] (in that God desired neither to have heathen in their worship[18] nor that they should learn the ceremonies of the heathen[19]—if they should learn them, however, he threateneth to do to them as he

164

thought to do to the heathen[1]) at the time of the apostles, unbelievers were likewise not permitted to join the believers.[2] Paul, too, separateth the believing from the unbelieving. Therefore we also desire in this matter, and in so far as is in us, in all things to follow Christ as our Master, and with his help keep his command and covenant[3] and turn from it neither to the right hand nor to the left;[4] that we may be worthy to receive with him the promise of the inheritance. May he give us and all who desire it with all their heart his grace to do this through

Jesus Christ our Lord,

Amen.

CONCERNING THE COVENANT OF GRACE GIVEN TO HIS PEOPLE IN CHRIST

When God the Almighty in accordance with his nature—for he is merciful and compassionate[5]—desired to have compassion on the ruined human race and free them from their ruin and harm;[6] and desired also to fulfil his promise of the coming Christ, he sent the Word of grace,[7] by whom all things were made[8] and are maintained, and he became man in Mary, the virgin chosen beforetime,[9] through the working of the Holy Spirit, that he might be like us in all things,[10] sin alone excepted,[11] as the scripture saith, "Forasmuch then as the children are partakers of flesh and blood, he also himself likewise took part of the same; that through death he might destroy him that had the power of death;[12] and deliver them[13] who through fear of death were all their lifetime subject to bondage."[14] He came,[15] as he was sent by the Father,[16] and he hath revealed and made known himself, that is the eternal will of the Father,[17] the Word of grace,[18] the name of the Father,[19] as it is

165

written, "I will declare thy name unto my brethren, in the midst of the Church will I sing praise unto thee,"[1] and again, "I have manifested thy name unto the men, which thou gavest me out of the world: thine they were, and thou gavest them me; and they have kept thy word. Now they know that all things whatsoever thou hast given me are of thee. For the word that thou gavest me have I given them, and they have received it and know surely that I came out from thee, and they believe that thou didst send me."[2]

From these words it is evident what Christ hath done here in the world, namely, to gather them who were previously the Father's and to lead them into the liberty of sons,[3] that they may become like unto and conformed to the image of Christ[4] in all obedience to the Father,[5] and that they may all come into the one fold of the divine promise and assurance,[6] as he proveth with the words, "And I have still other sheep, which are not of this fold: them also I must bring that there may be one flock and one fold."[7] Therefore doth he begin to search earnestly, first in Israel,[8] then also (when the fold had been fortified, that is, the covenant of grace had been ratified by the death of Christ[9]) in the whole world, as it is written, "I have given thee for a light to the Gentiles, that thou mayest be my salvation unto the end of the earth."[10] Since, however, this covenant, ratified or established in Christ,[11] leadeth not to a transitory but to an immortal hope,[12] the birth that leadeth thereto must also be such that it remaineth for ever and never ceaseth. Therefore also did Christ appear to bring about the same, proclaiming the gospel of God,[13] the word of the Father.[14] Those who believe the word,[15] write it in their hearts[16] and keep it,[17] are born as sons.[18] Peter agreeth, likewise, therewith when he saith, "Being born again, not of cor-

166

ruptible seed, but of incorruptible, by the word of truth."[1]

Thus, all they who are begotten through this seed are made eternal in nature and are led into the kingdom of Christ which abideth for ever,[2] since Peter saith, that they who do the will of God remain in eternity.[3] Thus, the bride becometh like the bridegroom. Now, because all this taketh place through the word, it is necessary that it be preached with diligence[4] in accordance with his word and command,[5] then he will give the increase and make the word living and active,[6] thereby cutting away from man old usages and habits, summa: the complete old life,[7] the old man with all his works.[8] Therefore is physical birth of no use in this connection. It hath naught to do with this,[9] as Paul saith, "They which are the children of the flesh, these are not the children of God: but the children of the promise are counted for seed."[10] Thus Christ giveth power to become sons of God not to them who are born of the will of man, of flesh and blood, but who are born of God.[11]

What need is there then of many words—but the devil loveth much dispute[12]—since the covenant of sonship, promised aforetime through the mouth of the prophets,[13] is established in Christ,[14] that the liberty of the children might be revealed[15] and that they, set free from bondage,[16] might be led into their inheritance and holiness[17] and make use, as children, of the good things of their Father,[18] which he hath given them in Christ.[19] Therefore let us allow truth to be truth,[20] as it will remain in all eternity;[21] and it will go evil with him who striveth against it,[22] and it will be hard to kick against the goad,[23] since the Lord hath commanded to add nothing to truth and diminish nothing from it.[24]

Therefore, since it is a covenant of sonship,[25] in

which God in Christ[1] hath separated the children from the slaves,[2] that they might all serve him in the one child-like Spirit—not in outward ceremonies,[3] but in the Spirit and in truth[4]—Paul saith, "So now there are no more slaves but all are sons through faith in Christ;"[5] as God also saith further, "Surely they are my people, children that will not lie: therefore was I their Saviour."[6] Now, since the distinction is made in Christ, it will remain eternally, and it will take place only as the Holy Spirit distinguisheth,[7] namely, that they who are urged by the Spirit of God are God's children, but they who have not the same are none of his.[8] And though it should displease the whole world, yet the Lord's counsel alone, and not ours, must stand; which we desire to hold, with his help, and to allow not ourselves to turn therefrom in all eternity.

Then if someone should say—as the world may well ask pointedly, because it knoweth naught of God,[9] "Are we then certain that all they whom we receive in our meetings have the Holy Spirit?" To this we give the answer, in so much as is given us to know and we should know, we are certain, namely, that everyone who believeth is sealed with the Holy Spirit.[10] But what God hath reserved for himself, namely, whether or not one believeth as he confesseth—that we leave to his power until the time that he reveal him, that he may be put away in accordance with the word of him who commandeth us to put away evil.[11] Therefore, if we want to be found faithful servants and messengers of him who hath sent us and ministers of our office, our duty here is to be watchful and not to use human presumption and opinion, that we misuse not the covenant of grace of the great God,[12] secured for us by Christ![13] For Christ saith, "As my Father hath sent me, even so send I you."[14]

Here we learn two things: firstly, how Christ's messengers should be, and secondly, what their office is, namely: As Christ, before he was sent by the Father was filled with his Spirit,[1] even so will he have his messengers,[2] that they tread and walk in the power of his Spirit[3] and are upright.[4] Secondly, their office, namely, that they should gather with or in Christ and lead into the fold of grace, that Christ's flock may be complete.[5]

Therefore Christ, when he desired to send his disciples, first commanded them not to leave Jerusalem till they should be endowed with power from on high.[6] From this we see what kind of messengers the Lord desireth to have, that they run not everyone as he himself pleaseth as the Lutherans and Papists do, where they know there is a fat living, with sheep to be shorn—how they care for the sheep, however, one seeth well— but that they are chosen beforehand, even as Aaron.[7] For if one is to go for the Lord, he must be chosen by him[8] and endowed with his power,[9] feel the same at work upon him,[10] above all let it rule over and lead him,[11] and act in accordance with his nature and character,[12] that he be conformed to his Master in word and life, that the disciples may have in him an example of blessedness,[13] even as Paul did when he saith, "Be ye followers of me, even as I also am of Christ."[14] For every one who would gather with Christ must be of his nature,[15] mind and spirit.[16] For whosoever hath not the Spirit of Christ is none of his,[17] how then can he gather with him, since he himself saith, "If a kingdom be divided against itself, that kingdom cannot stand."[18]

Thus, his kingdom would soon have to fall if he sent out servants other than of his nature and character. For he saith, "He that is not with me is against me; and he that gathereth not with me scattereth."[19] Therefore will he allow no one to go out, unless he be

169

first endowed with the power of his Spirit.[1] Now they who feel this power will heed the command of their Lord, who hath sent them, that they may proclaim to his good pleasure the tidings which they have to carry in his name.[2] When, however, Christ had won the victory and through his death had taken the power from him who had the power of death, and received all power from the Father,[3] he saith, "All power is given unto me in heaven and in earth. Go ye therefore, and teach all nations, baptizing them in the name of the Father, and of the Son and of the Holy Ghost: teaching them to observe all things whatsoever I have commanded you."[4]

Let us here observe well what is commanded us. For Christ giveth us here a two-fold command: firstly, that we should gather with him as they who have been sent by him;[5] and secondly, that we should strive diligently to keep those who are gathered, that they be not once more scattered and torn by wolves.[6] For Christ's sheep are very dear to him, for he hath bought them so dearly.[7] Therefore it is his will that they should also be dear to his shepherds, and he also committeth them to none but him who loveth him.[8]

Therefore doth he first command to gather diligently and saith, "Go and teach all nations." For, as is said above, since the Lord desireth to have a beautiful temple, an holy church, without spot or wrinkle,[9] yea, of his nature and purpose, therefore they must first be told by word of this nature and purpose and so led into the covenant of sonship.[10] For where the word is believed, there the Lord will give the increase and make the word living,[11] and plant those who believe into his nature through the gift of the child-like Spirit,[12] who assureth us that we are God's children and heirs of all his possessions.[13]

Therefore, after such teaching hath been given,

doth he command baptism, as a seal of the covenant of sonship, that all who have received and believed the word be baptized[1] and so accepted into the community of the saints, and after baptism he commandeth to continue to teach the observance of all things whatsoever the Lord hath commanded.[2] He desireth thereby that his servants should have zeal and diligence:[3] that they care for his sheep[4] and teach diligently,[5] that they hold to the Lord.[6] Now, all apostles, as true servants of their Master, have done this with the greatest diligence,[7] even as he commanded them,[8] and have done naught else, as one can clearly see and learn in Acts. Likewise also the other text, where the Lord saith, "Go ye into all the world, and preach the gospel to the whole creation. He that believeth and is baptized shall be blessed; but he that believeth not is damned." Here Christ showeth himself in accordance with his Father's nature, as he himself saith, "The Son can do nothing of himself: for what he seeth the Father do, that also doeth the Son."[9] Now, as the Father worked, in that he created heaven and earth with all that is therein, he placed everything in a proper order and desired not to do everything in one day, though he could well have done so, yet he made everything in six days,[10] and on the seventh day he rested from all his work.[11]

Mark in this the providence of God. When he wanted to make man, he created first all manner of cattle and what serveth man for food, that man when he was created should suffer no want. The same also did he for the creatures, that they were provided with their food before they were created. In the same way when he desired to make foliage, grass and all manner of green things, he first created the earth from which it should grow. Such order doth God observe in his work.[12]

171

Now, as the Son seeth the Father do, that doeth the Son likewise.[1] Hence, when he wanted to create a new man or to renew the same[2] into the likeness of him who hath created him,[3] he desired also to do everything in proper order, that we might learn of him as he of the Father,[4] and at all times hold ourselves in proper, true, holy and divine order;[5] and saith, "Go ye into all the world and preach the gospel to every creature. He that believeth and is baptized shall be saved; but he that believeth not shall be damned."[6]

Firstly, he saith, "Go ye into all the world!" for they could not carry out his charge before he had commanded them. For they would have known naught of mission, above all naught of going out into all the world, if he had not commanded them, as history showeth when the disciples murmured against Peter for entering a Gentile's house,[7] yea, Peter himself testifieth that it was an unusual thing for a Jew to enter the house of a heathen, but he did this through a revelation from the Lord.[8] Therefore it is clear, that if he had not had a special revelation he would not have gone to them, although the command had already been given to him, much less, that he would have gone there to preach without the command or mission.[9] For Paul saith, "How can they preach, when they are not sent."[10]

Now, since they cannot preach unless they are first sent, it is certain that God in the mission, that is in his command, placeth his word in his messenger's mouth, as the Lord himself testifieth when he saith, "Behold, I have put my words in thy mouth, and have set thee over the nations and over the kingdoms, to root out, to pull down and to destroy, and to throw down, and to build again, and to plant."[11] Therefore also all who are not sent have no word of God,[12] and they have no more than the one stealeth

172

from the other, or from the scriptures.[1] For this reason, in the first place, is the commission necessary. But it was not enough that they were sent. They had also to know why and for what purpose they were sent, or what they had to do. Therefore doth he give them the command to do his work and business and saith, "Teach all nations"[2] or, "Preach the gospel to every creature."[3]

In this command he placeth, as is said above, his word in their mouth,[4] even as to-day when a man sendeth a messenger he layeth in his mouth or commandeth how or what he should say and do. The messenger, also, if he will be faithful to him who sendeth him, doeth the same and taketh nothing from it and addeth nothing thereto. Even so doth Christ command to preach. That they may preach naught else than what is his will he sayeth expressly: the gospel. What is that other than a joyful message from God and Christ.

That they may not do the same according to their own pleasure, add naught thereto and diminish naught therefrom, and in no place do either too little or too much, that is, not praise where they should rebuke and rebuke him whom they should praise,[5] he saith in another place, "It shall not be ye that speak, but the Spirit of my Father shall speak in you."[6] For this reason he would not that they should leave Jerusalem until they should be endued with power from on high and thus go in the power of the Lord[7] and speak his word,[8] by means of which they should lead many into the true fold of grace if they received the same in faith,[9] as Paul also saith of several, "Ye received it not as the word of men, but as it is in truth, the word of God."[10] They were thereby renewed to sonship.

Since, however, they cannot believe without preaching, as Paul saith, "How can they believe in him of whom they have not heard? And how can they hear without a preacher? And how can they preach, except they be sent? So then faith cometh by hearing, and hearing from preaching, but preaching from the word of God."[1] Therefore doth he place faith after preaching, and saith, "He that believeth."[2] Now what is "to believe the word that is preached" but to write the same in one's heart, to keep it therein,[3] and to live accordingly,[4] from henceforth always letting oneself be led, ruled, guided and directed by the word.[5] Therefore doth Christ call the same blessed. Blessed are they who hear the word of God and keep it in a pure, clean and good heart. They are all led and brought to sonship.[6]

Now, they who attain sonship are then sealed into the testament of the promise through the covenant of grace as an assurance that they are certain joint-heirs of all the grace and gifts which are given to us from the Father in Christ.[7] Therefore doth he command baptism after faith as a sealing of the believing children of God, that a good conscience may unite with God.[8] "But he that believeth not is damned."[9] Here it is once more clear that not baptism without faith, but it is faith only, that maketh blessed, when it is sealed by baptism. Therefore is it a pure tom-foolery to baptize children before they have believed.

All the apostles have followed this order of Christ with the greatest diligence, as their history showeth, and have baptized none without his first believing or at least confessing his faith. Let us now regard some instances of their example and what they did. Firstly, we see that Peter after preaching for a long time, thereby piercing the hearts of the listening people so that they were moved to ask what they should do, gave the answer, "Repent, and be baptized every one of you in the name of Jesus Christ for the remission of sins, and ye shall receive

174

the gift of the Holy Spirit."[1] Here he pointeth them firstly, not to baptism but to repentance and improvement. Now what is to repent other than to lay aside sin, the old man with all his works,[2] and become like unto the death of Christ, into which all saints are baptized.[3]

And after he had pointed them to repentance, he told them that they should also be baptized to a new life, for it is a bath of new or re-birth, and promised also the benefit which shall follow therefrom, namely the gift of the Holy Spirit.[4] Therefore doth he say that they should let themselves be turned aside and led away from the perverse generation.[5] Now they who gladly accepted this word were baptized. Now what is to "accept gladly" other than to consent to the counsel given by God[6] and to submit oneself with one's whole heart thereto.[7] Others, however, rejected the counsel of God and were not baptized.[8] Here is distinguished once more who are led by the apostles into this fold, namely, they who have accepted their word with joy.

Secondly, let us look at the work of Philip, when he came to Samaria to preach to them about Christ. There the people with one accord gave heed unto those things which Philip spake. And when they believed Philip preaching the things concerning the kingdom of God, and the name of Jesus Christ, they were baptized, both men and women.[9] Note well, here he saith once more quite clearly who were baptized, namely, they who believed the preaching of Philip. It is not added, however, that he commanded them to bring their children and to have them also baptized. For, doubtless, they had also children, then as now, but he beginneth no such tomfoolery, as our falsely celebrated preachers now do. Or hath the devout apostle, perhaps, not understood enough, as they see it; or hath Christ forgotten it, that he did not command them to do so? But what happeneth when disciples seek to teach the master and reason seeketh to rule? Naught other than what happeneth now, and what befell Eve in Paradise.[1]

When Paul speaketh to the elders of Ephesus and testifieth powerfully to them that he is pure from the blood of all men—as though he would say, should evil arise afterwards and aught else break in, "For I have not shunned to declare unto you all the counsel of God."[2] I do not find that he saith one single word about child baptism, nor doth he in any of his epistles. Therefore, either it cannot be the counsel of God, or Paul omitted to declare or expound it to all. Moreover, he warneth them faithfully against any who teach other than they had received from him.[3] Therefore we intend to follow his counsel faithfully with the help of God, because he is a chosen instrument of God to proclaim his name,[4] and we intend to accept no other teaching than we have learned, from him, and no other method or order.

Likewise Philip was led by the angel to the eunuch's chariot on the way that goeth down from Jerusalem to Gaza, whom he found reading the prophet Esaias,[5] where he saith, "He was led as a sheep to the slaughter;"[6] beginning at which place in accordance with the eunuch's request the apostle began and testified to him of Christ. When thus speaking with one another they came to a stream, the eunuch spake to the apostle, "See, here is water; what doth hinder me to be baptized?" The apostle, although he had preached for long and knew most certainly that the Lord had led him to him, did not baptize him immediately at his request; though he could rest assured through the angel's information, he yet observed the order and first asked if he believed—then it might well be, as though he would say: For without faith it cannot be.

176

Then he began to confess his faith: that he believed that Christ was the Son of God. Whereupon he baptized him in the same water on confessing his faith. Therefore we still say that none is to be baptized without confession of his faith, preceded by preaching. That they themselves even confess in their ungodly baptism—if I do it no wrong in calling it baptism, for it is none—for when one bringeth a child to their puddle-bath or baptism he baptizeth it not immediately but first beginneth a long palaver and sermon, to show that one should first preach. After the same he calleth to deny the world, sin and the devil, and lastly, after all this, to have faith—of which they know little or nothing at all. Yet they testify thereby that our order is right, however much they strive against it, and testify to the truth, though not from their own knowledge but unwittingly like Caiaphas and thus make us the more certain. For they see that the apostles baptized believers.[1] This they want, like apes, to imitate, though they have received no command.

Thus we find also concerning Paul, who was baptized by Ananias at Damascus, who truly had seen the Lord on the way[2] and was caught up to the third heaven and heard unspeakable words,[3] yet was he not sealed to sonship till he had heard the preaching of Ananias and then he was baptized as the words show: "The Lord that appeared to thee in the way hath sent me, that thou mightest receive thy sight, and be filled with the Holy Ghost." And immediately there fell from his eyes as it had been scales: and he received sight forthwith, and arose, and was baptized.[4]

Here one seeth how God honoureth the office he hath ordained, and himself will not break his order,[5] therefore will he have it kept by us also. For though he (Paul) was, indeed, caught up into heaven[6] and saw Christ,[1] yet was his understanding only opened and the Holy Spirit given after the word of the Lord was proclaimed to him by Ananias.[2] Likewise also Cornelius, the centurion.[3] Notwithstanding that his prayers and his alms were come up before God and were pleasing to him—which thing is not possible without faith[4]—God sent his angel to inform him of Peter; to whom he sent, and when he came and spake with him of the word of the Lord, the Holy Spirit fell upon him. Here one seeth, how God useth his order and what he granteth to the word. For thus will he gather his bride. That is his counsel, which will stand eternally and never waver. For notwithstanding that Cornelius was pleasing before God, and heard also the voice of the angel, yet was he not sealed with the Holy Spirit until he heard also the word from Peter. Then God testified to his (Cornelius') faith with the gift of the Holy Spirit, whereupon he was baptized. Therefore is it great folly for man to oppose this order and act other than is commanded.[5]

Likewise also the keeper of the prison at Philippi, who believed with his whole house and was baptized; of whom they speak much and often thereby reveal their abominable nature—as though children also were baptized. Here the text stateth clearly that he took them into his house and set meat before them; also that they spake unto him the word of the Lord. Then he believed and his whole house and was baptized, and rejoiced greatly that he had come to believe in God.[6] Now, if children here understood the wonder of God, heard the preaching of Christ and believed, then they also were baptized, but if not, they were also not baptized, so nothing is to be proved thereby.

When Paul, however, passed through the upper coasts and found certain men, who were baptized

178

with the baptism of John, in whom he perhaps felt too much superficiality for men who were supposed to be brothers, he was moved to ask whether they had received the Holy Spirit or not; to whom they said that they had never heard of any Holy Spirit. Whereupon he asked whereunto they had then been baptized, and they gave answer: "Unto John's baptism."[1] Then he spake, "John baptized with the baptism of repentance[2] and pointed to Christ."[3] When they heard this they were baptized in the name of Jesus Christ. And when Paul laid his hands upon them they received the Holy Spirit.[4]

See, here the baptism of John had no validity for Paul, though it was of God, as Christ himself testifieth.[5] How much less must child baptism have validity for us—a thing not appointed by God, but by men. "For every plant, which my heavenly Father hath not planted, shall be rooted up,"[6] saith Christ. Therefore it must also have no validity for all his children. For what he ordaineth—and not what we of ourselves ordain—will stand and remain.

Likewise, someone may say, "But Paul saith that all our fathers under Moses were baptized with the cloud and with the sea[7]—wherein there were also children. Now, since they are included in the picture, you must still leave them therein." To this I say that if one regard the picture aright, one will find whether children were included therein or not. Now, note well: When Israel left Egypt and came to the sea and saw Pharaoh's men pursuing them and hard upon their backs; whom also, as they saw, they could not escape, they grew surly and began to murmur against God and moses, saying, "Were there no graves in Egypt, that thou hast led us away to die in the wilderness? Wherefore hast thou done this?[8] Is not this the word that we did tell thee in Egypt, saying, Let us alone, that we may serve the

Egyptians? For it had been better for us to serve the Egyptians than that we should die in the wilderness."[1] But when they saw the salvation of God, how he separated them and the others with the cloud, so that they could not come near one another; also how the Lord cleft the sea[2] and made them pass through dry-shod, but drowned all the enemy therein,[3] then they were shocked and feared because they had murmured against the Lord, so powerful a God, and against his servant Moses; they knew their sin and believed God their saviour, and submitted themselves to serve God aright under the hand of his servant Moses.[4] This Paul here calleth a baptism or submission, to which they were driven by the glorious wonder[5] which God performed with the cloud and with the sea before their eyes.[6]

Now if the newly born children also murmured against God and Moses, then they also blushed with shame together with the elders and committed themselves once more to serve God under Moses; if not, they could not have bowed and subjected themselves under Moses and blushed with shame, since they had not murmured. And this is Paul's real meaning in this passage.[7] Likewise in the ark, which is also a picture of the baptism, submersion, killing and dying of the old man, no children but eight souls who could all perceive and confess the work of God were saved.[8] Thus will God have it in his covenant: that each may know, sense and feel the working of the power of God and thus know to whom he should hold, that from henceforth he allow himself to be led astray by no strange teaching.[9] This the ark showeth us.

Then someone may say, "But children were circumcised on the eighth day,[10] who could also understand nothing, and yet they were accepted into the covenant.[11] Therefore why not also to-day?" To this I say, circumcision and baptism are two different things, and as Christ surpassed Abraham[1] doth baptism circumcision. For circumcision was commanded all men children in the house of Abraham, children and slaves.[2] But since in Christ sonship is distinguished from bondage, so that there are no more servants but all are children,[3] it is evident that baptism was not commanded to slaves but to children[4] —which children are conceived and born not of flesh and blood nor of the will of man but of God,[5] through his word.[6] Hence Paul saith, "For they are not all Israel, which are of Israel; neither, because they are the seed of Abraham, are they all children. For they are not God's children, which are children according to the flesh, but the children of the promise are counted for seed."[7] Therefore the people which came out of the loins of Abraham[8] is no more than an allegory of the true seed, who become children through faith in Christ,[9] of whom Paul saith, "If ye are Christ's, then ye are Abraham's seed, and heirs according to the promise."[10]

From these words it is clear with what seed God hath confirmed his covenant and to whom the promise applieth,[11] namely, they who walk in the footsteps of believing Abraham.[12] Because it was but an allegory of the true seed, which should be revealed in Christ, all children according to the promise may well be included in this covenant.[13] For that was the promise: that Christ should come of them,[14] through whom they and all peoples should receive blessing.[15] Not that they had already received it,[16] but that they should receive it and be blessed through Christ.[17]

Therefore, also, was there no distinction between servants and children,[18] but they were under the schoolmaster until Christ.[19] When he doth come, the former thing departeth like a shadow when the sunshine appeareth, as Paul also saith, "We establish the law"[20] from the semblance into the truth. Therefore doth circumcision cease in Christ, in whom the circumcision without hands appeareth, whose praise is not of men, but of God.[1] Thus, even as the covenant of circumcision was commanded Abraham, that he should circumcise himself, his seed and all in his house, being male, even so was it appointed by the Father concerning Christ in his house, that he himself and all his seed should be baptized,[2] as he proveth with the words which he spake to John, "Suffer it to be so, for thus it becometh us to fulfil all God's righteousness."[3]

Therefore let us consider the parable. Abraham was commanded to circumcise within his house, whether heirs by birth or slaves that had been bought.[4] And it was not commanded him outside his house. Now if Abraham was to circumcise his seed, he could not do so, unless it had first been born. Likewise also in the house of Christ no one will or can be marked with the covenant of grace or baptized, unless he is first born to Christ through the word of truth.[5]

Then they say the acceptance of God beareth anew and maketh children of God, and God accepteth children as well as old people, as Paul also saith, "For the promise is unto you, and to your children,"[6] therefore it is unjust to refuse them baptism. To this I say, That God accepteth children as well as the old we do not deny. For we also have the firm hope that he will look upon them with grace and accept them in their measure, as children. Nevertheless, God weakeneth not his order and diminisheth naught from his word; he who once gave through it new birth will not take this power from the word,[7] namely, that they who believe it[8] are born anew[9] and become children of God.[10] Now, since God himself honoureth this, his order, as is said above and is proved with Saul[11] and Cornelius,[12] this forceth me not to regard the acceptance of God as complete "new birth"—otherwise I diminish something from the word of God.[1] In addition, the acceptance of God of each individual is hidden from our eyes until it showeth itself in power, even as is also the fruit conceived in a woman until it is born. For who can know in truth what kind of fruit it will be, whether male or female, or what kind of figure and form it will have? Yet it is a fruit. Even so is it with the acceptance of God—that none knoweth how or wherefore. For the works of the Lord are incomprehensible.[2] Now, as the child before birth is hidden from our eyes in the mother's womb, even so in the matter of the acceptance and counsel of God, until it is born through the word.[3] Therefore just as little as a boy may be circumcised before birth, just as little may a man be baptized in the right way without it being preceded by preaching, and confessing his faith.[4]

He (Abraham) had to circumcise them on the eighth day, however, and not as soon as they were born, but allow them to grow a little that they might be able to bear the pain. So also God desireth in the house of Christ that before one maketh such a covenant with him, he should grow to some extent in faith and knowledge, that each may know what he doeth. This Christ testifieth with the words when he saith, "There is none who intendeth to build a house or a tower, which sitteth not down first and counteth the cost, whether he have sufficient to finish it, lest haply after he hath begun to build and is not able to finish it, all that behold it begin to mock him."[5] Thou seest, he desireth first consideration, yea, that a man test himself well,[6] examine and look within his heart and perceive what graces of God he findeth in him, whether he can rely on this and venture to finish this building, that he may not fail in the work and come to shame.[7]

He pictureth the same for us in another parable,

when he saith, "What king, going to make war against another king, sitteth not down first, and consulteth whether he be able with ten thousand to meet him that cometh against him with twenty thousand? Or else, while the other is yet a great way off, he sendeth an ambassage, and desireth conditions of peace. So likewise, whosoever he be of you, that forsaketh not all that he hath, he cannot be my disciple."[1] Note how clearly Christ here speaketh of "first growing," that each first test himself well whether he be able to do all this—as though he would say: He who cannot do it, namely, forsake all that he hath and deny himself, on no account let him venture, for he cannot be my disciple.[2]

Now, since in baptism such a denial of one's self and dying unto sin taketh place, in that we yield our members to God as instruments of righteousness and become disciples of Christ,[3] Christ desireth to portray for us through this parable that each individual should see well what he doeth, and not, once he hath put his hand to the plough, look back again and come to shame.[4] Therefore it is truly necessary that one should consider it a little better and regard the witness or truth aright, that he use it not to his own destruction,[5] for therein hath the Lord no pleasure.[6]

Further Peter proveth this in his epistle where he speaketh of the covenant of grace saying, "It is not the putting away of the filth of the flesh, but the covenant of a good conscience with God."[7] Now, if it must be the covenant of a good conscience it is necessary that he should first attain the same. For how could he make a covenant of a good conscience with God, who hath not yet apprehended this grace? Therefore is it rightly said in the parable that one should let it grow a little, that each may know how he buildeth on the foundation of truth, that he build

184

not thereon straw and hay which fire consumeth. For fire will test the building of each.[1]

But what is a good conscience towards God other than that I know that I have a gracious God,[2] who in Christ hath disregarded, remitted and forgiven me all sins and hath in Christ freely offered himself to me as Father,[3] yea, together with his manifold grace and riches;[4] that I, also, may know him as almighty and be moved and stirred to zeal thereby to bind myself to him, to submit to him and to trust him utterly as my dear Father[5] who at all times will seek good, yea, the very best, for me.[6] Hereupon I establish a covenant with him, in which I bind myself completely to him[7] and give him my members as instruments of his holy work, allow him from henceforth to bring about, work and do all things in me; while I, as an instrument suffer his work and let myself be used by the Master for whatsoever he will,[8] yea, at all times, like an obedient child, serve and observe his gracious will and turn not from it to the right hand or to the left as long as I live. As a proof of this I accept the pure water, that from henceforth through his inspiration I desire to lead a holy life.[9]

Again God uniteth in this way with man: that he desireth to be his God and Father,[10] to care for him as a father for his son, yea, to give him everything in Christ.[11] As an assurance of this he desireth to witness from heaven and give him the grace of his Spirit, who leadeth him into all truth, doeth everything in him and accomplisheth his will whereby man beginneth a new life in his power,[12] as Paul saith, "If any man be in Christ, he is a new creature."[13] Now consider here if a child can make such a covenant of a good conscience with God, since it knoweth neither good nor evil.[14] Now since it knoweth neither good nor evil, how can it then know this glorious wealth of the grace of the Almighty? Now, since it knoweth this not, much less can it bind itself to walk therein. Therefore is it great folly on the part of any who profess the same, and naught other than a leading away from God and annulling of the true order and command of Christ.

But whence cometh this knowledge and good conscience other than where the heart is awakened through the word of God, and God giveth the increase and maketh it living in him,[1] heweth out the carnal mind and implanteth the mind of God.[2] From this cometh the new birth of which Christ saith, "Except a man be born again of water and of the Spirit, he cannot enter into the kingdom of God."[3] And this is the meaning: that whosoever is instructed by the word of God and believeth the same, will have his faith sealed by the outpouring of the Holy Spirit,[4] whereby he, renewed or born anew, is led into a holy, divine life, whereupon he receiveth the water[5] as a sign of the death of the old man.[6]

Then they say, "But here water is placed first, therefore one can first baptize, if faith but cometh afterward." So I ask whether water can bear anew? Of course they will say, "No." Then they say, "Water doeth it not, but the word which is put into the water hath this power." I say that the word is nowhere put into water or bound to the water, on the contrary, the water is bound to the word, since the word commandeth the water. For the command is not bound to the work, but the work to the command. Neither doth the command adjust itself to the work, but the work must be adjusted in accordance with the command.[7] Where this is the case the command sanctifieth the work, otherwise it remaineth fruitless. Therefore not the water will bring, require and demand the word, but the word the water. Thus, it becometh clear that the word must go first and not

186

the water, for the water is demanded by the word and not the word by the water.

Thus, the three witnesses follow, of whom John saith, "There are three that bear record in heaven, the Father, the Word, and the Holy Ghost: and these three are one."[1] Thus, whosoever lacketh one of them, hath none; but whosoever hath one hath them all.[2] Therefore the Word showeth us what the Father requireth and demandeth. And what the same showeth, the Holy Spirit accomplisheth with effectual power. Now, whosoever suffereth this his work, hath with him God's testimony and, thus preserved,[3] will be found a son of God.[4]

Now, as they are three that witness in heaven, we likewise have three on earth, namely, the Spirit, water and blood: and these three serve likewise in one.[5] Now, if any desire to contend with the former text that water is placed first, here the Spirit is placed foremost. This, then, is the first witness of a godly life, for there it must begin to work in us a new life, divine in nature, and lead us to sonship, as Paul also saith, "The same Spirit assureth us that we are God's children."[6] He saith not, however, that water doeth this. But since God desireth to have a people separate from the world, he hath commanded his children that all who have apprehended sonship should be inscribed with baptism into the covenant of sonship, wherein they should have killed the old man and become like unto the death of Christ; deny the world utterly and completely and henceforth serve Christ alone in a holy life.[7]

Now, whosoever hath attained this second witness, will soon be followed by the third, namely, that in accordance with the word of Christ he will be hated of all, as he saith, "The time cometh, that whosoever killeth you will think that he doeth God service."[8] But whosoever endureth in all this, faithful and devout to the end, turning neither to the right hand nor to the left,[1] and daunted by nothing, setteth his seal that God is true,[2] therefore is he also loved by God and accepted as heir with all the saints.[3]

Moreover, Paul saith, "According to his mercy he saved us by the washing of regeneration and renewing of the Holy Ghost; which he shed on us abundantly through Jesus Christ that being justified by his grace we should be made heirs of eternal life."[4] With this he agreeth when he saith, "He gave himself for his church, that he might sanctify her, and hath cleansed her with the washing of water by the word, that he might present her to himself a glorious church, not having spot or wrinkle."[5] Now, if this must take place by the word, it will be necessary first to preach the word and to baptize after the gospel hath been believed. So much now of this matter.

CONCERNING THE SUPPER OF OUR LORD JESUS CHRIST, WHEREIN HE SHOWETH US HOW HIS SUFFERING SERVETH FOR OUR SALVATION

Now, since we have come to treat of the gracious mystery which the Lord Christ holdeth before us in his last supper taken with his disciples,[6] let us pass over the misusages of those falsely called Christians, who have deceitfully taken upon themselves this practice. For who can recount the manifold abuses that they have practised, and made of light darkness[7] to their own harm![8] Yet must I mention the grossest of them, not because I have pleasure in speaking ill of it, but because it hath led so far astray from the right use that an abomination hath actually been made of it, and now one who is not instructed can with difficulty understand the right use, where the misuse is not first wiped out.

Now, they have thereby pointed from life to death and from the Creator to the creature,[1] and with that which was given to all believers for salvation,[2] comfort and delight they have wrought death, that it may appear how cruel and pernicious their turning away and seduction is and like carnal Israel in the wilderness, which spake to Aaron, "We know not what is become of Moses on the mountain. Up, make us gods, which shall go before us!" Then he answered them, "Break off the golden earrings of your wives, sons and daughters, and bring them unto me!" This they did, and he received them at their hand, and he fashioned it with a graving-tool, and they made a calf and spake, "These be thy gods, O Israel, which brought thee up out of the land of Egypt."[3] Thus, they took the honour from God, their Redeemer, and gave it to a molten image, the likeness of an ox that eateth grass.[4]

Even as Israel used against God their best treasure and adornment, which was given them by God, even so doth this people its best treasure, given by God for their adornment, namely, they have misused his holy word to their own destruction.[5] For as those set up a golden calf,[6] these have set up a baked loaf, of which they say, "This is Christ, who hath redeemed us with his flesh and blood," though it hath neither flesh nor blood, neither life nor breath,[7] nor can it be of use to itself,[8] much less help another, yet none taketh this to heart and considereth that perhaps there is here some deception.

Indeed, sundry come and desire to hide it a little better and cover their deceit and say, "The bread is not flesh and blood, for it is a simple loaf like any other. But Christ is enjoyed therein to the comfort of us all." Then, if one asketh where that is written, they point to Matthew 26, Mark 14, Luke 22, I Corinthians 11.

From these they conclude this. O the foolish attacks brought forward by reason! What better game could the devil have started than to distort this, as well as more, and, indeed, his servants are also divided, split and disunited in this, as is said above. One will that the loaf is the body, the other that it is not, and they all seek to support themselves with the scriptures.

The first saith the bread is not bread but the body of Christ and supporteth himself with the words: "This is my body,"[1] and thus setteth up an abomination in place of the comforting institution of Christ and saith, "This is Christ, as sure as he hung on the cross and redeemed us with his flesh and blood," though it hath truly neither flesh nor blood, neither breath nor life, can neither stand nor walk, and the mice eat it; yet they do not perceive, and have thus a dead Christ. How, then, can he give others life? And that will have to take place, which Christ saith, "Whatsoever entereth in at the mouth goeth into the belly, and is cast out into the draught."[2] Thus, this would have to take place also with him, and he should come at last to the sows. There he would meet with fine honour!—so that all other peoples, Jews and Turks mock at such folly.

Then they answer, "The bread is cast out into the draught, but Christ remaineth in the heart." I say, if Christ once became bread, then he must remain bread eternally, for he cannot leave himself, and what he hath become he must remain. He once became man.[3] Now he remaineth for ever and ever true man and God. Thus, if he once became bread, he would also have to remain bread for ever and ever. Moreover, then must bread have suffered for us and not Christ apart from the bread, for the words were already spoken. That would indeed be to deny the faith, for not bread but Christ died for us.

The other now saith the bread is not Christ but a simple loaf, but Christ is therein. He desireth also to prove this with the words: "This is my body." Thus doth reason deceive, where human wisdom is reckoned as divine wisdom. Now, it is not written: "Herein is my body," but, "This is my body." Thus they change the words of Christ simply to defend their folly. But if the words were spoken of bread, as they say, then the Pope must be right and not Luther, according to the words, for "This" is written and not, "Herein." Now, if the Pope's opinion is naught, as it is, indeed, naught, Luther's is just as little. That both are naught, however, is proved for us by the apostle, when he saith to the Hebrews, "He was found in fashion like other men, sin alone excepted."[1] Now if naught but sin was excepted, ubiquity was not excepted. If this be not excepted, then truly he will not be in every morsel of bread, even as, when he walked upon the earth and taught, he was not at the same time in every place, but went from one place to another.[2]

Then sundry say, "It is true that he was not present everywhere. Now, however, he is transfigured, so he is present everywhere. For what otherwise should transfiguration be?" To this I say: But he was not transfigured when he kept the supper with his disciples.[3] Thus, if he was not present everywhere before the transfiguration, then he was likewise not in every piece of bread which he gave his disciples. If at that time he was not therein, still less is he now. Therefore this was truly not Christ's meaning, nor did it come into his mind that he should give us his body to eat. For he was not sent by his Father for this purpose.[4] This he himself denieth when the disciples misunderstood his words and were horrified and said, "This is a hard saying; who can hear it?"[5] as though they would say: "Who can eat thy flesh? That will be a hard

191

thing if none are to receive life unless they eat thy flesh." Then he gave them answer, "It is the Spirit that quickeneth; the flesh profiteth nothing," that implieth, "to eat." But he was born for us, preached, was scourged for us, was killed, rose and ascended up into heaven—that is of the greatest profit to us. For this purpose was he sent, and not as food.[1] But as we have already said, let us now pass over the abuse and speak shortly of the truth.

For in the night in which our Lord Christ was betrayed, he took bread, thanked God his Father, brake it and gave it to his disciples and said, "Take, eat; this is my body, which is broken for you!" After the same manner also he took the cup and said, "Share it among you, for this is the cup, the new covenant in my blood. Do this, as oft as ye do it, in remembrance of me!"[2] Herein Christ doth not at all profess that he or his body desireth to be eaten, but he treateth of something quite other herein, which it is truly necessary that each should well understand. For Christ had been sent by God the Father, that through him the covenant of the promise might be ratified.[3] Christ desired to explain this to his disciples in this meal, for now the time appointed by the Father had come, when this should take place and he should give of the promised grace to everyone who believed in his name,[4] through which they would be planted into the divine nature.[5]

Therefore, when he would teach them this he took the loaf, thanked his Father, brake it and gave it to his disciples and said, "Take and eat it; this is my body which is given for you."[6] Here Christ desireth naught else than to show us how he with his death redeemeth us from sin, hell, the devil and death and hath now planted us into the true divine nature and character[7] that we, all, who eat of the loaf with him are one loaf and body with him,[8] he the head[9] and we members one of another,[1] in so far as we become like unto his death and suffer with him that we also may be raised to glory with him.[2]

This he proveth in that he telleth them to eat the broken bread, and thus every member doth identify himself with the head and fulfil in his measure as a member of the body his suffering, as Paul also saith, "I fill up that which was behind of the afflictions of Christ with my body for his body—which body ye are."[3] Now, it is Christ's will that they do this, that they become one body, one plant and one tree with him, and this his purpose, he showeth later right gloriously in another parable, when Judas had left them,[4] in that he saith, "I am a true vine, ye are the branches, and the Father is the husbandman."[5] For when Christ desired to take leave of his disciples, seeing their sorrow, he sought to comfort them with this, that they might know what he had given them and to what he had led them, that they, after his departure, might find comfort therein, and thereby revive their hearts to take care of this grace and not to be negligent, but continually to bear in mind all the benefits shown us by the Father through Christ.[6]

Therefore doth he say, "As often as ye do this, do it in remembrance of me." That is as though he would say, Now when you remember this divine grace, that ye are planted into the divine promise and made partakers of the divine nature,[7] heirs of all the Father owns, that God hath become ours in Christ and we his, that we have become one bread and one body with Christ, out of many brought and led into one,[8] and have become one plant with him[9]— then we should bear in mind that he hath obtained this for us through his death and so dearly bought us, that we strive earnestly to keep the same and be found grateful to him for this benefit.[10]

Now that is the meaning in this act. He who useth it other maketh of it idolatry, which it is not. Therefore Paul saith, "Let a man examine himself before he eat of this bread and drink of this cup."[1] Here the Holy Spirit desireth that a man heed him well, retire into his heart and behold if he be a partaker of this nature and grace of Christ and a true member of Christ. For in this the one sheweth himself to the others as a member of Christ, partaking of his grace, of his nature and of one heart, mind and soul with all believers and, with them, one body and one bread, as though out of many grains of corn was now one loaf, one matter and substance.[2]

He, however, who findeth not this in himself, doth eat and drink judgment to himself.[3] Herewith doth Paul show clearly, if one hath eyes to see, what Christ's meaning is in this matter. Let him who wantonly will not see bear his own sentence. Enough, herewith, of this matter.

CONCERNING SWEARING, ABOUT WHICH THERE IS NOW MUCH CONTROVERSY

Since now there is much controversy about swearing and each bringeth forward his opinion, yet are they destitute of truth and seek to lead astray many through their mad conceptions, to burden their hearts and to lead them into sin,[4] I, too, was moved to point out the truth and to reveal their falsehood, deceit and lack of understanding. Not that I delight to quarrel with them (for that is neither my custom nor that of the Church of God[5]), but I do it solely that certain devout hearts may keep themselves unspotted from them and from their false teaching.[6]

They say, firstly, that God, himself, in the old covenant commanded his people to swear by his name; now the Son is not against the Father, therefore what the Father once commanded, the Son hath not changed.[1] To this we say, we know well that the Son is not against the Father, otherwise his kingdom could not stand.[2] But they are one, and for this reason they will that we likewise should be one in him.[3] Now, because he is one with the Father, he in the Father, and the Father in him,[4] not he but the Father in him hath now not annulled his word or law but actually established it, as Paul saith, from the shadow into the truth.[5] Therefore, since Moses' vail is taken away,[6] the light of divine grace,[7] the brightness of God's glory is[8] discovered and revealed to us in Christ.[9] Then the shadows flee away[10] that the sun of divine understanding may shine and give us light,[11] for in him lie hidden all the treasures of wisdom and of knowledge.[12]

Therefore in the old covenant, God meant naught else by the command to swear by his name than that they should show through his name that they had learned to know, fear and honour him. He desireth thus to draw them away from abominations, therefore did he command that they swear not by the name of heathen gods, for they are but vain.[13] Therefore also is a heavy penalty promised those who do this, as he saith especially through the prophet Amos, "Behold, the days come, saith the Lord, that I will send a famine in the land, not a famine of bread, nor a thirst for water, but of hearing the words of the Lord: and they shall wander from sea to sea, and from the north even to the east they shall run to and fro to seek the word of the Lord, and shall not find it. In that day shall fair virgins and young men faint for thirst, who swear by the sin of Samaria and say: As truly thy god, O Dan, liveth; as truly thy god, O Beersheba, liveth. For they shall fall, and never rise up again."[14]

The sins of Samaria, however, were the idols with which they committed sin,[1] for they were all vain and useless, of naught and had to come to nothing.[2] Therefore was everything testified by them completely useless and had no being, and was an abomination before the eyes of God. For, since they themselves—the idols—were a lying device, no truth could be testified to by them. For truth cannot be confirmed by a lie.[3] Moreover, whosoever calleth them God, which they are not,[4] speaketh an untruth and doth lie. Therefore in forbidding them to swear by the idols of the heathen he would forbid them all lying, untruth and vain gossip, which thing is later expressed more clearly by the apostle, for no vail hangeth before his face,[5] "Wherefore lay lying now aside and speak every man truth with his neighbour: for ye are members one of another."[6]

This speaking of the truth, God calleth in the old covenant swearing by his name, as David also testifieth, "He that sweareth by God shall be honoured: but the mouth of them that speak lies shall be stopped."[7] Now since the light of divine truth hath appeared more brightly in Christ, who hath revealed to us the real will of the Father,[8] he is not against but with the Father.[9] Israel, however, who bore the name of the people of God, though more in outward appearance than in power and truth, could not grasp the glory, for the vail still hangeth before their eyes[10]—which vail indicateth that the way to holiness was not yet made manifest.[11] For the time of grace had not yet come. Now, however, it hath been revealed in Christ,[12] so we see that that radiance or knowledge was as nothing to this superabundant clarity revealed to us in Christ.[13] For the law was given by Moses, but truth came by Christ.[14]

For this reason doth Paul say that he counted all that had formerly been gain to him as loss and filth

196

for the excellency of the knowledge of Christ.[1] Therefore God, to whom they clove in hope of what should come and not of what they had already received, that they might not continue to ruin themselves with the abomination of the heathen, placed his name in their mouth, though he was not yet known in the heart,[2] as the word that the Lord spake to Moses showeth, "All that the people hath spoken unto thee is good: O that there were such an heart in them, that they would fear me, and keep my commandments."[3]

These words show that they had truly not known him in their heart. Though certain of them knew him, like the prophets, there was as yet no distinction between child and servant, until the time determined by the Father when Christ came,[4] through whom we have received grace for grace.[5] Now, however, since the truth hath come through Christ, that is, hath been revealed, he desireth no ceremonial pomp, but, as he is Spirit, that men serve him in spirit and in truth.[6] Therefore Christ, in order to drive away the shadows that the light of truth—which light he is himself—may shine upon us,[7] cometh and saith, "Ye have heard that it hath been said to them of old: Thou shalt swear no false oath but shalt perform thine oath unto God. But I say unto you that ye swear not at all; neither by heaven; for it is God's throne: nor by the earth; for it is his footstool: nor by Jerusalem; for it is the city of the great King. Neither shalt thou swear by thy head, because thou canst not make one hair white or black.[8] But let your yea be yea; and your nay, nay: for whatsoever is more than these cometh of evil"—that is the devil.[9]

Now, if one should say, as they all interpret it, false and superficial swearing is forbidden, but when one sweareth out of love, necessity and the profit of one's neighbour, it is well done and not wrong—this happeneth when human reason goeth before the

197

knowledge of God, and where human cleverness desireth to rule over the Spirit of God, and not allow itself to be controlled by the same. For just so did Eve look at the forbidden fruit, and chose the same at the counsel of the serpent, which she followed more than the counsel of God, therefore was she deceived by its cunning and led into death.[1] So it is still: whosoever will please men cannot be Christ's servant.[2] For truly here one cannot let reason rule or twist the scriptures in accordance with human presumption or opinion, for that is futile, but one must give God the honour and leave his command unaltered.

If then someone saith: "Must one then only understand the scriptures literally?"—we say: No! But here in this place and everywhere, as the scripture came by the Holy Spirit we must let it be judged by the same.[3] Who, however, can attain this judgment, apart from him who hath the Holy Spirit, for the carnal man receiveth naught of the things of the Spirit of God, but the spiritual man judgeth all things spiritually?[4] And those who have him will easily recognize what is meant here concerning Christ, and will find that Christ here bringeth forth the truth out of the shadow[5] and saith, "To the men of old was said: Thou shalt not swear falsely.[6] But I say unto you: Swear not at all."[7] And it is primarily Christ's purpose, as the whole chapter showeth, to lead us to a more perfect righteousness than that to which God's people of old was led, when he saith, "Thou shalt not kill.[8] But I say unto you: Ye shall also not be angry."[9]

Likewise: "To the men of old is said: Thou shalt not commit adultery.[10] But I say unto you: Whosoever looketh on a woman to lust after her hath committed adultery with her already in his heart."[11] Likewise: "To the men of old is said: Thou shalt love

198

thy friend and hate thine enemy. But I say unto you: Love your enemies, do good to them that hate you, bless them that curse you, pray for them that persecute you; that ye may be children of your Father in heaven." Summa: "Except your righteousness shall exceed the righteousness of the scribes and Pharisees," saith Christ, "ye shall not enter into the kingdom of heaven."[1]

That, now, is one reason why Christ here forbiddeth swearing. For shortly, it is his will that his people, who are called by Christ, walk in a better righteousness and observe his testimony more diligently than his people of old, because the truth is revealed and hath come more fully to light in Christ.[2] The other reason is our weakness: that we in our own strength are able to do neither what is small nor what is great, without the working of God in us, as the words show: "Thou shalt not swear by thy head, because thou canst not make a single hair white or black,"[3] and as he saith in another place, "Which of you by being anxious can add one cubit unto his stature?"[4]

Now because there is no strength or capacity in us, of ourselves, it is his desire that we give and allow honour to him who can do and work all things. For he is a jealous God and giveth his glory to none other.[5] Now, whosoever sweareth to do this or that encroacheth upon God's honour and robbeth God of what is his, for he sweareth to do this, though he can do nothing and doth not even know if God desireth to do it in him.[6] Therefore doth James say, "For that ye ought to say: If God will, I shall do this or that."[7] Therefore all God-fearing men will keep themselves from such, and though the world crieth much against them, will heed it not.

The third reason is this, that now the truth hath come or hath been revealed through Christ and we have been planted therein,[8] now not we, but the truth, which is Christ, liveth in us.[1] He doeth and proveth, yea also speaketh all things in us, as Christ saith, "For it is not ye that speak, but the Spirit of my Father which speaketh in you."[2] Now, since this is so, all that a believer saith is placed in God, confirmed and steadfast; nor will it waver, for he speaketh it in or through God, or God through him. Therefore doth James say, "Let your yea be yea, and your nay, nay,"[3] as though he would say: See that ye are not men of superficial words and thoughtless gossip, who grieve the Holy Spirit of God, who dwelleth in you;[4] but mark and heed what he speaketh in you or moveth you to say, that he may also carry it out and give power to your speech, that ye may walk in the truth and your words be truth—your yea, yea and your nay, nay.[5] Beyond this swear no other oath.[6]

Then Paul also saith, "God who is faithful hath brought it to pass that our word to you was not yea and nay. For the Son of God, Jesus Christ, who was preached among you by us, was not yea and nay, but in him was yea. For all God's promises are yea in him and amen in him, unto the praise of God."[7] As though he would say: He, who hath left nothing undone, but hath brought to pass all that he hath spoken to you through me, and hath borne witness to his word himself in power and truth, revealeth thereby that it was the word not of men but of God that I proclaimed to you.[8]

Now, since God speaketh all things in believers or giveth them all things to speak,[9] it must be that he, who will not believe such words and desireth first to have an oath, hath not the same Spirit. Now he who hath him not, is none of his.[10] Wherefore doth he, who urgeth one to swear, testify that the truth of God is not in him. And again, he that sweareth testifieth that he heedeth and observeth not the same. For if he knew his word to stand in God, wherein all things become firm, he would seek no farther, but hold to that which the truth hath spoken and testified through him. He, however, who standeth in the truth and hath placed his word in the truth, which is God himself,[1] and then seeketh another testification with swearing, turneth himself from the Creator to the creature and weakeneth the truth in him, for he desireth first to testify to it more strongly through himself than God hath already testified to it in him. For that is to rob God of what is his and to refuse to give him the honour that he doeth it and must do it.[2] Therefore, saith James, "To him that knoweth to do good and doeth it not, to him it is sin."[3]

Now if one should say, "All manner of swearing is, indeed, forbidden,[4] but to testify to the truth with God, who is truth,[5] is not forbidden us," I answer as follows: That to which Israel had power to swear, in accordance with the Lord's command, was also truth and not lying;[6] for they were forbidden to swear to lying and wrong, but if they swore to the truth, that was allowed them.[7] Thus, if such were allowed us, Christ would have let the first command remain (according to thy words), since to swear falsely was forbidden. He said clearly, however, "To the men of old it was said: Thou shalt not swear falsely,[8] but I say unto you: Swear not at all."[9]

Therefore weigh up the words of Christ carefully. He said, "To the men of old was said: Ye shall not swear falsely, but I say unto you: Swear not at all." Moreover, he said, "To the men of old was said: Thou shalt hate thine enemy, but I say unto you: Love your enemies."[10] Now, if I hate my enemy and repay him evil for evil, give him curse for curse and blow for blow, would I also thereby be doing right? No truly, for that would be to forsake the command[11] and nature of our Master.[12] Just as little doth he do right who sweareth, even though he sweareth to what is in itself truth, for that is likewise forbidden.[1] For it is enough that the truth itself testifieth, in so far as it is in us, for that is better, nobler and surer than all the witness of men.

Therefore Christ himself saith, "I receive not testimony from men, for I have a better witness than that of John. For the works that I do testify of me and the Father who hath sent me testifieth also."[2] Thus, he will himself testify in each, to what extent he will. Therefore is all swearing vain, however it may be done, for in doing it he heedeth not the testimony borne by God in him.

Then when one saith, "But love doeth all things,[3] therefore to serve and profit one's neighbour one may, indeed, swear—that is not wrong," we say, love truly doeth all things, but it neither will nor can act against its nature,[4] for it is no doer of sins but of righteousness,[5] and never faileth.[6] So, on the contrary, it would act for the betterment of its neighbour, and with all earnestness seek to turn him away from what he is about to do, if it is wrong. That is its function, and that for which God hath chosen and accepted his people,[7] for this purpose also hath he given his Holy Spirit into our hearts:[8] that he witness in us against sins[9] and therefore reprove the world.[10] Now, whosoever complieth with them and testifieth not against them forsaketh the witness of the Spirit of God in him.

To their saying, however, that God hath himself sworn,[11] therefore it truly cannot be wrong, we answer, none denieth that God and Christ hath sworn. But that proveth not that men have also the right to do so. For what God promiseth he can perform, not with the help of another, but completely of himself, in his own strength, therefore can he truly pledge and promise of himself. Now he hath never gone above this nor sworn by any one higher, for there is no one higher, as the apostle testifieth, "Because God could swear by no greater, he sware by himself,[1] saying: Surely I will multiply thee."[2]

Now because God is the truth, he promiseth to do such through himself and to bring it about. Therefore if one will understand the position it is as though the man saith, "I will do it," yet there is the difference that what God promiseth he is able to do of himself, but man is not able. Now, since he can do nothing, he will rightly and dutifully leave the honour to him who must do everything in him,[3] as James teacheth, and will say, "If God will I shall do it."[4] If he doeth this not, he depriveth God of the honour[5] that he oweth him and that it is his duty to give.[6] Now, since he can do nothing,[7] neither hath he power to swear by himself,[8] for he cannot of himself keep it, how should he then have power to swear by one who is greater? For he who hath not power to swear by the very least may still less touch what is greater,[9] as Christ himself showeth with the words: "Woe unto you, ye blind guides, which say: Whosoever shall swear by the temple, it is nothing; but whosoever shall swear by the gold of the temple he is a debtor. Ye fools and blind; for whether is greater, the gold, or the temple that sanctifieth the gold? And, Whosoever shall swear by the altar it is nothing; but whosoever sweareth by the gift that is upon it, he is guilty. Ye fools and blind: for whether is greater, the gift, or the altar that sanctifieth the gift? Whoso therefore shall swear by the altar, sweareth by it, and by all things thereon. And whoso shall swear by the temple, sweareth by it, and by him that dwelleth therein. And he that shall swear by heaven, sweareth by the throne of God, and by him that sitteth thereon."[10]

From these words it is clear that God desireth still less that one swear by what is great than by what is small. For the priests regarded it not as wrong to swear by the altar, but they regarded it as wrong to swear by the sacrifice, because it was now a sweet savour unto the Lord.[1] Here Christ showeth their folly and lack of understanding. He calleth them fools, because they know not that the altar is more than the sacrifice, and ought truly to know that because he that sweareth by the sacrifice doeth wrong, he that actually sweareth by the altar, doeth still greater wrong; and that if he doeth wrong who sweareth by the gold of the temple, he doeth still greater wrong who actually sweareth by the temple, since he sweareth not only by the same, but by him who dwelleth therein, that is by God.[2] Since they knew this not, he rebuked them for their blindness of heart, for they presumed to be teachers of others[3] and held themselves to be wise,[4] and yet were fools, without knowledge of God.[5]

From these words it is evident that just as little as God desireth men to swear by the temple, the altar, heaven, earth, their own head or any created thing, just as little, and still less, doth he desire the same by his name. Therefore saith James, "Above all things, dear brothers, swear not, neither by heaven, neither by the earth, neither by any other oath: but let your yea be yea; and your nay, nay; lest ye fall into hypocrisy."[6] Here James will have no oath at all, whether small or great, to avoid hypocrisy. Therefore, let men twist it as they will and dress it up and adorn it as they may, no good will be found in human swearing, for Christ himself saith, "Let your speech be, Yea, yea; Nay, nay: for whatsoever is more than these cometh of evil."[7] The evil one, however, is the devil, that teareth good from the heart of men and planteth evil.[8]

Therefore the devout will walk in the truth, allow it to rule and guide them and hold to the same;[9]

whatsoever it stirreth, speaketh and doeth within them, believe and observe the same;[1] and this for the sake of the truth which is God himself,[2] which dwelleth in them.[3] Therefore they neither need nor desire any oath.[4] It is not our duty, for the sake of those who are outside, to copy them, but on the contrary to testify against their sin, for God hath given his Spirit for this purpose: to reprove the world for sin.[5] Therefore let us look a little better at the dear apostle Paul, and not use his writings as a cloak for wickedness and distort none of them to our own destruction.[6] For the moment, we desire to say no more about swearing.

CONCERNING GOVERNMENTAL AUTHORITY AND ITS APPOINTED SERVICE

Because we are so much attacked concerning governmental authority, and asked what we think about it: whether it was appointed by God or not, whether rulers can be Christians or not—we do not desire to hold back the truth, and we desire to bring forward nothing without or apart from the basis of truth, that one may see that we have not departed from the truth, but that all we do is founded therein and that we walk in the truth. Therefore we desire to say nothing to harm any, nor to keep silence to oblige any—not even ourselves—but to bear witness to the truth as God hath placed it in us, because the Lord commandeth us, saying, "Ye shall be my witnesses to the people."[7] Therefore do we desire to speak according to his word. Let him who hath ears to hear, hear!

It is clear and evident that because God the Almighty, in his grace desired not so completely to cast man off that he would no more remember or have mercy on the human race and receive them to grace, therefore even in the midst of his wrath he remembered his grace and promised blessing from the woman's seed; yet man had to lose the Garden of Eden.[1] Thus, since God did not completely take away the mercy that he felt, he was himself ruler over men and punished him who did evil, but loved the devout, as is clearly to be seen in Abel and Cain. God loved Abel, but when Cain acted wrongly, God punished him himself, when he said, "Cain, what hast thou done? Behold, the voice of thy brother's blood crieth unto me from the ground. And now art thou cursed from the earth, which hath opened her mouth to receive thy brother's blood from thy hands. When thou tillest the ground it shall not henceforth yield unto thee her strength; a fugitive and a vagabond shalt thou be in the earth."[2]

Now that was the rule of the Lord, thus did he punish the evildoer, as is also to be seen in Adam and Eve.[3] But the devout he loved, and when they were hard pressed by unjust men, God was judge, and left not innocent blood unavenged,[4] as he will do still, as he promised through the mouth of his prophets: "When I remit men all their sins, yet will I not remit them the innocent blood that they have shed."[5] Therefore saith Christ, "That upon them may come all the righteous blood shed, from Abel unto the blood of Zacharias."[6] Thus did God himself rule and judge men through his Spirit, until men completely ruined themselves and the carnal mind took the upper hand in them, which each did follow.

God spake, "My Spirit shall not always be at strife with men, for they are flesh."[7] Observe here what moved God to take away the rule of his Spirit from men: naught else than the corrupt nature and carnal mind of men. For, because they would no longer obey, but allowed themselves to be overruled by sin, the Spirit of God went from them.[8] Yet it was

206

not his will to cast them off eternally, therefore did he give them their ruler after the flood, as the wise man also saith, "He set a ruler over every people."[1] Paul agreeth with this, "All government, everywhere, is ordained of God."[2] But to what purpose? To be a servant of God for the punishment of evildoers.[3]

For, since God no longer wanted to let his Spirit strive with carnal-minded man,[4] yet did not want the earth to be completely stained with blood and evildoers to remain unpunished, he had to have an instrument of punishment.[5] That, as was said above, was the ruling power,[6] which he also commanded, "Whoso sheddeth man's blood, by man shall his blood be shed."[7] From this it is seen that power and government have grown rather from the wrath and punishment of God than from blessing. Moreover, when he gave them power over all flesh, he yet reserved the highest power for himself, from which it is clear that he desireth that they look to him and heed him,[8] that they do naught of themselves, that they act not on their own initiative, wantonly, but allow themselves to be used as a rod by him who guideth them in accordance with his will and pleasure.[9]

All this is the long-suffering of the Almighty, who desireth not that any should perish, but that all should come to repentance.[10] For, although men have ruined themselves in his sight, so that he could have rightly exterminated them all, yet did he remember his mercy and desireth them well, therefore at all times doth he seek their good,[11] that they may recognize this in time to come and turn to him[12] and be healed.[13] Where this is not done, the Lord will not lie. He will turn about, tear down and destroy and there shall be none to deliver, for the mouth of the Lord hath spoken it.[14]

Therefore, wherever the ruling power presumeth to act of itself, or wantonly, the stick rebelleth against him that useth it, the axe against him that heweth therewith and the saw against him that saweth therewith. Hereby it becometh quite clear that they are naught else than an instrument by means of which God desireth to punish evil men. Now the tool can of itself do no good, except it alloweth the master to use it according to his will. Where that is the case, work is done; otherwise it remaineth undone.[1]

Even so is it with ruling powers: though they for long act wantonly, they achieve no good, for they allow not themselves to be used by him who hath appointed them thereto, but desire to act of themselves, according to their wanton wills. So God punisheth the rods together with those who were to be beaten, in that those who are subject rebel against the authority.[2] For as they (the rulers) rebel against him who should guide them, it is their just sentence that God should punish them with their own sins and give them a disobedient people, that they might hate one another and become hated, that they may thereby know they have neglected their office and allow him to have the honour, who hath appointed them thereto.[3]

If, however, they will not consider this, but turn to the extermination and wiping out of nations, then the Lord will punish the fruit of their arrogant hearts and eyes (in that they ascribe to themselves power, strength and ability, not only in this world, but also in that which is to come)[4] as the wise man doth show: "Give ear, ye that rule the people and raise yourselves over the nations, for power is given you of the Lord and sovereignty from the Highest, who shall try your works and search out your counsels. Because, being ministers of his kingdom, ye have not judged aright, nor kept the law, nor walked after the counsel of God; horribly and speedily shall he come upon you: for a sharp judgment shall be to them that be in high places. For the lowly experience grace, but the mighty shall be mightily punished."[1] Enough of the punishment of governmental authority.

As there is none, however, who desireth right with all his heart,[2] it is rightly their punishment to have children to be their princes, and effeminate or foolish people to rule over them, as he hath said he would give them.[3] For God trieth all things for the betterment of man. But when all is of no avail, he letteth go his wrath as he hath said. Thus he let all peoples be and chose for himself one single people,[4] namely Israel, whose God and King he desired to be, as he expresseth clearly through the wise man: "In all lands hath he set a ruler, but over Israel he is himself Lord."[5] Therefore did he keep watch over them as sheep[6] and led them from one place to another and suffered no man to do them wrong.[7]

For their sakes he reproved kings and mighty nations and said, "Touch not mine anointed, and do my prophets no harm." These also he called his inheritance[8] and children,[9] thus he is their Father,[10] Lord and King and reigneth over them, ruleth and leadeth them.[11] Though they sinned greatly against him, he forsook them not for his name's sake,[12] until after committing many sins they asked for a king and spake to Samuel, "Set a king over us, to judge us, as all the nations have."[13]

When, however, Samuel laid before them the right of the king—to deter them from such an undertaking —they followed him not and refused to obey the faithful counsel of Samuel, saying, "Nay; but we will have a king over us; that we also may be like all the nations; and that our king may judge us, and go out before us, and fight our battles."[14] The Lord, however, spake to Samuel, "Hearken unto the voice of the people in all that they say unto thee: for they have not rejected thee, but they have rejected me, that I should not reign over them. According to all the works which they have done since the day that I brought them up out of Egypt even unto this day, wherewith they have forsaken me, and served other gods, so do they also unto thee. Now therefore obey their voice."[1] Because they time and again forsook the Almighty and beyond that desired yet a king, Samuel said, "Thus saith the Lord: I have brought you out of Egypt, and delivered you out of the hand of the Egyptians, and out of the hand of all kings and of them that oppressed you: And ye have this day rejected your God, who himself saved you out of all your adversities and your tribulations; and ye have said unto him: Set a king over us,"[2] as though he would say: It is all too little that ye have done against God to provoke him! Therefore is his wrath kindled against you and he giveth you a king. Behold, there is your king![3] Further saith the Lord, "Thou saidst: Give us a king and princes. I gave thee a king in mine anger, and took him away in my wrath."[4] From all these words it is evident that God hath appointed men as rulers out of wrath only and not out of favour. It was only after the transgression, when they forsook God and gave themselves up to carnal lusts and sins, that he gave them a man to rule over them, that his Spirit might not continually be at strife with them.[5] This he did not only to the nations, but also to the Jews, as is said above, the Lord said, "They have rejected me, that I should not reign over them."[6] Therefore is temporal power a sign, picture and reminder of departure from God, and should truly be to all men an occasion to look within and to consider to what they have come, and thus to take the opportunity to turn back the more quickly to God, from whom they have fallen away. Who, however, regardeth it thus? Now, since none desire to take it to heart, that will at last come upon them that rightly should come.[1]

Thus, we see from whence temporal power first came and what moved God to give the same. That for which it is appointed hath also been told; namely, for the punishment of evil men.[2] For, since men desired not to allow themselves to be ruled by the Spirit of the Lord, God had to use another rod to force them to preserve themselves from harm, that the land might not be completely polluted with blood-guilty men, that he would not have to destroy the whole earth on their account,[3] but that it might be preserved to the time of the promised seed in whom all things would be brought to rights;[4] who, when he cometh to establish a new kingdom, cometh not with great pomp in the way of the world, but as it is written: "Rejoice greatly, O daughter of Zion; shout, O daughter of Jerusalem: behold, thy King cometh unto thee: he is just and having salvation; poor, and riding upon an ass, and upon a colt, the foal of an ass."[5] He cometh not for wrath, not for vengeance, not for destruction, but to make blessed.[6] He calleth men to himself and saith, "Come and learn of me, for I am meek and humble in heart."[7] Hence, all who desire to come into his kingdom must become of his nature and of his mind and spirit.[8] Therefore, also, did he rebuke his disciples, when they desired to practise vengeance and asked that fire might fall from heaven and consume those who received them not, and said, "Know ye not of what Spirit ye are the children? The Son of man is not come to destroy men's souls, but to make them blessed."[9] As though he would say: What would ye then do? That is not my purpose! If ye would be my disciples, ye must not do thus, for I have not been sent to practise vengeance.

Behold, here doth Christ do away with vengeance in his kingdom. He will not use outward vengeance and destruction of men, hence also doth he command in the Church of his kingdom, saying, "To the men of old was said: A hand for a hand, an eye for an eye, a tooth for a tooth: but I say unto you, that ye resist not evil: but whosoever shall smite thee on thy right cheek, turn to him the other also. And if any man will sue thee at the law, and take away thy coat, let him have thy cloak also."[1] Behold, how Christ doth here encroach upon the office of governmental authority, for it was commanded to shed blood for blood,[2] to destroy a hand for a hand, an eye for an eye and a tooth for a tooth.[3]

But Christ in his kingdom giveth us a different picture and desireth not that vengeance be taken, as also Paul teacheth us, "Avenge not yourselves, dear brothers, but give place unto the wrath of God."[4] Thus Christ here desireth that not only subjects, but all men who come to his kingdom, should not resist evil.[5] For, since he encroacheth upon the office of governmental authority and desireth not that it be used in his kingdom, truly he saith not alone to those who previously had no power, but much more to those who used it, that they should set it aside and leave vengeance to God alone, when they come to his kingdom. The others he leaveth in their authority and custom.

Therefore saith he, "My kingdom is not of this world: if my kingdom were of this world, then would my servants fight for me, that I should not be delivered to the Jews."[6] Note well—the King of heaven and earth, what power, magnificence and glory he hath![7] Note the battle he wageth against those who would kill him! See how with a powerful host he goeth out against them, how he smiteth the enemy, in that he saith to Peter, "Put up again thy sword into his place:[1] knowest thou not that I can pray to the Father to send me sundry legions of angels to fight for me?"[2] Behold, how he practiseth vengeance, in that he took the ear of Malchus that had been struck off and put it on again for him![3]

"Whosoever would be my disciple," saith he, "let him take his cross upon him and follow me."[4] Therefore doth he command further, saying, "Resist not evil. Do good to them that hate you, and pray for them that persecute you, bless them that curse you, that ye may be the children of your Father which is in heaven: for he maketh his sun to rise and his rain to fall on the good and on the evil."[5]

Here it is evident, since he saith particularly that they are not children of vengeance, that Christ will not have in his house or kingdom servants of vengeance, but of blessing, love and good action, as he himself was.[6] Now, he who hath not this spirit is none of his.[7]

Now if one should say, "But Paul calleth them servants of God.[8] How then can that be—that they are not Christians, yet are they servants of God?" Then we say, it may well be, both to-day and in times past. For who doth not know that in times past Israel alone was the Lord's people, whom he had chosen for himself out of all nations,[9] and all the Gentiles were as nothing before him. Yet doth he call Nebuchadnezzar his servant, when he saith, "I will send and take Nebuchadnezzar, the king of Babylon, my servant, and will set his throne upon these stones."[10] Even so doth he call the king of Assyria a staff or rod of his wrath and his hand the strength of his indignation, that he might therewith smite the hypocrites, the people that had deserved his wrath.[11]

Now they were servants of God, yet not Jews. Even so is it to-day. For God hath two kinds of servants, servants of vengeance to execute wrath

213

upon him that doeth evil,[1] for they were also given in wrath;[2] Christ, however, is not come for vengeance, but for blessing,[3] hence those who are planted in him and are his servants must no longer serve for vengeance but for blessing, that the one might be built up and edified by the other[4] and we all grow together and increase in the knowledge of Christ and become a perfect man in the perfect maturity of Christ;[5] that is, that we may receive a holy,[6] blameless and unspotted life,[7] that we may be holy, as he is holy.[8]

Then they say, "Now the Son is not against the Father, therefore doth he neither break down nor do away with that which the Father hath once ordained. The Father hath appointed ruling authority,[9] therefore it must also remain in Christ—otherwise the Son would be against the Father." It is true that the Son is not against the Father, for they are both one.[10] It followeth not from this, however, that what the Father hath appointed everywhere must remain in Christ, for then the grace of Christ would be in vain. Reason: after the transgression[11] the Father appointed death in all men;[12] Christ, however, through his death,[13] hath destroyed the power and might of death and hath appointed life[14] in all who believe in his name.[15] Therefore he is not against the Father, but he hath fulfilled the Father's promise.[16]

Further, God appointed and gave Abraham circumcision, commanding it so sternly that the soul of any boy who was not circumcised was to be destroyed from among his people. Yet, it ceaseth in Christ.[17] The Father also commanded to love one's friend and hate one's enemy,[18] regarding which thing, for Saul did it not, but spared the life of his enemy, the king of the Amalekites, and left him alive, he was rejected from being king over Israel.[19] Yet Christ commandeth to love not only the friend but also the enemy.[20] Thus, there is much that the Father appointed, such

214

as sacrifices, sabbaths and the like, which in Christ, in whom the essential itself is, cease and come to an end.[1] But one must not say so presumptuously, that therefore is the Son against the Father. On the contrary, one must say, what the Father appointed in Christ will remain in him and is not changed, such as love,[2] peace,[3] unity[4] and community.[5] What he hath appointed outside Christ, however, such as death,[6] wrath,[7] disfavour,[8] curse,[9] malediction,[10] vengeance[11] and their servants—that is not fitting in Christ.

Through this every man can instruct himself. But those who do not see and heed this distinction can reach no true understanding. Just this is what the whole world lacketh. Christ, however, is the full blessing of the Father,[12] thus whosoever will inherit the blessing of God must receive it through Christ.[13] Now, since the full blessing of God is in Christ[14]— yea, Christ is himself the blessing,[15] promised to the fathers,[16] but fulfilled and given to us[17]—what was given and ordained in wrath, curse, disfavour and anger[18] neither can nor may be fitting in Christ.[19] For because blessing cometh or hath come,[20] wrath ceaseth.[21] Now governmental authority was given in wrath[22] and its office appointed in anger,[23] for they rejected the Lord, that he should not reign over them.[24] Thus the child of blessing cannot[25] be the servant of wrath[26] and vengeance.[27]

Then they say, "But David was a ruler and king, yet he was devout and pleased God—why should that not be so now?" We say, it is true that David, who was devout and pleasing to God, was a king,[28] but the reason why that age could bear it while the present time will not suffer it is that at that time the way to holiness had not been revealed.[29] And although Israel did much evil,[30] so that God could rightly have cast them off from before his face,[31] yet he refrained

215

for his name's sake,[1] and suffered their ways until the time that Christ was sent,[2] as Paul also testifieth, "This time of ignorance God overlooked; but now he commandeth all men everywhere to repent."[3]

Also, at that time, vengeance had not yet been abolished, but was allowed them, as Christ himself saith, "To the men of old was said: Thou shalt love thy friend and hate thine enemy."[4] Now, since this was allowed them, although vengeance belonged to God[5] then as today, they could have a hand therein,[6] as one seeth oft here and there in the Scriptures that they executed vengeance at God's command.[7] Therefore, in olden times the devout man was more rightly king over Israel than the godless man, for he was also a figure of Christ, who is the true king of the holy hill,[8] for whom they, who were under the yoke of bondage, waited.[9] Now, however, he hath come,[10] hath received[11] and prepared the kingdom[12] and separated the children from the slaves,[13] so that they have received the freedom promised them[14] (which king was not given us in wrath,[15] but out of the blessing, grace and love of God[16]) thus that which was given in anger, wrath and displeasure ceaseth.[17]

After this they say: "Then according to your words no ruler can be blessed, yet it is not God's will that a man should be lost, but that all should come unto the knowledge of the truth[18]—this, however, would be closed to the ruler." To this we say with Paul, "God willeth that all men come unto the knowledge of truth and are healed and saved."[19] That many do not follow his will, however,[20] and obey not his voice,[21] is their own fault, for Christ saith, "Come unto me all ye that are heavy laden."[22] He maketh here no exception. Whosoever desireth to come to him he will not cast out.[23] Therefore rulers can also come to him—the way is just as free to them as to subjects,[24] though they find it more difficult[25]—if only they allow

216

and suffer Christ to work. But where he is at work[1] he worketh naught else than what is of his nature and character, even as the vine giveth fruit that is not foreign to its nature, and all its branches show themselves like the vine.[2]

Thus also in Christ: whosoever is placed in him,[3] planted[4] and grafted into him[5] will prove himself to be not foreign to his nature,[6] namely, will empty himself of himself and of his glory.[7] Therefore doth he say to his disciples, "The kings of the nations are called gracious lords, and they that are powerful rule over the people. But it shall not be so among you, but let the greatest among you be the servant of all."[8] Why? For this reason: that such was his mind[9] and nature[10] and he himself also did so. He came not to be served, but because he wished to serve,[11] and he hath thereby given us an example, that we might follow in his footsteps.[12]

For whosoever will be Christ's[13] must surrender himself utterly to him[14] so that he can say with Paul, "I live not now, but Christ liveth in me,"[15] and, "Christ is my life."[16] Now in whomsoever Christ now liveth and not he himself, even though he were a ruler,[17] Christ would show in him just that which he himself also did,[18] and that his Kingdom was not of this world.[19] For Christ fled when men wanted to make him a king.[20] How, then, should the members desire to rebel[21] against the head[22] and the branches against the roots,[23] since truly the servant is not above his Lord?[24] For Christ useth in his saints to-day just as little worldly pomp as he did at the time of his pilgrimage here on earth.[25] For whosoever will be exalted with him[26] must first humble himself with him[27] and empty himself of all things.[28]

Now, if any ruler leaveth, with him, pomp and glory and taketh upon him the poor,[29] lowly[30] and humble form of a servant,[31] serving all men,[32] obeying[33]

217

and subject to all men in Christ,[1] so that he can say with Paul, "Though I was free, yet have I made myself a servant unto all for Christ's sake"[2]—then entrance into the Kingdom of Christ is not closed to him.[3] As long, however, as that doth not take place, and he remaineth unbroken and in his glory, he cannot be a disciple of Christ.[4]

To sum up: Because governmental authority was given in wrath,[5] for the punishment of evildoers,[6] whosoever incurreth its penalty hath fallen under the curse,[7] therefore God's wrath, anger and vengeance cometh upon him, namely, the punishment of the ruling authority, which is the servant of the vengeance, anger and wrath of God[8]—from which wrath, anger, vengeance and curse, Christ hath redeemed us and set us free,[9] and hath made us children of grace,[10] who cannot now be servants of vengeance.[11] Thus, a ruler can be no Christian, or no Christian can be a ruler. For one is our king—Christ, who hath been appointed by his Father upon his holy hill.[12]

What then is his office? To shed blood? O no, for he saith, "The Son of man is not come to destroy men's lives, but to save them."[13] Or hath he come to wage war? Yea, a very great war against hell, the devil and the world, all of which he hath overcome;[14] but this is a struggle in which neither spear nor sword is used.[15] This battle we ought also to fight and arm ourselves with God's armour[16] that we may overcome with him[17]—but the wars of the world he would condemn.

What, then, is his office, since he neither warreth, sueth at law nor sheddeth blood? This David showeth us, in that he saith, "I will proclaim the law of the Lord, as the Lord hath commanded me."[18] And again, "I will declare thy name unto my brethren: in the midst of the congregation will I sing praise unto thee."[19] This he (Christ) also showeth in the temple at

Jerusalem, when he spake to his mother, saying, "Wist ye not that I must be about my Father's business?"[1] For, for this purpose was he sent by God,[2] and to this he also held. Therefore when he appointed helpers and sent them out he did not command them to sue at law or to shed blood,[3] but said, "As my Father hath sent me, even so send I you."[4]

For what then was he sent? Namely, to preach the gospel.[5] He gave them also a sword, wherewith they should smite and punish evildoers—even the following: "If thy brother commit sin punish him."[6] That is the rule that holdeth sway in the kingdom or house of Christ. Yet are they subject to the human ordinances of the ruling authority[7] and ready to every good work[8] and so wait for the glory that shall be revealed in them,[9] when they shall be like him,[10] and willingly waive their rights, with Christ, for the hope of their salvation,[11] that they may also be glorified with him.[12]

Thus we consider that enough hath been said concerning governmental authority and that it is clear that it is a sign of the turning away from God,[13] therefore is its office none other than that God should punish through it, as with a rod, those who have deserted him[14] and those who do evil;[15] but not the devout. As Paul saith, "Wilt thou then not be afraid of the power? do that which is good, for rulers are not a terror to them that do good, but to them that do evil, and they are God's servants to execute vengeance and punishment upon them that do evil."[16] Thus God in Christ is alone Lord over the devout,[17] even as the law was given by the Father and yet is done away in Christ, as Paul saith, "Christ is the end of the law for righteousness to every one that believeth." And again, "The law was our schoolmaster until Christ came, that we might become devout through faith. Now, however, that faith is come, we are no longer under the law, for we are all children of God through faith in Christ,"[1] and again, "If ye walk in the Spirit, ye are not under the law."[2]

Now, although the law, in so far as it is drawn up in writing, is done away in Christ, yet man, immediately he leaveth the work of the Spirit,[3] becometh a transgressor of the same[4] and cometh again under its punishment.[5] Thus, we are free from governmental authority in Christ, that is from its punishment, which is God's vengeance;[6] since we are reconciled to him.[7] As soon, however, as a man beginneth again to sin[8] and doeth wrong,[9] he falleth under wrath[10] and the curse and will fall into the hands of the ruling power,[11] that it may execute God's vengeance upon him.[12] That is the punishment outside Christ, into which all they who forsake God fall,[13] and they are under the curse or malediction.[14] For outside Christ the power of government hath still its place as a certain sign that God's wrath doth still continue against sinners and godless men,[15] and only the devout are reconciled with God through Christ and are under his blessing.[16]

To continue, however, God, who is faithful, hath ordained for every office, whether outside or in Christ, its dues and purtenances, that it may act unhampered, therefore hath he also ordained for governmental authority its dues and taxes, which one should give without reserve, and not resist it in this.[17] For he who doeth so, resisteth God's ordinance,[18] because Christ himself also gave it its dues[19] and also commanded others to give.[20]

Therefore we also desire to give the ruler willingly that which is ordained for his office, call it what one will—taxes, revenue, payment in kind, tribute, customs, toll or service—and to show our willing subjection therein,[21] and to be ready to every good work.[22] If, however, he goeth beyond this wilfully, then he executeth not the office of the Lord, but his own office. For, as is said already, the ruling power is a staff, stick, rod and instrument of God's vengeance,[1] through which God himself punisheth evildoers in anger.[2] It is for this office that taxes and duties are appointed[3] and not for wanton warfare and bloodshed. Therefore hath one no obligation to them for the same: yea, on the contrary, we are forbidden to give, not commanded, because we are not children of vengeance,[4] and must no more yield our members to be weapons of unrighteousness,[5] and serve no unrighteousness.

Thus, it is always wrong that they turn to the extermination of nations.[6] Now, whosoever payeth them taxes for this, helpeth them in their iniquity and maketh himself a partaker of their sins. Therefore, though they should strive to force us to this, we say with Peter, "We must obey God rather than man,"[7] and obey them not in the same and give them nothing, that we be not partakers of other men's sins.[8] Though many of them defend these taxes with Paul's saying[9] and support themselves with the words of Christ, "Render unto Caesar the things which are Caesar's,"[10] it is to be feared they do so only that they be not persecuted with the cross of Christ, and desire the friendship of men which is enmity with God.[11] For these words are said neither by Christ nor Paul with a view to permitting rulers to carry out every caprice, but they are spoken regarding the appointed appurtenances, such as services, payment in kind, revenue, etc., which are appointed them by God for the execution of their office.[12] For, since this office is not done away by Christ for the unjust, its appointed service must remain. When the rulers are also evil, the punishment of the people is yet greater.[13]

Now, because we are also subject to the human order for the Lord's sake,[14] Paul commandeth to give it that which is its due, that is its appointed service or tax. It appeareth in this passage of Paul that there were certain brothers in Rome who wanted to be free from governing authority in all things and neither obey it nor pay tribute (even as men in Münster in our own days, deceived by the devil, revolted against authority) whom Paul here desireth to oppose, or rather desireth to lay before them the full and proper Christian order, as the whole epistle showeth.

Now, let that be as it may, he teacheth them that they should give the taxes, tribute and revenue due to the state and not revolt against it, but be obedient. That he speaketh, however, of the taxes due to the state, those which have been appointed by God, and not of such wanton wickedness as the wars of the state, is shown by the words: "Give them their dues," as though he would say: Give what is appointed for their office—what is to be given annually. For what is not appointed and commanded by God, one giveth not out of duty, but because one desireth to do so, or on such occasions, rather because one is driven and coerced by the ruling power.

Therefore the words make a distinction, "Give what duty ye owe," and, "To whom it is due,"[1]—not, "Whosoever will have it and whatsoever he will have." Thus Christ also commandeth to give to Caesar what is Caesar's,[2] but he speaketh not at all, as many interpret it, of such taxes for warfare and bloodshed. For the tax which the Jews then gave, for which reason Christ was asked if it were right to give or not, was given annually, and began when Christ was born, under the rule of the emperor Augustus,[3] when in all the world there was peace and no war, as the chronicles say. Therefore it was given neither for war nor for bloodshed, but was even, as to-day the lord of the manor doth appoint to them who cart or carry wood from the forest, to each his appointed sum to be

222

given yearly, as, as I understand, whosoever carteth wood in a wagon, one gulden per year, whosoever taketh wood in a barrow, half a gulden, and whosoever doth carry it, a quarter gulden. Of this, Christ saith one should give, not of blood taxes.

Then someone may say, "But they use it all wrongly in any case, so, from this point of view, one should give nothing." That they use all for evil—that is something for which they shall bear their own sentence.[1] We, however, give it not for their wrong use, but for their appointed office.[2] But because wars and the destruction of nations is more against their office than with it,[3] nothing is ordained them for this purpose, and we can give nothing for this for the sake of the office, since it is not appointed. But everything wherein and whereby we can serve man for his betterment, we desire to do diligently. But whatsoever is against God, the conscience and our calling[4]—there we want to obey God more than man,[5] and in the meantime to await God's will that he may lend and give us his grace to do this through Jesus Christ. Amen.

CONCLUSION OF THIS BOOK

Thus we have brought forward, through the grace of God, the truth concerning the points which are most questioned in this land; firstly, why God desireth to have a separate people,[6] which is holy,[7] blameless and unblemished[8] and without spot or wrinkle;[9] and how God himself divideth and separateth the devout from the evil,[10] and also in the end will do;[11] and what the Lord doth promise both, the devout and the evil.[12] Also concerning the house of God, how it should be built up,[13] and what kind of messengers he sendeth to build it,[14] that none run of himself, but that they should be chosen of God[15]—as

Aaron was[1] to gather to the Lord his people[2]—with whom he maketh[3] the covenant of his grace;[4] and what kind of covenant it is,[5] what we should do[6] and receive therein,[7] whereby it is evident who should receive it.[8] Likewise concerning the Supper[9] and swearing,[10] whereby every man may learn what is right. We speak also of governmental authority and its appointed service,[11] and in our opinion prove sufficiently for what God useth it[12] and how far it is God's servant and what its office is.[13]

We speak, in addition, of the appurtenances that are its dues or the appointed taxes of its office, how far they are to be given[14] and not to be given,[15] and that in the shortest form of which we have been able, for the comfort of the devout[16] and for a testimony against the ungodly.[17] It is our desire thereby to have warned every man that he oppose not so wantonly the truth and be found as those that fight against God,[18] and that he bind not one sin upon another, for he will not remain unpunished for the one;[19] or make himself a partaker of other men's sins.[20] But if any will do this, he may know that it will be hard for him to kick against the pricks,[21] and a battle that he cannot win.[22] For the word of Christ will not fail: "What ye have done to mine, ye have done to me, myself."[23] And God the Lord, who hath promised it, will not lie, namely, that he will avenge the blood of his saints.[24] Moreover, if the filthy continueth to be filthy, let him bear his sentence. The judge is God.[25] Who hath ears to hear, let him hear.[26]

Thus, we have given an account, with sufficient reason, of the truth concerning the points and articles most called in question in the land of Hesse. May God the Almighty grant us and all his chosen children to walk in his truth as we have begun through his Christ, that we may continue, remain and endure therein unto the end, to the eternal praise of his holy name, and allow no tribulation or tyrannical force or any manner of cunning of the falsely famed preachers to turn us away or move us, that we may appear with all his saints in joy before him, holy and unblemished, on the day of his coming and receive the promise in Christ Jesus.

Amen, Yea Amen

OF this Christian Church, which was built up by God through Christ and gathered by his Holy Spirit recently in Germany, the following have been appointed servants [to whom the Church of God was entrusted up till this year 1565], apart from their helpers: Jakob Hutter from the country of Tirol, Hans Amon from Bavaria, Peter Rideman from Silesia, who made this Confession, Leonhard Lanzenstil from Bavaria as mentioned above, and Peter Walbot also from the country of Tirol.

This year this Confession was reprinted by Philips Vollanndt.

REFERENCES

The scriptural texts used by Peter Rideman in his work were derived from translations of the Bible into German either contemporary with or earlier than Luther's translation. Among those known to have been widely used among the Hutterians of the first half of the sixteenth century were the *Froschauer* or *Züricher Bibel* and a so-called Anabaptist Bible, by Ludwig Hetzer, both of which were printed during the early period of the Reformation. There were also fourteen translations of the Bible into German, all from the Vulgate, prior to 1522 when Luther's translation appeared, and with some of these or parts of them Peter Rideman would, doubtless, have been familiar. In order to remain as faithful as possible to the original it has been thought advisable to translate the texts used by Peter Rideman direct from the German. Thus they will be found to differ in the main from any of the current English versions of the Bible.

It will be noted that among the references appear the names of the following books: I Esdras, II Esdras, Tobit, The Wisdom of Solomon (Wisdom), Ecclesiasticus, Baruch, and I Maccabees. These books are located in the "Old Testament Apocrypha." In the sixteenth century they were regarded as having equal or nearly equal weight and authority as the books of what is now known as the Old Testament.

228

REFERENCES

THE FIRST PART

PAGE

9 (1) Romans 10, 10   (2) Zechariah 2, 8

11 (1) Titus 2, 12   (2) James 1, 17

15 (1) I Corinthians 8, 5
   (2) Genesis 1-2, 1
   (3) Deuteronomy 32, 39
   (4) Exodus 20
   (5) Deuteronomy 4, 35
   (6) Isaiah 43, 11
   (7) Isaiah 6, 3; Psalms 33, 6-7
   (8) Romans 1, 20

16 (1) Genesis 1, 1-10
   (2) John 14, 1-14
   (3) Wisdom 7, 7
   (4) II John, 4-6
   (5) John 8, 39-47
   (6) Malachi 1, 6
   (7) Deuteronomy 32, 5
   (8) John 4, 24
   (9) Romans 8, 1-8
  (10) Psalms 50, 16-17
  (11) John 9, 30-41

17 (1) Deuteronomy 32
   (2) I John 2, 18-24
   (3) John 8, 41-44
   (4) John 1, 12
   (5) Matthew 6, 7-13
   (6) John 15, 16-20

18 (1) John 16, 26-27
   (2) I Peter 2, 6-10
   (3) Ephesians 2, 1-13
   (4) I Peter 1, 3-5
   (5) II Peter 1, 3-4
   (6) Ephesians 1, 13-23
   (7) Romans 8, 11-17
   (8) John 16, 25-33
   (9) Romans 8, 26-34
  (10) I Peter 3, 8-12

19 (1) Galatians 2, 17-21
   (2) II Corinthians 6, 14-18
   (3) Genesis 1, 1-10
   (4) Genesis 1
   (5) Isaiah 66, 1
   (6) Romans 1, 20
   (7) Ecclesiasticus 39, 26-27

20 (1) Wisdom 13, 1-3
   (2) Romans 1, 20-32
   (3) Genesis 1, 25-31

21 (1) I Peter **2**, 21-25
   (2) James **1**, 9-20
   (3) Revelation **21**, 1-6

   (4) Ephesians **1**, 13-23
   (5) Hebrews **6**, 10-16
   (6) Psalms **44**, 22

22 (1) Romans **8**, 35-39
   (2) Deuteronomy **6**, 4
   (3) Deuteronomy **4**, 29-39
   (4) John **14**, 1-14
   (5) John **1**, 1-2

   (6) Colossians **1**, 16-22
   (7) John **14**, 15-24
   (8) Genesis **3**, 6-11
   (9) John **1**, 14

23 (1) I Corinthians **15**, 20-28
   (2) Acts **4**, 12
   (3) Luke **2**, 21
   (4) Isaiah **25**, 6-8; Hosea **13**, 14; I Corinthians **15**, 51-58; Hebrews **2**, 12-18

   (5) John **1**, 1
   (6) John **1**, 14
   (7) Colossians **2**, 9
   (8) Isaiah **61**, 1-2; Luke **4**, 18-19
   (9) John **5**, 21
  (10) John **1**, 16

24 (1) John **1**, 1-13
   (2) Isaiah **9**, 2; Matthew **4**, 12-16
   (3) John **8**, 12
   (4) Hebrews **1**, 1-4

   (5) Philippians **2**, 5-11
   (6) John **8**, 36-47
   (7) John **14**, 1-11
   (8) John **16**, 12-15

25 (1) John **1**, 9-14
   (2) Colossians **1**, 12-17
   (3) Acts **17**, 24-28
   (4) Hebrews **1**, 3
   (5) I Corinthians **12**, 3

   (6) Matthew **28**, 18
   (7) Hebrews **2**, 12-16
   (8) Mark **5**, 1-13
   (9) I John **2**, 1-6
  (10) I Corinthians **12**, 3

26 (1) I Peter **1**, 13-21
   (2) II Corinthians **5**, 18-21
   (3) I Peter **2**, 9-12
   (4) II Corinthians **6**, 14-16

   (5) John **8**, 24-32
   (6) Romans **6**, 16-18
   (7) II Corinthians **3**, 3-6
   (8) John **13**, 13

27 (1) John **1**, 1-2
   (2) Luke **1**, 26-28
   (3) Ephesians **1**, 13
   (4) Luke **1**, 28-35
   (5) Hebrews **2**, 11-16
   (6) Genesis **3**, 15; **12**, 1-3; Isaiah **7**, 14-16

   (7) Genesis **3**, 6
   (8) Romans **5**, 12-14
   (9) Genesis **1**, 28
  (10) I John **3**, 1-6
  (11) Luke **1**, 34-38
  (12) Romans **1**, 1-4

28 (1) II Corinthians **5**, 21 ;
    Hebrews **4**, 14-15
  (2) Colossians **2**, 9
  (3) Isaiah **53**, 1-5; I Peter
    2, 21-24
  (4) II Corinthians **5**, 18-21
  (5) I Peter **2**, 24
  (6) Isaiah **7**, 14

  (7) Matthew **1**, 18-25
  (8) Luke **2**, 8-11
  (9) Luke **3**, 2-6
(10) Philippians **2**, 5-8
(11) Hebrews **4**, 15
(12) Hebrews **2**, 17-18
(13) John **17**, 20-26
(14) Matthew **4**, 12-17

29 (1) Matthew **27**, 27-56;
    Mark **15**, 16-41; Luke
    22, 31-46; John **19**,
    1-37
  (2) I Peter **3**, 18
  (3) Romans **1**, 3
  (4) Luke **2**, 4-7
  (5) Psalms **8**, 5
  (6) Hebrews **2**, 5-10
  (7) Genesis **3**, 4-6

  (8) Isaiah **53**, 5
  (9) Hebrews **6**, 4-6
(10) I John **3**, 5-8
(11) Hebrews **10**, 26-31
(12) Matthew **27**, 57-61;
    Mark **15**, 42-47; Luke
    23, 50-55; John **19**,
    38-42
(13) John **12**, 24-26

30 (1) John **5**, 28-29
  (2) Ephesians **4**, 8-10
  (3) I Peter **3**, 18-21
  (4) I Peter **1**, 3-5
  (5) Genesis **3**, 14-15; **12**, 1-4

  (6) Hebrews **2**, 14-15
  (7) Isaiah **25**, 6-9; Hosea
    13, 14; I Corinthians
    15, 53-58
  (8) Acts **2**, 33-39; **3**, 12-16

31 (1) Psalms **16**, 8-11
  (2) Romans **14**, 9
  (3) Hebrews **2**, 14-15
  (4) Daniel **7**, 27-28
  (5) Matthew **28**, 18
  (6) Luke **24**, 13-35; John
    20, 1-9; **21**, 1-7; I
    Corinthians **15**, 3-9
  (7) Acts **10**, 37-43

  (8) Matthew **28**, 18-20;
    Mark **16**, 15-16
  (9) Romans **1**, 1-5; **16**, 17-
    20
(10) Ephesians **4**, 7-8
(11) Acts **7**, 55-56
(12) John **17**, 1-5
(13) Philippians **2**, 5-8

32 (1) John **17**, 1-5
  (2) John **1**, 14; Luke **2**,
    1-12; Hebrews **2**, 14-
    18
  (3) John **5**, 21-29
  (4) John **6**, 38-40
  (5) Hebrews **5**, 1-2

  (6) I Timothy **2**, 3-5
  (7) I John **2**, 1-2
  (8) I Corinthians **15**, 12-20
  (9) John **5**, 22
(10) II Thessalonians **1**, 6-10
(11) Romans **2**, 1-8

233

57 (1) II Esdras **3**, 21-22
(2) John **3**, 3-5
(3) II Corinthians **12**, 7
(4) I John **1**, 8-10
(5) II Esdras **3**, 4-8; **7**, 21-24

(6) Psalms **51**, 5
(7) Romans **5**, 15-19
(8) Wisdom **1**, 13-15
(9) I Peter **1**, 3-5

58 (1) I John **2**, 1-2
(2) Ezekiel **18**, 20; **33**, 10-19
(3) I John **2**, 1, 2
(4) Romans **7**, 13
(5) I Corinthians **15**, 21, 22

(6) Psalms **52**, 3-7; Isaiah **1**, 1-4
(7) Romans **3**, 10-18
(8) Genesis **3**, 6
(9) Luke **16**, 14-31

59 (1) Matthew **10**, 21-25
(2) I John **2**, 15-17
(3) Matthew **10**, 5-10; Luke **14**, 33
(4) Romans **1**, 16-32
(5) I Peter **2**, 19-25
(6) Matthew **3**, 1-12; Luke **3**, 1-10; Acts **2**, 39-40; **17**, 30-31

(7) Romans **7**, 7-13
(8) II Samuel **12**, 13-17
(9) Psalms **51**, 1-13
(10) I Peter **4**, 1-3
(11) Deuteronomy **32**, 15-18
(12) Ecclesiasticus **21**, 1-4

60 (1) Romans **6**, 16-23
(2) Ecclesiasticus **21**, 1-4; II Esdras **3**, 4-7; Romans **5**, 14-17
(3) Psalms **101**, 1-4

(4) Tobit **4**, 1-6
(5) Deuteronomy **32**, 19-25
(6) Genesis **3**, 8-10
(7) Psalms **51**, 1-14
(8) I Corinthians **9**, 24-27

61 (1) Psalms **121**
(2) Isaiah **66**, 2
(3) James **4**, 1-10
(4) Isaiah **58**, 6-10
(5) Matthew **11**, 28

(6) John **15**, 16
(7) Acts **1**, 7-8
(8) John **6**, 28-37
(9) I Timothy **1**, 15
(10) John **6**, 39-40

62 (1) Ephesians **1**, 10-14
(2) Joel **2**, 27-29; Acts **2**, 14-21; Romans **8**, 1-10
(3) I Corinthians **2**, 10-16; II Peter **1**, 2-4
(4) John **15**, 1-6
(5) I Corinthians **10**, 14-21
(6) Romans **12**, 1-5; I Corinthians **12**, 20-27

(7) Romans **11**, 16-24
(8) Matthew **7**, 16-23; **12**, 33-35; Luke **6**, 43-46
(9) John **15**, 1-9; Romans **11**, 16-18
(10) Ephesians **2**
(11) Acts **3**, 19-25

63 (1) Genesis **17**, 3-10; Leviticus **26**, 9-13; Ezekiel **37**; II Corinthians **6**, 14-18
(2) Genesis **1**, 26-27
(3) Wisdom **1**, 12-14
(4) Genesis **3**, 1-6
(5) Hebrews **6**, 17-20
(6) II Corinthians **6**, 16

(7) Genesis **14** and **15**
(8) John **1**, 12; Ephesians **1**, 3-5
(9) Genesis **3**, 8-15
(10) Genesis **17**, 19; **28**, 10-15
(11) Hebrews **7**, 18-28
(12) Hebrews **9**, 11-16
(13) Acts **3**, 17-26

64 (1) Acts **7**, 51-53
(2) Hebrews **10**, 4
(3) II Esdras **3**, 17-20

(4) Galatians **4**, 21-26; Exodus **20**, 1-17
(5) Hebrews **7**, 18-19
(6) II Corinthians **3**, 11-18

65 (1) Hebrews **8**, 10-13; II Corinthians **5**, 17
(2) Hebrews **7**, 22
(3) Philippians **3**, 7-8
(4) Galatians **4**, 21-24
(5) Galatians **5**, 1-5
(6) Romans **8**, 3; Hebrews **7**, 28

(7) Romans **3**, 19-20
(8) Romans **7**, 7-14
(9) Galatians **3**, 21-24
(10) John **14**, 26; Acts **1**, 1-8; **2**, 1-21; **2**, 32-33
(11) Ephesians **1**, 12-14
(12) Galatians **5**, 16-18
(13) Romans **10**, 4

66 (1) Romans **3**, 31
(2) Romans **7**, 14-16
(3) Ephesians **2**, 8-16
(4) II Corinthians **3**, 6-9
(5) I Corinthians **9**, 19-21; II Corinthians **3**, 7-18
(6) Romans **7**, 6-25
(7) Romans **8**, 1-9

(8) Isaiah **61**, 1-2; Luke **4**, 16-19
(9) Romans **8**, 1-2
(10) Romans **1**, 16; I Corinthians **1**, 18
(11) I Corinthians **15**, 1-2
(12) Genesis **3**, 14-15; **17**, 1-5

67 (1) I John **1**, 5-10
(2) Romans **8**, 2-4
(3) James **1**, 17-18
(4) II Corinthians **5**, 14-17
(5) II Peter **1**, 3-4
(6) II Corinthians **3**, 3-11
(7) Jeremiah **31**, 33-34; Hebrews **8**, 6-11; **10**, 15-17

(8) Hebrews **4**, 12
(9) II Corinthians **3**, 14-18
(10) Jeremiah **8**, 1-3; Hebrews **7**, 18-28
(11) Jeremiah **31**, 31-34
(12) Jeremiah **31**, 34; Hebrews **8**, 6-12
(13) John **16**, 12-15

68
(1) Hebrews **9**, 14-15
(2) Joel **2**, 28, 29; Acts **2**, 17-21
(3) Galatians **4**, 4-7
(4) Romans **8**, 2
(5) John **8**, 36
(6) Galatians **5**, 1-4
(7) Romans **8**, 8, 9

(8) James **1**, 17-18; I Peter **1**, 3-5
(9) II Esdras **3**, 10-11; **7**, 48-53; Romans **5**, 12-15
(10) Matthew **28**, 18-20; Mark **16**, 15-16

69
(1) Luke **1**, 30-38
(2) Matthew **1**, 18-25; Luke **2**, 4-7
(3) Ephesians **1**, 12-14
(4) Acts **8**, 36-38

(5) Matthew **15**, 13
(6) I Peter **3**, 18-21
(7) Jeremiah **31**, 34
(8) Deuteronomy **1**, 39

70
(1) Matthew **28**, 19-20
(2) Matthew **28**, 19-20
(3) Acts **8**, 36-38

(4) Acts **2**, 22-41; **8**, 29-38; **10**, 44-48; **16**, 13-15; **16**, 27-34
(5) Matthew **28**, 19-20

71
(1) II Thessalonians **3**, 10
(2) II Thessalonians **3**, 10-12
(3) Exodus **7**, 9-13;

II Timothy **3**, 8
(4) Acts **2**, 38-39
(5) Acts **2**, 38-41

72
(1) Acts **2**, 15-17
(2) Joel **2**, 28-29
(3) John **4**, 25-42; **16**, 12-15
(4) Romans **9**, 30-33
(5) Acts **2**, 37-39
(6) Joel **2**, 28-29

(7) John **14**, 26
(8) Luke **24**, 45-49
(9) Acts **2**, 39
(10) Genesis **17**, 1-7
(11) Acts **3**, 25

73
(1) Romans **9**, 3-5
(2) Acts **2**, 38-41
(3) Matthew **19**, 14; Mark **10**, 14; Luke **18**, 16

(4) Jeremiah **31**, 33-34
(5) Matthew **19**, 13-15; Mark **10**, 13-16; Luke **18**, 15-17

74
(1) Matthew **28**, 18-20
(2) Acts **8**, 14-17; **19**, 4-6
(3) Acts **13**, 1-3; I Timothy **4**, 14

(4) Matthew **19**, 13-15
(5) John **3**, 5

75
(1) John **3**, 1-5
(2) II Corinthians **5**, 17
(3) John **1**, 33; I Peter **1**, 23; James **1**, 17-18
(4) Isaiah **40**, 3; Malachi **3**, 1

(5) Romans **6**, 3-6
(6) Philippians **3**, 8-10
(7) Matthew **3**, 1-11; Mark **1**, 2-8; Luke **3**, 1-18
(8) I Corinthians **15**, 29-36
(*continued*)

(5) Acts **13**, 1-3

(6) Hebrews **5**, 4

81 (1) Acts **1**, 21-26

(2) Acts **6**, 1-6; I Timothy **4**, 14; II Timothy **1**, 6

(3) I Timothy **3**, 2-10

(4) Judges **2**, 16-18

(5) Romans **9**, 29-33

82 (1) I Corinthians **12**, 28; Ephesians **4**, 11-14

(2) Matthew **28**, 16-20; Mark **16**, 14-16

(3) Romans **1**, 1-5; **16**, 25-27

(4) I Timothy **3**, 1-7; Titus **1**, 5-9

(5) I Corinthians **12**, 28

(6) Romans **12**, 4-8;

83 (1) Deuteronomy **32**, 15-22

(2) Exodus **32**, 1-6

(3) Exodus **32**, 1-6; Psalms **105**, 26-37

(4) Matthew **26**, 19-29; Mark **14**, 22-25; Luke **22**, 14-30; I Corinthians **11**, 20-26

(5) Exodus **20**, 4-6; Baruch **4**, 6-7

84 (1) Matthew **26**, 26-29; Mark **14**, 22-25

(2) John **17**, 24-26

(3) Luke **22**, 19

(4) Matthew **26**, 11; Mark **14**, 6-7; John **12**, 7-8

85 (1) Matthew **26**, 47-50; Mark **14**, 43-46; Luke **22**, 47-48; John **13**, 27-30

(2) Isaiah **62**, 11

(7) Acts **2**, 42-47; **13**, 1-3

(6) John **2**, 19-22; Luke **24**, 45-49; Acts **1**, 4-8; **2**, 1-4

(7) Jeremiah **1**, 9; Luke **21**, 14-15

I Corinthians **12**, 1-11

(7) Acts **6**, 2-6; I Timothy **3**, 8-10; Titus **1**, 5-9

(8) Acts **15**, 2-6

(9) Ecclesiasticus **39**, 20-32

(10) Matthew **26**, 17-29; Mark **14**, 12-31; Luke **22**, 14-30; I Corinthians **11**, 20-29

(6) I Kings **8**, 27; Isaiah **66**, 1; Acts **7**, 48-49; **17**, 24-25

(7) Luke **2**, 42-46

(8) Acts **7**, 48-50

(9) Philippians **2**, 5-8; Hebrews **5**, 5-9

(10) Mark **1**, 35-37

(11) Philippians **2**, 5-8

(12) Hebrews **4**, 15

(5) I Corinthians **3**, 16; **6**, 19; II Corinthians **6**, 16-18

(6) Hebrews **10**, 8-14

(7) Hebrews **9**, 14

(3) John **6**, 29-40; **20**, 30-31

(4) Ephesians **4**, 20-24; Colossians **3**, 1-10

(5) II Peter **1**, 2-4

(6) Ephesians **2**, 17-22

(*continued*)

(7) John **14**, 1-3
(8) John **15**, 1-11
(9) I Thessalonians **4**, 13
(10) Matthew **26**, 26-29;

86 (1) John **15**, 1-9
(2) I Corinthians **10**, 17
(3) John **6**, 29-37
(4) I Corinthians **10**, 1-4;
12, 12-20; Romans
12, 4, 5
(5) Romans **11**, 17-24
(6) I Corinthians **6**, 15-20

87 (1) Jeremiah **31**, 33; Hebrews **8**, 10
(2) Wisdom **7**, 18, 1-4
(3) II Peter **1**, 2-4
(4) Romans **12**, 1, 2;
I Corinthians **2**
(5) Luke **22**, 20
(6) Hebrews **9**, 14-15
(7) I Corinthians **10**, 16-17

88 (1) I John **1**, 1-3
(2) Romans **1**, 16, 17
(3) Philippians **2**, 1-8
(4) I Corinthians **12**, 12-27
(5) Acts **2**, 42-47; **4**, 32-37
(6) II Corinthians **8**, 7-15

89 (1) Genesis **1**, 25-31
(2) Genesis **3**, 2-6; II Esdras
3, 4-7; **7**, 21-25;
Romans **5**, 12-14
(3) I Timothy **6**, 6-9
(4) Luke **16**, 9-13
(5) Exodus **20**, 17; Deuteronomy **5**, 21
(6) Luke **16**, 11-12

90 (1) Luke **12**, 33-40
(2) Acts **2**, 44, 45; **4**, 32-37
(3) I John **1**, 3
(4) Luke **16**, 11-13

Mark **14**, 22-25; Luke
22, 14-20; I Corin-
thians **11**, 23-26
(11) Luke **22**, 20

(7) Romans **12**, 1-3; Philippians **2**, 1-5
(8) John **15**, 1-8
(9) Matthew **26**, 26; Luke
22, 19
(10) Romans **8**, 16-17
(11) Luke **22**, 20

(8) Acts **2**, 42-47; **4**, 32
(9) John **13**, 35
(10) I Corinthians **10**, 16-31
(11) I Corinthians **11**, 28-32
(12) John **14**; **16**, 13-20;
Acts **2**, 22, 23
(13) I Corinthians **6**, 12-20;
10, 11-24; Romans
12, 1-5

(7) Exodus **16**, 16-18
(8) Genesis **1**, 26-29
(9) Genesis **3**, 2-12
(10) Romans **1**, 18-25
(11) Wisdom **13**, 1-3; **15**,
14-19

(7) Matthew **10**, 32-39;
Luke **9**, 23-26;
Mark **8**, 34-38
(8) Luke **14**, 33
(9) Ephesians **4**, 20-32;
Colossians **3**, 1-11
(10) Mark **10**, 15; Luke **18**,
17
(11) Matthew **18**, 1-4

(5) I Corinthians **10**, 16
(6) Ephesians **4**, 22-24;
Colossians **3**, 1-10
(*continued*)

243

105 (1) Romans **13**, 3-4; I Peter **2**, 13-17
(2) Genesis **49**, 10
(3) Psalms **2**, 1-7
(4) Matthew **28**, 18; Philippians **2**, 9-11

106 (1) Ecclesiasticus **17**, 17
(2) Hebrews **4**, 12
(3) Matthew **28**, 18; Philippians **2**, 9-11
(4) Psalms **2**, 6
(5) Hosea **13**, 10-11
(6) Genesis **12**, 1-3; Galatians **3**, 8
(7) Genesis **9**, 6
(8) John **12**, 47

107 (1) Colossians **1**, 19-23
(2) Galatians **3**, 8-9
(3) Hosea **13**, 11
(4) Luke **9**, 51-56
(5) Romans **13**, 7-10
(6) I Corinthians **5**, 12
(7) Matthew **11**, 28

108 (1) Matthew **19**, 27-30
(2) Luke **2**, 8-20; Ephesians **5**, 23-27
(3) Isaiah **2**, 1-4; Micah **4**, 1-4
(4) Romans **12**, 14-21; Deuteronomy **32**, 35;

109 (1) Luke **22**, 47-53
(2) Matthew **16**, 24-25; Mark **8**, 34-35
(3) Matthew **5**, 38-48
(4) Isaiah **50**, 6
(5) Deuteronomy **32**, 35-36; Joel **3**, 1-2
(6) Genesis **14**, 14-16; Numbers **31**, 1-8; Joshua **6**; **8**, 1-29; **9**, 1-2;

(5) Hebrews **4**, 12-13
(6) John **16**, 13-15; Romans **8**, 1-17
(7) Romans **13**; Titus **3**, 1-7; I Peter **2**, 6-18

(9) Exodus **21**, 12-27
(10) Matthew **5**, 21-24
(11) John **18**, 36
(12) Philippians **2**, 5-11
(13) Matthew **10**, 37-39; Luke **14**, 26-27
(14) Matthew **20**, 25-28; Luke **22**, 25-27
(15) Mark **9**, 33-35; I Peter **5**, 5-6

(8) John **6**, 37
(9) Philippians **2**, 5-8
(10) Galatians **2**, 20
(11) John **6**, 15
(12) Matthew **10**, 37-39; Luke **14**, 33

Hebrews **10**, 30
(5) I Peter **2**, 19-23
(6) John **18**
(7) Matthew **26**, 51-54; Mark **14**, 47; John **18**, 10-11

Judges **4**; I Samuel **17**, 20-52
(7) Matthew **5**, 38-39
(8) Luke **9**, 51-56; Romans **12**, 19
(9) Romans **13**, 1-7; I Peter **2**, 13-17; Ecclesiasticus **17**, 17; I Samuel **8**, 22

110 (1) Matthew **17**, 24-27
(2) Matthew **22**, 15-21;
Mark **12**, 13-17; Luke
20, 20-25
(3) I Timothy **5**, 22
(4) Romans **13**, 7

(5) I Samuel **8**, 7-18
(6) Romans **13**, 6-7
(7) I Samuel **8**, 11-17
(8) Matthew **22**, 15-21;
Mark **12**, 13-17;
Luke **20**, 20-25

111 (1) Luke **2**, 1-5
(2) Acts **5**, 29
(3) Isaiah **2**, 1-4; Micah **4**,
1-3
(4) John **12**, 47; Luke **9**, 55

(5) Galatians **3**, 2-14
(6) Romans **8**, 6-8
(7) Matthew **5**, 21-24; Romans **12**, 14
(8) I Timothy **5**, 22

112 (1) Ezekiel **33**, 18-20; Galatians **5**, 16-21
(2) Ephesians **4**, 15-24;
II Thessalonians **3**,
3-12

(3) Ephesians **6**, 5-8; Isaiah
3, 16-24
(4) John **16**, 7-11
(5) James **1**, 27
(6) Luke **16**, 19-26

113 (1) I Corinthians **6**, 7
(2) Matthew **5**, 39-42
(3) I Corinthians **5**, 12
(4) Genesis **6**, 3
(5) Luke **12**, 13-14

(6) Isaiah **61**, 1-2; Luke **4**,
16-19
(7) John **7**, 38
(8) Ecclesiasticus **17**, 17

114 (1) Matthew **5**, 40-41
(2) Luke **16**, 19-25
(3) Colossians **3**, 1-2
(4) Galatians **3**, 21-24; Hebrews **7**, 18-28
(5) Deuteronomy **10**, 20-22

(6) Deuteronomy **32**, 39-40
(7) Deuteronomy **10**, 20
(8) Exodus **20**, 7; Deuteronomy **5**, 11
(9) John **1**, 1-18

115 (1) Psalms **63**, 11
(2) Isaiah **45**, 23-24
(3) Romans **14**, 11
(4) Jeremiah **31**, 31-34
(5) Hebrews **7**, 18-19
(6) II Corinthians **3**, 11-18

(7) Ephesians **4**, 25
(8) Psalms **15**, 1-3
(9) Romans **8**, 1-15
(10) II John **1**, 4-6
(11) John **8**, 12-47

116 (1) Galatians **3**, 21-26
(2) Galatians **4**, 1-7
(3) Colossians **2**, 13-17
(4) Galatians **4**, 4-8
(5) Hebrews **9**, 11-15
(6) Romans **8**, 10-17; Jeremiah **31**, 33-34;

Hebrews **8**, 7-10; **10**,
8-17
(7) Deuteronomy **10**, 20;
Psalms **63**, 11
(8) John **1**, 1-18
(9) Matthew **5**, 33-37
(10) Matthew **13**, 39

245

117 (1) Luke 1, 5-17
(2) Matthew 5, 34-37
(3) John 15, 4-7
(4) James 5, 12

(5) Genesis 22, 15-18; Ezekiel 33, 11
(6) Psalms 110, 4
(7) Deuteronomy 32, 40
(8) Matthew 5, 34

118 (1) Matthew 23, 16-22
(2) Matthew 23, 16-24;
Luke 11, 42

(3) James 5, 12
(4) John 15, 5
(5) James 4, 13-15

119 (1) Luke 1, 28, 39-45;
Matthew 10, 11-13;
Luke 10, 5-9
(2) John 14, 27
(3) Matthew 10, 13; Luke
10, 1-12

(4) Mark 13, 11; Luke 12,
11-12; 21, 9-15
(5) Judges 6, 12-23
(6) Matthew 28, 19-20
(7) Luke 1, 41
(8) Exodus 20, 7; Deuteronomy 5, 11

120 (1) Acts 2, 42-46; 4, 32
(2) Galatians 2, 9
(3) Philippians 2, 29
(4) Romans 12, 1-10; I
Peter 1, 22

(5) John 3, 16-18
(6) Proverbs 17, 18
(7) Matthew 18, 6-10;
I Corinthians 11, 17-
19

121 (1) John 4, 23
(2) Ecclesiasticus 18, 23-24
(3) John 9, 31
(4) Romans 12, 4-5; Hebrews 12, 1-6

(5) Matthew 5, 21-24
(6) Mark 11, 25-26
(7) James 1, 5-8
(8) I John 5, 13-15

122 (1) Matthew 7, 7-11
(2) Jeremiah 29, 10-13;
Matthew 7, 7-11; 21,
21-22; Mark 11, 22-
24; Luke 22, 39-46;
John 14, 10-14; 15,
7; 16, 23-27

(3) James 1, 5-8
(4) Luke 9, 52-56
(5) Romans 8, 26-27
(6) John 4, 21-24
(7) I John 5, 14-15

123 (1) Ephesians 5, 19; Colossians 3, 16
(2) II Peter 1, 19-21

(3) Psalms 50, 14-23
(4) II Timothy 3, 14-17

246

247

253

(*continued*)

176 (1) Genesis **3**, 1-6
    (2) Acts **20**, 26-27
    (3) Galatians **1**, 6-9

    (4) Acts **9**, 10-15
    (5) Acts **8**, 26-28
    (6) Isaiah **53**, 7

177 (1) Acts **2**, 41; **8**, 12-15; **9**, 17, 18; **10**, 44-48; **16**, 14-15
    (2) Acts **9**, 1-18; I Corinthians **15**, 8

    (3) II Corinthians **12**, 1-4
    (4) Acts **9**, 17, 18
    (5) Matthew **28**, 18-20
    (6) II Corinthians **12**, 1-4

178 (1) I Corinthians **15**, 3-9
    (2) Acts **9**, 10-20
    (3) Acts **10**, 1-8
    (4) Hebrews **11**, 6

    (5) Matthew **28**, 18-20; Mark **16**, 15, 16
    (6) Acts **16**, 25-34

179 (1) Acts **19**, 1-5
    (2) Matthew **3**; Mark **1**, 4; Luke **3**, 15-18
    (3) John **1**, 19-34
    (4) Acts **19**, 6

    (5) Matthew **21**, 23-32
    (6) Matthew **15**, 13
    (7) I Corinthians **10**, 1-4
    (8) Exodus **14**, 9-11

180 (1) Exodus **14**, 11, 12
    (2) Psalms **106**, 6-12
    (3) Psalms **136**, 10-26
    (4) Exodus **14**, 31
    (5) I Corinthians **10**, 1-6
    (6) Exodus **14**, 19-31

    (7) I Corinthians **10**, 1-6
    (8) Genesis **7**, 13
    (9) Hebrews **13**, 7-9
  (10) Genesis **17**, 10-12
  (11) Genesis **17**, 3-12; **26**, 1-5; **28**, 10-15; **48**, 14-16

181 (1) Hebrews **7**
    (2) Genesis **17**, 10-13
    (3) Galatians **4**, 4-7
    (4) Matthew **28**, 19-20; Mark **16**, 15, 16
    (5) John **1**, 12, 13
    (6) I Peter **1**, 3-5
    (7) Romans **9**, 6-8
    (8) Genesis **15**, 1-5
    (9) Galatians **4**, 22-28
  (10) Romans **9**, 6-8; Galatians **3**, 16-18

  (11) Luke **1**, 41-55
  (12) Romans **4**, 9-17
  (13) Galatians **3**, 7-14; **4**, 22-28
  (14) Romans **9**, 1-8
  (15) Genesis **12**, 1-3; **22**, 15-18
  (16) Hebrews **11**, 39, 40
  (17) Psalms **132**, 12-18
  (18) Galatians **4**, 1
  (19) Galatians **4**, 2
  (20) Romans **3**, 31

182 (1) Romans **2**, 17-29
    (2) Matthew **28**, 18-20; Mark **16**, 15, 16

    (3) Matthew **3**, 13-15
    (4) Genesis **17**, 9-12
    (5) I Peter **1**, 22, 23
    (*continued*)

261

(continued)

PETER RIDEMAN AND THE
HUTTERIAN MOVEMENT

Peter Rideman was an elder of the Church of the Brothers known as Hutterians. He wrote this book "in the dry summer of the year 1540, as he lay a prisoner in Hesse."[1] In the *Chronicles* of the Hutterian Church there are references to a printed confession of faith sent to the nobility of Moravia in 1545,[2] and in 1547 it was recorded: "Our whole religion, teaching and faith and its grounds one can find in our printed Account."[3] These entries clearly refer to the work of Peter Rideman, and two actual specimens of these editions have been found. There are also six extant copies of the second edition, printed in 1565. It was from one of these latter copies that the present translation was made in 1950.

Rideman's *Rechenschaft unserer Religion, Lehr und Glaubens* (*Account of our Religion, Doctrine and Faith*) has remained the fundamental confession of that faith which the Hutterian movement has expressed throughout four centuries; the faith by which the Hutterian brotherhood-communities still live today. It is an authentic account of the basis on which they maintain their community of goods, their attitude of complete non-violence and of non-participation in politics.

The present volume is a translation of the revised edition in the German language, published by the

[1] From a marginal note in the Hutterian *Greater Church Chronicle* (*Das grosse Gemeinde-Geschichtbuch*, by Dr. Rudolf Wolkan, Vienna, 1923, p.167).
[2] *Die Geschichtsbücher der Wiedertäufer in Österreich-Ungarn in der Zeit von 1526 bis 1785*, by Dr. Josef von Beck. Vienna, 1883.
[3] *Greater Chronicle*, Wolkan edition, p. 241.

Society of Brothers in 1938. The translation is of special significance, because the Hutterian communities are established today in the United States and Canada.

The Hutterian brotherhood sprang from the so-called Anabaptist movement of the early sixteenth century in Moravia and the Tyrol. The name "Anabaptist" or "Wiedertäufer" was given by their opponents, meaning "those who baptize again." It has always been refuted by the Hutterians on the grounds that infant baptism is no baptism and it is therefore not a repetition when a person is baptized on confession of faith. A more fitting name would have been "Baptizers," a term which is being used by modern German writers. The Hutterians called themselves simply the Brothers, later adding the words "known as Hutterians." The name Hutterian, or *Hutterisch,* was given them by their opponents and persecutors, after Jakob Hutter, an early leader of this group. The Hutterians always remained numerically a minor group of the Anabaptist movement, and literature of the Reformation period down to modern times makes little mention of them. Their history, however, is a distinct and consistent thread.

Attention should be drawn to the fact that the Hutterians are distinct from, and had nothing to do with, the ill-famed Anabaptist regime in Münster, of which much more historical notice is taken. The Hutterian attitude towards temporal power and secular authority, an attitude founded on the Bible and contrasting with the Münster regime, is expounded by Peter Rideman in this work.

"In Switzerland, in the year 1525, several scholars met to talk over matters of faith. Among them were Conrad Grebel, a nobleman, Felix Manz, Ulrich Zwingli, and a clergyman called Georg vom Haus Jakob [afterwards called Blaurock]. They found that
268

child baptism has no scriptural foundation. On the contrary, from the teaching of Romans 10, one must first have a living faith active in love, and then, on the recognition and confession of the faith, receive the Christian baptism of a good conscience, and continue to serve God in the godliness of a Christian life, standing steadfast to the end through all suffering."[1]

Ulrich Zwingli shrank back from the obvious consequences of such a radical faith, and later became one of the persecutors of this new movement. The movement grew, and the followers of it became known as Anabaptists. As the movement spread over large parts of central Europe, it was most cruelly persecuted, both by the Roman Catholics and by the new State Churches of Luther and Zwingli. Manz and Blaurock each died a martyr's death, Grebel was condemned to death, but died of the plague at Maienfeld in 1526.[2] The Anabaptists suffered fierce persecution in the Tyrolese Alps, and many families sought a new home around Nikolsburg in Moravia.

Here, after many struggles, emerged the distinct Church of the Brothers known as Hutterians, which still exists today. This story is told by Eberhard Arnold in the essay appearing on the following pages.

In 1529, at the age of twenty-three, Peter Rideman was elected a Servant of the Word. Between 1529 and 1532, as he lay for three years and four weeks in prison, he wrote his first "Account and Confession of our Faith," which is also preserved and still used by the Brothers. On his release from prison in Gmünden in 1532 he joined the Brothers in Moravia, and in 1533 was sent out on mission in Franconia, where, together

[1] Extract from a letter by Johannes Waldner to Christian Friedrich Gregor, March 22, 1811. Printed in *The Plough,* published in English and German by the Society of Brothers at the Cotswold Bruderhof during 1938, 1939 and 1940.
[2] *Mennonite Lexicon.*

with his companion, Six Breitfuss, he was again cast into prison. During an imprisonment of over four years, all efforts failed to turn him from the faith. The Nuremberg Council sent picked theologians and jurists to contend with him in prison. For the 14th of September, 1536 there is a minute of the Council which states "Peter Rideman still lying in *Lug ins Land* (the tower prison) because he still remains stubborn."[1]

On the 14th of July, 1537 he was released and rejoined the Brothers. During the time of his imprisonment a split had taken place in the Church, and two groups under the leadership of Philipp Plener and Gabriel Ascherham had broken away. These two groups were unable to maintain their own unity, and during the next two years Peter Rideman was able to reunite some of them with the Mother Church.

In 1539 Peter Rideman was sent on mission to Hesse in answer to an appeal from seeking and zealous circles there that Servants of the Word be sent to them to clear up many confused matters. In the same year he returned to Steinabrunn in Austria, the chief gathering place of the Brothers. From here, about this time, one hundred and fifty brothers were led off to prison in the castle of Falkenstein, a happening which is reported in detail in the chronicles of the Brothers. Letters of comfort written by Peter Rideman to the Brothers in prison are among his numerous preserved epistles.

At the beginning of 1540 he was again sent to Hesse, his chief task being to strengthen the contact between the Anabaptist circles there and the Church in Moravia. He was soon captured and imprisoned. The chronicles of the year 1541 report that at that time he had lain for almost a year in prison in Marburg,

[1] Footnote by Eberhard Arnold, in the manuscript of the Hutterian *Smaller Church Chronicle (Kleines Geschichtsbuch)*.

Hesse. It was during this imprisonment that he wrote the *Account of our Religion, Doctrine and Faith* translated in this volume.

From the time of his appointment as Elder of the Church on his release from prison in 1542, Peter Rideman's name is seldom mentioned in the chronicles of the Hutterians, but very many of his writings have been handed down to the present day. Still in existence and use are forty-six songs and thirty-five epistles.

Peter Rideman died a natural death in peace in the Church on the 1st of December, 1556. It is reported in the *Greater Church Chronicle*: "He had served the Church of God in the Service of the Word of God for twenty-seven years, including imprisonments which he suffered and which amounted to nine years."[1]

Much the same life is lived in all Hutterian communities today as in the sixteenth century: full community of goods, communal work and worship, and a common table. There are no class distinctions, no race distinctions. An order of social justice is built up arising from love for one's neighbor. Community is the fruit of this faith and the necessary expression of it.

This is the value of the *Account* and *Confession* of Peter Rideman to the Hutterian Brotherhood today and its challenge to the world at large. It is embodied and finds its meaning in a practical life. The way of life which the Hutterians represent would be impossible without the faith behind it.

To Peter Rideman was given the clarity to express this faith, to render an account, to hand down a witness which has remained valid, and which after 400 years is still regarded as the clearest and most comprehensive "Account and Confession of our Faith and Religion" by the Hutterian Brotherhood.

[1] *Greater Church Chronicle*, p. 269.

THE HUTTERIAN
BROTHERS

FOUR CENTURIES OF COMMON LIFE
AND WORK

by
EBERHARD ARNOLD

The following pages contain a review of the whole history of the Hutterian movement, which goes back for a little more than four hundred years. It is an essay written by Eberhard Arnold in 1931, shortly after he had visited the Hutterian communities in America. Eberhard Arnold died in 1935 and was thus unable to write the history of the Hutterian Church in preparation for which he had done a great deal of research work; but this essay clearly reflects his profound knowledge of the subject.

First published in English in 1940 in the form of a pamphlet, this essay was for many years an important source of information on the Hutterians, in the absence of much else in the English language. It is fitting that it can now be published anew within the same covers as Peter Rideman's great *Confession of Faith* in its second English edition.

THE HUTTERIAN BROTHERS

Four Centuries of Common
Life and Work

by

EBERHARD ARNOLD

The Hutterian Brothers are a community on a Christian communal basis which has a common source of origin with the Mennonites. In the first seven years of their existence their teachings were almost exactly the same, as indeed, with a few exceptions, they are still today. As in the first epistles of Jakob Hutter, Hans Ammon and Peter Rideman, and especially in the teaching of Ulrich Stadler, they emphasize especially the working of the Spirit in the Church of complete community as an effect of the indissoluble unity between the Creator and Father, the Redeemer and Son and the Holy Spirit.

Regarding the fact of the humanity of Jesus, they emphasize in their confessions of faith and teachings that Christ did not bring His flesh from Heaven but received it from Mary. In them the redemption of Christ does away with the original sin inherited by children, in that Christ died for the sins of the whole world. All that remain of original sin are physical death and the inclination to evil.

For the Brothers, governmental authority as a God-given order belongs to the revelation of the wrath of God, whereas the Church never has any part in the bloody judgment of God, only in His loving heart, in the absolute love of Jesus Christ and in the discipline purely of mind and spirit through the Holy Spirit. So to them the Church of complete community is the ark of the last days. The expectation of the coming day of judgment has always been very living and effective among them.

The first messenger sent out by the Mother Church at Zurich to work in the Alpine lands, from which nearly the whole Hutterian Church had its origin, was Georg Blaurock. He suffered martyrdom in the Tyrol in 1529. He was succeeded immediately by Jakob Hutter, who proclaimed the same teaching, in essence, as Blaurock had spread. As persecution was unusually fierce in the Tyrolean Alps, and as hundreds of the adherents of the so-called Anabaptist movement fell a prey to it, many families sought a new home in Moravia. In the early years of the movement, Nikolsburg—the scene of the last activity of Dr. Balthasar Hubmaier—was the center in Moravia around which they gathered.

Here, owing to the threatened attacks of the Turks, the decisive question arose as to whether in the face of expected violence an attitude of non-violence could be maintained. A group of about two hundred adults under the guidance of Jakob Widemann and other friends of Hans Hut decided in favor of unconditional non-violence and for community of goods in accordance with the spirit and example of the Early Christians. To realize their ideals they had to form a Church of their own. In 1528 they left Nikolsburg and found a place in the neighboring town of Austerlitz on the lands of the von Kaunitz family, which had in 1511 allowed Picards to settle there. In the village of Bogenitz, where they spent a night on the way, they chose four reliable men to support their leader, Jakob Widemann, amongst whom was Jakob Mändl, who was formerly steward of a large estate in Nikolsburg. Even before they reached the site of their new home, they introduced community of goods. The leaders laid a coat on the open field, and on it each placed what he possessed.

Thus here in 1528 (after several previous beginnings in the circles influenced by Hans Hut in Nikolsburg and Lintz) a community was founded on a Christian communal basis which has outlived all persecutions. Jakob Hutter came repeatedly from the Tyrol to visit the Church-community at Austerlitz, whose way of life attracted him strongly. For this reason he directed "Anabaptists," fleeing from the Tyrol, to Austerlitz and Auspitz, and in 1533 settled there himself with a large number of adherents.

Jakob Widemann found himself unable to cope with the leadership of a community which had grown so enormously. The new arrivals from the Tyrol had more confidence in Jakob Hutter than in all the other leaders and entrusted him with the chief responsibility of leadership.

With circumspection and energy he brought order to the life of the young community. The strict discipline of complete community which he introduced did not meet with the approval of all who, first in Austerlitz and then in Auspitz, had sought community or at least mutual understanding with Jakob Hutter's Tyroleans. Now many kept at a distance and formed separate groups with a more modified administration of the communal way of life. None of these, however, lasted long, whereas the stricter community of Jakob Hutter grew ever stronger, as it constantly received new members from the German-speaking countries, in which the persecution of the Baptizers continued with increasing fierceness, and especially from the Tyrol. As well as this, many who had estranged themselves returned. In more than eighty places in Moravia common households, known as *Haushaben* were formed, which soon took an outstanding place in the economic life of the land. Some Hutterian households had more than a thousand inhabitants, and nearly all had over five hundred. Their opponents asserted that there were soon seventeen thousand Hutterians (Erhart). Some even spoke towards the end of the century of seventy thousand (Ottius, *Annalen*). They developed an industrial activity which in its far-sighted organization can almost be compared to a factory today, rationally worked on the endless belt system: only one must not forget that these working communities were large and joyous spiritual units, such as one would seek in vain today in a factory.

Because of their diligence and industry the Hutterian Brothers were very highly esteemed by the feudal lords who benefited greatly through them; on the other hand one part of the population fought against them because of their competition. They were also opposed by the clergy who sought to crush their teaching and confused the brotherly community of the Hutterians with the utterly different revolution of Münster. Thus they were in a difficult position in spite of outward tolerance which for some time enabled them to let their economic and religious powers develop fully. With them economic and religious life went hand in hand, for it seemed to them that only so could love to God be realized as love to one's neighbor. For their faith in its actual and effective application reached its peak in the following polemic and positive principles: All faith in God and in Christ is a counterfeit and is no reality unless it is active in love. The love of God, as the work of the Holy Spirit, demands, not only in spiritual things but just as much in earthly matters, the giving up of property into the full community of justice and brotherliness, and especially in the giving of all one's powers in work.

All their striving was to live as nearly as possible as the Early Church had lived; this they did as the

278

Pentecostal expression of the Holy Spirit, the working of which they saw to be the same throughout the centuries, and not out of slavery to the written word, for against this they constantly fought. Even after Jakob Hutter's death, their teaching, generally speaking, differed from that of the other Baptizers only in the principles mentioned. Community of goods and the more clear-cut conception of the Church formed the main line of division. Where this separation was overcome it was not hard for the Hutterian communities—thanks to their organization, their thorough preparation, and above all thanks to the fiery strength of the Spirit amongst them in the times of persecution of the sixteenth century—to win adherents from the ranks of the Baptizers in general, and above all from the Swiss Brothers. As was the case with the Swiss Brothers, the Schlatten Conclusions of 1527[1] remained with the Hutterians in high respect as decisive of the direction given by the "Beginners" for their attitude to the Church. But to the Hutterian communities the teaching of community of goods remained the highest norm. On it their whole religious and social life is built.

A flexible division of labor was introduced for all belonging to the community. In doing this certain orders were established to which each member, as he

[1] The Schlatten Articles or Conclusions are the first known points upon which the Baptizer movement differs from both the Roman Catholic and Protestant tenets. Michael Sattler, a learned monk and one of the first martyrs of the movement, drew up seven points in 1527 in answer to nine accusations made against him and his followers by the Roman Catholic Church. With the exception of life in community they contain the essential attitude of faith of the Hutterians to baptism, the Lord's Supper, Church discipline, non-violence, the refusal to take oaths, etc. Upon this confession Michael Sattler and a number of men and women were put to death by fire, water and the sword.

was incorporated in the Body of Christ, submitted and surrendered himself. The division of labor was not applied only to the activities for production, but also to the work in the house and family life. It began with the education of the smallest children and maintained this community education until they were fully capable of working. Only one must not overlook the fact that the parents were in the same intensive community life in which their children were brought up, so that there can be no thought of abolishing family life. But in this way the mothers (in so far as they were not occupied, because of their special gifts in this direction, in the school and children's house) were set free for many hours' work for the common good. The older children received regular instruction from school teachers in the subjects taught today in a German village school. Above all, however, they received instruction in the deepening of their life of faith and prayer, and regarding the objects of the Church's faith. Education, which in those days in all lands touched only a small portion of the young people who lived in towns, was so highly developed by the Hutterian Brothers that hardly an illiterate person was to be found among them, and their art in hand-writing evokes the admiration of specialists today as an example of a rare culture. Even such difficult matter as the answer of the Hutterians to the Process at Worms[2] in 1557 was excellently written by the bigger children under the guidance of their teacher, Bärthel Fliegel.[3] The School Order of the Hutterians, dated

[2] In the Process at Worms in 1557 the Hutterians were attacked by the Lutheran Church represented by Melanchthon on account of the Schlatten Articles of faith with the addition of life in common and the community's education of children.

[3] The original, dated 1637, containing 355 pages, is in the Eberhard Arnold collection of manuscripts.

1568, is one of the oldest to be found in the German language. (Hege, *Die Taeufer in der Kurpfalz*, p. 116). Their educational institutions were so advanced that like private boarding schools today, they were attended by children of other confessions. Great value was put upon the general well-being of the pupils, as well as on their mental education. Their schools were the first in Europe in which scientific methods were employed to hinder the spreading of infectious diseases (Wolkan, *Hutterer*, p. 74).

Vocational training began, not after schooling had ended, but with the bigger school children. Each boy and each girl had to undergo such a training. The modern technical schools were preceded by the Hutterian Brothers by four hundred years. This is the reason that their handicraft reached such maturity, and the products of the Hutterian communities were desired because of their genuineness, and were famed far and wide. Their handicraft covered nearly all the needs of general use. Nothing was made that served purposes of war. Neither were articles of luxury—especially as regards clothing—produced. In certain branches of handicraft, such as pottery and knife-making, an artistic direction was fostered similar to that in hand-writing.

Farming took a large place in the economic life of the Hutterians. It not only provided for the needs of daily life, but also produced the raw material for a series of crafts—for grinding grain, brewing, leather-work, spinning and weaving, and for the branches of work which carried still further the processes to which the products of farming are subject, like the bakery, saddlery, shoe-maker's shop and smithy. Other crafts that were fostered were those of the smith, the carpenter, the potter and builder. The business of procuring raw material and selling the finished articles lay in the hands of special buyers and sellers, who had to take special care that only the best wares were delivered. The community drew up rules for each handicraft guild which were amended on the grounds of experience.

The needs of all the inhabitants of the household were met from the common purse, into which all income flowed. Through the industry of the inhabitants and the thrift practiced generally, the Hutterian households in the second generation attained such well-being that it aroused the envy of the surrounding population and also led to hostility because of their religious views.

The whole life of the Hutterian community was pervaded by the spirit of its faith. The highest aim (both for the individuals and for the whole) was a life in fellowship with God. Therefore everything was avoided that contradicted this ultimate aim of their life. The thousands of martyrs from their ranks who suffered death for their faith testify to the earnestness with which they sought to fulfill the commands of Jesus, according to their spirit and in the love of faith. Witness is also borne to this by the surrender of their common property when the government exercised pressure on their conscience, and ultimately by wandering from one land to another when the authorities ceased to tolerate even a single one of their teachings.

Even in the twentieth century two Hutterian Brothers suffered martyrdom in an American prison because they refused to give up the principle of defenselessness. Of nearly fifty, mostly very young men, who came under the power of the military authorities, in spite of the strongest pressure not a single one departed one iota from the position of faith of their fathers. Nearly three hundred and fifty years had passed since in 1573 the governor of the prison of Wittlingen in Württemberg testified openly to the fortitude of the Brothers, in that he said he had never heard of a Hutterian Brother in the country departing from his faith. (From the letter of the Brothers Matthes Binder and Paul Prele to Peter Walpot, May 16, 1573. Brünn, Mährisches Landesarchiv, Becks Abschrift.)

The epistles written by persecuted members in other lands, giving wonderful witnesses of joyous confidence in faith, brought ever-new zeal for the faith to the Brothers in Moravia in the sixteenth century. Their messengers, who carried on an extensive missionary activity in the German-speaking lands, were exposed to the same, and even more constant, dangers as the Christians of the first centuries and later the Catholic and Protestant missions among heathen people outside Europe. They went to the Tyrol, Upper Austria, Bohemia, Styria, Silesia, Bavaria, Swabia, Hesse, Switzerland, the lower Rhine and the Palatinate "to gather the zealous for the Lord," as they said, and in so doing shrunk from neither torture nor imprisonment. Only a few Hutterian missionaries in the sixteenth century died a natural death; most of their lives ended in prison or at the place of execution (Beck, p. 39).

The literature of the Hutterian Brothers in the first fifty years, and also to a great extent later, originated in prisons—especially numerous epistles, confessions of faith and letters of encouragement in endurance, as well as many religious songs. All their writings, including the great concordances of the first fifty years, were copied by hand, and are all still in the most living use in the Hutterian Church. Next to the Bible, of decisive importance for their religious and moral faith and conduct was Peter Rideman's *Account of our Religion, Doctrine and Faith* of 1540, one of the very few Hutterian books that was printed while still in Moravia. Two copies of the edition of 1565 are still extant in America, one being at Rockport, Alexandria, South Dakota in the charge of the elder and

Minister of the Word, David Hofer.[4] The manuscripts dating from 1545 to 1620 in the hands of the Hutterian Brothers of America consist of seventy-three different books, of which twenty contain over two hundred and fifty leaves, that is over five hundred pages; the manuscripts from 1620 to 1700 number one hundred and eighteen. Later, also, and especially since 1763, these were copied with amazing diligence. There are at the Bruderhof communities in America more than two hundred and nine such manuscripts written between 1760 and 1824. As copies are made year by year, there are today several thousand handwritten books in the possession of the Brothers. In *Das kleine Geschichts-Buch: Geschichtsbücher der Hutterischen Brüder* which was published under the scholarly guidance of Johann Loserth in cooperation with Eberhard Arnold; as well as in Eberhard Arnold's book, *Die völlige Gemeinschaft der Brüder, die man die Hutterischen nennt,* published by the Hochweg-Verlag, a publishing house in Berlin, an exact description and account is given of these manuscripts. They consist of epistles, confessions of faith, songs, concordances, "Article Books" and writings both of an explanatory and militant character, mainly dating from the first eighty years; and very numerous expositions of the Scriptures, teachings, addresses, prologues and orders dating from 1585 to 1700. Two very old medical books are also extant.

J akob Hutter was leader of the communal life for only three years. On a missionary journey to the Tyrol at the end of 1535 he fell into the hands of the persecutors at Klausen on the Eisack. After the most

[4] This and the following information about extant writings was current in 1931 when this essay was written. For up-to-date information about extant Hutterian books and manuscripts see *The Mennonite Quarterly Review* XLIV:1, January 1970.

cruel torture, which failed to move him from his faith or make him betray his host and brothers, he suffered martyrdom at Innsbruck on March 3rd, 1536, being burnt at the stake. From the first this community in Moravia and Hungary was called "Hutterian Brothers" after him, and in more recent times they have signed themselves "Hutterian Brothers." Among themselves they called, and call, themselves "The Brothers," but never reject the term "The Hutterian Brothers." They like best to use the expression "The Brothers, known as the Hutterians."

The history of the Hutterian community is full of movement. When in the year 1535 the Parliament of Moravia, urged by the Government, decided to eject the "Anabaptists," the lords were in no hurry to comply as they did not want to lose industrious tenants who had brought them great benefit. It was not till 1547, after the end of the Smalkaldic War, that the nobles and feudal lords were forced to submit to the decree of ejection. The ejected Baptizers tried to live in woods and caves. Every door was closed to them, as King Ferdinand had decreed that no one was to shelter them. Several families, communities and what remained of communities had in 1546 found a place of refuge in Hungary.

After the Treaty of Passau between the Emperor and the Protestant princes in 1552 and the religious peace at Augsburg in 1555, it was possible for the Baptizers to risk returning to their old homes in Moravia. Oppression and persecution gradually subsided. The following years, until 1565, were for them a time of gathering and reconstruction. Through the energetic action of their friends in influencing the Emperor it was possible for them to remain in the country. One can see with what respect they were regarded by their protectors at the court at Vienna from the fact that the Hutterian doctor, Georg Zobel,

285

was repeatedly called to Vienna—once to treat the Emperor in person, and another time to suggest measures for combating an epidemic. Thanks to their good education and earnest conception of life they were in demand far and wide as workmen and as leaders in different departments of work. From 1565 to 1592 it was possible for them to develop their powers to the full. Their chronicles speak of this period, which began under the leadership of Peter Walpot, as "The Golden Age." Later their great success in economic matters awoke opposition in part of the remaining population. At the same time the Catholic clergy began to make a strong attack; and their position was undermined especially by the activity of the priest Ehrhard, the Jesuit Cardanus and later by the priest Fischer. To begin with higher taxes were imposed on the crafts of the Hutterians than on other crafts, and special taxes were imposed on the nobles who let Hutterian families settle on their estates. To all this came the tendency, which had grown slowly since 1592 when persecution began anew, and especially since the Thirty Years' War and the war with the Turks, to relax the strict order of the Hutterian households. So that although the leaders had fought successfully for more than a hundred and thirty years against this tendency, yet even towards the end of the sixteenth century a decline could be felt in their influence on the surrounding world which till then had been unparalleled. The community suffered a hard blow when in 1575 the estate of Nikolsburg, which was in its immediate neighborhood, came into the possession of Adam von Dietrichstein, the father of Cardinal Franz von Dietrichstein, as a result of the extravagance of Christoph von Liechtenstein. Conditions there suffered so fundamental a change that all who did not wish to become Roman Catholic had to leave their homes.

The victory of the Roman Catholics in the Battle of the White Mountain in 1620 resulted in mass ejections. An imperial mandate of September 28, 1622, declared that any inhabitant of the land who associated with the Hutterian Brotherhood had to leave Moravia within four weeks, and return was punishable with mutilation and death.

Over twenty thousand adherents of the Hutterian community were driven from Moravia to Hungary, having to leave all their possessions behind. Some of these refugees went to Slovakia, then belonging to Hungary, and to Transylvania; others were scattered in all directions and never came together again. After this blow they were not able to recover their former significance. Only miserable remnants were left after the time of persecution of the next forty years, which included the attacks of the Turks, with their economically destructive and demoralizing effects, and the billeting of soldiers. A Kesselsdorf "teaching" of about the year 1665, in the possession of the Brothers, has a statement in the handwriting of the Servant of the Word, Hans Friedrich Kuentsch, that at that time within a few years only a thousand members of the Church were left out of many thousands (twelve thousand).

Though they were able to establish households in the East, these never reached the significance of those in Moravia. In Hungary some thirty households arose, the largest of which consisted of about five hundred families; Sabatisch and Lewär for a considerable time even after 1620 had several thousand members, but after the time of their last important bishop, Andreas Ehrenpreis (1662), their power of resistance was gradually broken. They had to suffer very badly during the Thirty Years' War and the Turkish War succeeding it from the pillage of troops in search of forage, for to these their large storehouses were a welcome goal. Between 1639 and 1665 they turned in their need for help to the Mennonites in Holland, and received liberal support from them. That their communal storehouses might not be constantly subject to the attacks of troops, in 1685 they partly gave up their communal economy in Hungary. In 1695 they did the same in Transylvania, and in 1699 their last household left each family to care for itself. The land and buildings remained under communal administration. The Brothers have still original notes of the last episcopal elders of this time, Kaspar Eglauch and Tobias Bertsch, which show that they too regarded full community, including that of goods, as the most important thing for their Service of the Word. The Hutterian Brothers of today also have evidence that in the further time of decline, from 1700 to 1763, the direction of the faith and life of the Hutterians was represented, though the way was not found to carry it out fully anew. When the plundering of the troops came to an end, religious persecution began again. Jesuits made repeated attempts to get the Hutterian Brothers to join the Roman Catholic Church. Upon the failure of gentle measures, the Jesuits received permission from the Empress Maria Theresa in the year 1760 to use firm means against the Hutterians. One ordinance commanded all Hutterian children to be baptized by Catholic priests. Their religious books were collected and taken to Catholic libraries, in many cases in filled wagons drawn by two horses. The greater number were burnt and the Hutterians were given Catholic books to take their place. The Hutterian Servants of the Word were thrown into prison and were given regular instruction in the teaching of the Catholic Church by the Jesuits. Catholic religious services were held in the dormitories of the Hutterians, whose members were coerced by

288

military force to take part. The soldiers had to be supported by the households. After the troops had burdened their households for months, the proposal was made to them to attend special, separate services of the Catholic Church and to teach their children through their own schoolteachers. As well as this they were assured of different privileges; they were to be exempt from military service and from taxes and to get their own local government. The Hutterian farms that had been handed over to the Catholic Church were left to them for their common use. What the Catholic Church strove for in vain in other lands, it succeeded in attaining here to a very large extent through power and cunning. Most of the inhabitants went over to Catholicism. They received the name *Habaner* or "New Christians" and most were submerged in the rest of the population. Two small close-knit groups, each consisting of about two hundred souls and having thirty to forty families, have remained until the present day at Sabatisch and Lewär as well as some single families at St. Johann in Slovakia. In 1848, the year of the Revolution, the privileges lost their validity. The Habaner were made subject to the State authorities; the common estate was from now on rented and managed by the elder or leader in the name of the still existing "brotherhoods," the rent being divided amongst all the members.

Only a small remnant was able to save itself and a good part of the Hutterian writings. It was strengthened by a little group from Kärnten, which had left the Catholic Church in 1752 and wanted to form a Lutheran Church as a result of reading the writings of Luther and Johann Arndt, and other spiritual writings based on the Bible. As they would not return to Catholicism they were banished with a heavy loss of property, and brought by ship to Transylvania. They were turned out at a village near the place where the Hutterian Brothers lived. Those among them who took the words of the Sermon on the Mount especially earnestly to heart did not find in the local Lutheran Church what they were seeking; soon afterwards they joined the Hutterian community, and in 1763 their first Servant of the Word was ordained and confirmed in his ministry by the Hutterians, who faithfully supplied them with their old writings. Community of goods, which had been given up between 1685 and 1699 under the misery and oppression of war, was reintroduced in 1763 at Kreuz. Also here the Hutterian Brothers were continually harassed by the Jesuits. Their Servants of the Word and other leading brothers and sisters were imprisoned or forced to take part in Catholic services. Several members were carried away to different villages and towns. But they soon came together again. In the year 1767 their children were to be taken from them and brought up in a Jesuit orphanage. When the shocked parents got news of this intention they decided to flee. A group of sixty-seven souls succeeded in crossing the Carpathians. They rented a piece of land in Wallachia, in the neighborhood of Bucharest, and again established a household. They had to suffer heavily here later from the pillaging of the troops in the war between Russia and Turkey. Thus an offer made in 1770 by Czarina Katharine of Russia, assuring exemption from military service, control of their own schools and far-reaching administrative independence, was very welcome. All the Hutterian families emigrated to Russia and founded a Bruderhof in Wischenka about a hundred and twenty miles north of Kiev. This Bruderhof was greatly enlarged through the addition of Habaner from Hungary. When the Brothers who had remained in Hungary and gone over to the Catholic Church learned that in Russia they were not subject to oppression on account of their faith, many families likewise decided to emigrate. Thus there arose in Russia a community of faith and goods consisting of a hundred and forty souls, of whom half were New Hutterians from Kärnten and the other half Old Hutterians, some of whom had taken part in the refounding of community in Transylvania, while some had been won for the new Church-community as a result of the sending out of Brothers from Wischenka. In a short time they became prosperous, which, however, resulted in the second and third generation in sapping of spiritual life. In spite of all the efforts and opposition of their leader Johannes Waldner, who was now an old man, they gave up their communal household economy in 1819; their school was given up—a thing that until then had never happened, even in times of the worst persecution —and the community grew poor. In 1842 they left the settlement and founded two villages, Hutterthal and Johannisruh, in a fertile district to the north of the Crimean Peninsula, near Melitopol, where Mennonites from West Prussia had already established the Molotschna Colony. Here they soon once more became prosperous. Communal life, which in spite of constantly repeated applications was for a long time opposed by the Government, was at last successfully introduced by two groups in 1857 and 1859-60, after many attempts had been made since 1850 which had not proved capable of lasting. In Hutterdorf and Scheromet they founded two households like those in Moravia, whereas the remaining inhabitants of Hutterthal and Johannisruh continued having private property. A third community of goods, which was reintroduced by some well-to-do inhabitants of Johannisruh, was temporarily given up after several years, and was only successfully renewed in America, in 1877.

The introduction of general conscription in Russia faced the Hutterian communities, as it did the Mennonites, with the alternative of dropping their principle of non-violence or emigrating to a land in which they could remain exempt from military service. The alternative offered by the Russian Government—forestry service—did not satisfy them. In 1873 the trusted Brothers whom they had sent to America received from the governments in Washington and Ottawa (as did the envoys of the Mennonites) the assurance that their religious faith regarding war would be respected.

Thus in 1874 and 1877 the Hutterian Brothers decided to emigrate to the United States of America, and founded three Bruderhof communities in South Dakota.

The first Bruderhof was founded in Tabor County, South Dakota, on the Missouri. By 1918 it had founded five daughter settlements which were sold during the First World War owing to the fact that the Government withdrew the exemption from military service which it had once assured them. All emigrated to Canada between 1918 and 1922, and settled in Manitoba. These communities were called the *Schmiedegruppe* or "Smith Group" because they came to America under the leadership of Michael Waldner, who was a smith, with the cooperation of other smiths.

In 1874 and in 1875 a second group settled in South Dakota. Its members were called *Dariusleute* (Darius People) as they came under the leadership of Darius Walter. Though founding in South Dakota they transferred to Alberta, Canada in 1918 for the same reasons as the "Smith Group."

A third group, known as *Lehrerleute* (Teacher People) because those who led them to America, Jakob

292

Wipf and Peter Hofer, were teachers, also moved to Canada.

The Hutterian Brothers in Russia, who had given up community of goods and lived in Hutterthal and Johannisruh to the north of the Crimea, also emigrated to America. They settled in South Dakota, North Dakota, California and Saskatchewan. They did not introduce community of goods after emigrating to America, and soon formed part of the Crimean Mennonite Brethren Church and other colonies.

The old writings of the sixteenth and seventeenth centuries are read, discussed and explained, and the very old songs sung in the Bruderhof Communities in the United States and Canada as is rarely to be found in another fellowship. The old orders also are practically all maintained organically in strength by the Brothers today. They live today in the New World as their forefathers lived in Moravia in the sixteenth century. Even their costume has barely changed. The men of the Smith and Darius Groups still wear hooks and eyes in accordance with the old custom. Together with the refusal of military service and community of goods, Church discipline, from brotherly admonition to exclusion, is in full force today as it was four hundred years ago. The Bruderhof communities have until today retained love for and in the common life and devotion and surrender to the common work.

The main occupation of the Hutterian Brothers today is farming. Industry had reached such a state of development in America at the time of their immigration that handicraft had no hope of competing with it. The workshops which they maintain serve in practice only the needs of the Bruderhof itself. Laziness is not tolerated among them. Every member who is capable of work must work for the whole. The work is planned and divided among all the inhabitants of the Bruderhof. Overwork is avoided by means of well-planned cooperation. At the head of each Bruderhof are one or two Ministers of the Word and the steward, who receive their task, usually for life, through the votes of the men members. They are helped and advised by some—often about five—older members. The leadership of the communal work is in the hands of the steward, who is constantly helped by the distributor of work (*Weinzedel*) and the housemother. He has charge of the common purse and sees to the storage and distribution of stores. The leaders of the individual departments are under him and responsible to him.

No one in a Bruderhof has money except the steward. The needs of individuals are met out of the common purse. No one has personal property. Whoever joins the community must give up all he has to it; he cannot demand it back should he want to leave. The individual communities are economically independent of each other. Community of goods is to a certain degree limited to the members of the same Bruderhof. When a Bruderhof exchanges goods with another, the transaction often takes place by means of money. When, as often happens, a Bruderhof helps another materially it does so as a gift. Savings are used mainly to extend a Bruderhof already in existence or to establish a new one. When an older community founds a new Bruderhof, to which the children of its members, to a large extent, move, no claim is made for the repayment of expenses. The new Bruderhof usually stands in very close relationship to the parent community, both sometimes forming one corporation. Though each Bruderhof is to a certain degree independent, there is a very close kinship in religious matters and also in practical work and life. The leadership of the whole Brotherhood by one elder, as was formerly always the case, has not yet been reached in America. Sometimes the responsible Ministers of the Word of all three, or at least of two, of the family-unions meet for a common consultation; generally, however, only those belonging to one of these family-unions, the "Smith," "Darius" or the "Teacher" groups. At certain intervals of time the different Bruderhof communities send their representatives to conferences to consult with each other and discuss matters concerning the whole community and religious questions; and their decisions are binding on the whole. The Hutterian Brothers have not wavered from the conviction of their fathers in the sixteenth century. They present a unique example in world history of an intimate common life built up on a Christian communal basis that has stood throughout four centuries. Heroism, such as is to be found in but a few religious communities, finds expression in the overcoming of the most difficult situations in times of persecution, and in the devotion and surrender of life and property for the faith.

BIBLIOGRAPHY

For a complete bibliography of English Language materials on the Hutterian Brethren see *The Mennonite Quarterly Review* XLIV: 1, Jan. 1970, 106-113.

Beck, Joseph von., ed. *Die Geschichtsbücher der Wiedertäufer in Österreich-Ungarn in der Zeit von 1526 bis 1785*. Vienna, 1883.

Clark, Bertha W. "The Hutterian Communities." *Journal of Political Economy*, XXXII, 1924.

Die Lieder der Hutterischen Brüder. Scottdale, Pa.: Mennonite Publishing House, 1914.

Hege, Christian. *Die Täufer in der Kurpfalz*. Frankfurt, 1908.

Horsch, John. *The Hutterian Brethren, 1528-1931*. Goshen, Ind.: Mennonite Historical Society, 1931.

Hrubn, Frau. *Die Wiedertäufer in Mähren*. Leipzig, 1935.

Liefmann, Robert. *Die kommunistschen Gemeinden in Nordamerika*. Jena, 1922.

Loserth, Johannes. *Der Anabaptismus in Tirol vom Jahre 1536 bis zu seinem Erlöschen*. Vienna, 1892.

―――. *Der Anabaptismus in Tirol von seinen Anfängen bis zum Tode Jakob Huters (1526-1536)*. Vienna, 1892.

―――. *Der Communismus der mährischen Wiedertäufer im 16 und 17 Jahrhundert*. Vienna, 1894.

―――. *Dr. Balthasar Hubmaier und die Anfänge der Wiedertaufe in Mähren*. Brunn, 1893.

Mennonite Encyclopedia. Scottdale, Pa.: Mennonite Publishing House.

Mennonitisches Lexikon. Frankfurt, 1913, 1938.

Müller, Lydia, ed. *Der Kommunismus der mährischen Wiedertäufer*. Leipzig, 1927.

―――. *Glaubenszeugnisse oberdeutscher Taufgesinnter. In "Quellen und Forschungen zur Reformationsgeschichte"*. Leipzig, 1938.

Walter, Elias, ed. *Lieder der Hutterischen Brüder*. Scottdale, Pa., 1914.

Wiswedel, Wilhelm. *Bilder und Führergestalten aus dem Täufertum* I-II. Kassel, 1928, 1930.

Wolkan, Rudolf. *Die Hutterer*. Vienna, 1918.

———. *Die Lieder der Wiedertäufer*. Berlin, 1913.

———. *Geschicht-Buch der hutterischen Brüder* (known as *Das grosse Gemeinde-Geschichtbuch, The Greater Church Chronicle*). Vienna, 1923.

———. *Österreichische Wiedertäufer und Kommunisten in Amerika*. Vienna, 1918.

Zieglschmid, A.J.F., ed. *Die älteste Chronik der hutterischen Brüder*. Vienna, 1943.